Dimensions of Creativity

Dimensions of Creativity

edited by *Margaret A. Boden*

A Bradford Book
The MIT Press
Cambridge, Massachusetts
London, England

This book was set in Palatino by DEKR Corporation and was printed and bound in the United States of America.

Library of Congress Cataloging-in-Publication Data

Dimensions of creativity / edited by Margaret A. Boden.
   p.   cm.
"A Bradford book."
Includes index.
ISBN 0-262-02368-7
1. Creative ability. 2. Creative thinking. I. Boden, Margaret A.
BF408.D56   1994
153.3'5—dc20   93-44754
                                                    CIP

Contents

Contributors   vi
Acknowledgments   vii

Chapter 1
Introduction   1
Margaret A. Boden

Chapter 2
Making Up Discovery   13
Simon Schaffer

Chapter 3
Where Do New Ideas Come From?   53
Gerd Gigerenzer

Chapter 4
What Is Creativity?   75
Margaret A. Boden

Chapter 5
Creativity: Beyond the Darwinian Paradigm   119
David N. Perkins

Chapter 6
The Creators' Patterns   143
Howard Gardner

Chapter 7
How Can We Measure a Society's Creativity?   159
Colin Martindale

Chapter 8
The Measurement of Creativity   199
Hans J. Eysenck

Index   243

Contributors

Margaret A. Boden
School of Cognitive and
Computing Sciences
University of Sussex
Brighton BN1 9QH
ENGLAND
Phone: 0273-678386
FAX: 0273-671320

Hans Eysenck
Institute of Psychiatry
De Crespigny Park
London SE5 8EF
ENGLAND
Phone: 071-703-5411

Howard Gardner
The Development Group/
Project Zero
Harvard Graduate School of
Education
323 Longfellow Hall
Appian Way
Cambridge, Massachusetts 02138
USA
Phone: (617) 495-4342
FAX: (617) 495-9709
Telex: (1) 921 496

Gerd Gigerenzer
Department of Psychology
University of Chicago
5848 S. University Avenue
Chicago, Illinois 60637
USA
Phone: (312) 702-8859
FAX: (312) 702-0886

Colin Martindale
Department of Psychology
Clarence Cook Little Hall
University of Maine
Orono, Maine 04469-0140
USA
Phone: (207) 581-2032

David Perkins
Harvard Graduate School of
Education
323 Longfellow Hall
Appian Way
Cambridge, Massachusetts 02138
USA
Phone: (617) 495-4342/4376
FAX: (617) 496-4288

Simon Schaffer
Department of the History
and Philosophy of Science
Free School Lane
Cambridge CB2 3RH
ENGLAND
Phone: (0223) 334543

Acknowledgments

This book arose from the work of The Achievement Project, a research group sponsored for five years by the Renaissance Trust. All the papers were presented at research meetings of this group, in Windsor (December 1990) and Ashford, Kent (December 1991). The authors thanks Mr. T. L. Martin, sponsor of the Renaissance Trust, for his encouragement and support.

The Achievement Project is interdisciplinary, bringing together academics in the history of science and economics, the philosophy and sociology of science, anthropology, and psychology. It studies the factors important in cultural and economic achievements of diverse kinds, and in its historical aspects is primarily focused on intellectual and material culture in modern Europe.

Anyone wishing to know more about the activities of the Project may receive copies of the *Newsletter* by writing to Mrs. Priscilla Frost, The Achievement Project, 10B Littlegate Street, Oxford, OX1 1QT, England.

Chapter 1

Introduction

Margaret Boden

Creativity is a prized feature of the human mind, but prizes can coexist with puzzlement. The concept of creativity may trail clouds of glory, but it brings along also a host of controversial questions. The first of these is: *What is it?* How should creativity be defined? Is every novel idea a creative one? If not, what's the difference? If positive evaluation is essential, what sort of evaluation (and by whom) is relevant? Is creativity a psychological category, or a social one?

Is the creative process much the same in the arts and the sciences, or are these forms of originality fundamentally distinct? What about artists and scientists themselves: do they have (do they need) personalities different from the average person's, and perhaps also different from each other's?

Can creativity be measured, and if so, how? Is it in principle possible to compare two novel ideas to show that one is more creative than the other? Or is this sort of judgment, familiar though it is, something that cannot be justified in objective, still less quantitative, terms?

Last, but not least: assuming that we can recognize creativity when we see it, can we explain how it comes about? In other words, can anything systematic be said about the context of discovery, as opposed to the context of justification?

Such questions are not new. Some were raised by Plato, who thought a rational understanding of creativity to be impossible: "A poet is holy, and never able to compose until he has become inspired, and is beside himself and reason is no longer in him . . . for not by art does he utter these, but by power divine." Plato's successors have not always been so pessimistic. But that is not to say that they are united. The questions listed above have been asked by people with significantly different interests: by psychologists, historians, philosophers of science, musicologists, aestheticians, anxious parents—indeed, by virtually every thinking person. It is hardly surprising that they have offered diverse answers.

The chapters collected here reflect a variety of professional concerns and theoretical approaches. The individual authors did not aim to offer a mutually harmonious account of creativity. Yet despite their very different emphases, their insights are to a large extent complementary.

In chapters 2 and 3, two historians of science stress the social aspects of creativity, including the importance of a new idea's being positively valued by a certain social group if it is to be generally recognized as creative. The other five authors focus more on the psychological aspects, asking how it is that new ideas arise in individual minds and what sorts of personality are involved. But historical and psychological approaches are not mutually exclusive.

For example, the notions of "conceptual space" and "Klondike space" (developed in chapters 4 and 5 respectively) are used to describe cognitive dimensions within individual minds. But since these are the person's currently accepted styles of thinking, their origin is largely social, not purely idiosyncratic. In attempting to define the conceptual spaces within a given individual's mind, we must rely heavily on our knowledge of the cultural influences on the person concerned. Historical as well as psychological evidence is likewise needed to identify the Klondike spaces inhabited by a particular person or group.

Similarly, a psychologist's "individualistic" emphasis on creative personalities (chapters 6 and 8) may stress motivational factors that enable an original thinker to survive despite a largely uncomprehending society. Because the label "creative" is a socially sanctioned honorific, it may not be ascribed to an idea until long after its initial occurrence. We therefore need to understand what personal characteristics help someone to persevere in thinking unorthodox thoughts, even though only a few people—if any—recognize their value.

A historian shows (in chapter 3) that the availability of certain measuring tools can mold the theories about what is to be measured. But this is, in part, to remind us that accepted group practices will very likely inform the minds of group members. In other words, conceptual spaces can be—and normally are—shared by many individuals. No psychologist, however interested in individuals' thinking or personality, need deny the pervasive effects of cultural style and social evaluation.

Even when authors disagree considerably in their overall theoretical approach, there may be useful common ground to be admitted, as well as intriguing challenges to be met. Chapter 4, for instance, is the only one that addresses creativity in computational terms. But its account of the exploration and transformation of conceptual spaces is consistent not only with the other "psychological" chapters, but also with the social-historical concerns of chapters 2 and 3.

Again, the final two chapters adopt an operationalist, positivist approach very different from that of most of the others—especially the first. But the empirical results reported in these final chapters are consistent with the claims of other authors. Behavioristic and physiological evidence (see chapter 8) is relevant to the phenomena described elsewhere in structural or social terms. For example, the ability to combine two seemingly unrelated ideas may be influenced by varying levels of a particular neurochemical, even if the *selection* of the two ideas to be combined must be explained in a different way. Similarly, if an apparently crude "measure" of creativity (like that described in chapter 7) correlates with acceptable judgments of creativity—and provides surprising empirical data to boot—then this is interesting. If the critic cannot accept the author's interpretation, some other explanation of the unexpected data must be found.

In short, there are many differences among the themes and approaches of the chapters in this volume. But most can be fruitfully reconciled. Difference need not imply contradiction.

One common view of creativity, however, is contradicted by several chapters included here. Karl Popper's philosophy of science makes a rigid distinction between "discovery" and "justification." The context of discovery—the generation of the novel idea within some individual's mind—is said to be irrelevant to the philosophy of science, which focuses on rational justification. Who cares if Kepler's ideas sprang from a superstitious numerology, or if Kekulé's arose within a dream? All that matters is that they turned out to be justified. The context of discovery is said to be irrelevant also to theoretical psychology. According to Popper, creative "inspiration" is fundamentally irrational. So nothing systematic can be said about how it is possible for new ideas to arise. A psychology of creativity is not merely philosophically uninteresting, but impossible.

This Popperian view of creativity is as pessimistic as Plato's, to which indeed it is significantly similar. It is rejected explicitly in chapters 2 and 3, and implicitly in chapters 4 and 5. Popper insists that scientific discovery (and artistic creativity too) cannot be predicted. There are a number of reasons why this is true. But it does not follow that nothing can be said, in general terms, about the mental processes by which new ideas arise.

Simon Schaffer's "Making Up Discovery" (chapter 2) addresses both the occurrence of a new idea and its positive evaluation: authorship and authorization. He argues that a list of famous scientists is a roll call of intellectual heroes, whose heroic status is not a simple consequence of unique individual merit but is socially ascribed. Discovery involves "a lengthy process of hard work and negotiation within a set of complex social networks."

Some influential social group has to value an idea if it is to be recognized, preserved, and communicated. In science, the evaluation often involves the explicit identification of the idea as a "discovery," together with the naming of some person as the "discoverer." Schaffer shows that this social process is a form of mythmaking, which typically obscures the facts in two ways. First, it suggests that the idea, the discovery, happened at one specific instant—rather than being a gradual development over time (perhaps over a lifetime). Second, it suggests that only one person (or perhaps a majestic duo, like Crick and Watson) had the idea. The facts are usually very different.

The point of labeling a scientific idea a "discovery" is to mark it— and the associated research practices—as something of which the relevant scientific community approves. The historian may be able to point to similar ideas that would have merited the accolade but that— for a large variety of reasons—did not receive it. In other words, a scientific discovery (an example of what in chapter 4 is called H-creativity) is identified as such not intrinsically, in terms only of the properties of the idea itself, but largely extrinsically, in terms of what relevant people think of it.

Schaffer shows that Popper's distinction between discovery and justification is oversimple, and that the valuation of new ideas by scientists is a less rational process than he implies. In addition, Schaffer rejects another widely held view: Robert Merton's sociology of science. This approach underplays the role of the creative individual, claiming that "the same" discovery is often made simultaneously. For Merton, scientific discoveries are not unique but multiple, and also inevitable: if one person hadn't thought of it, another would have—and almost certainly did.

The glorification of individuals is indeed misleading. (Schaffer remarks that although the crucial contributions of other researchers are sometimes recognized, those of a researcher's technicians are rarely mentioned.) However, Mertonians ignore the role of specific scientific groups in producing and naming discovery. Detailed consideration of alleged multiple discoveries show that there are crucial differences, due more to historical contingency than to sociological determinism.

The examples discussed in chapter 2 include the discoveries of dinosaurs, magneto-optic rotation, and the planet Neptune. Each of these is commonly described in Mertonian or heroic-Popperian terms. Dinosaurs and Neptune, for example, often figure in stories of multiple discovery and the inevitability of scientific advance. But the truth is more complex. What was to be counted by astronomers as "the same" discovery was a matter of extended (and politically influenced) negotiation. As for the effect of electromagnetism on light, Faraday was canonized (by Clerk Maxwell, for instance) as the heroic discoverer of this phenomenon. But the standard narrative concerning Faraday's achievement obscures important aspects and alternative interpretations of his work.

For each of these cases, the relevant scientific community (including institutions such as museums, societies, and laboratories) defined in retrospect just what the "discovery" was. They decided its character, its author, and its timing. A similar case could be made for examples drawn from the arts. In that sense, creativity—of the sort that is recorded in the history books ("H-creativity")—is not a purely psychological category, but largely a matter of social attribution.

Gerd Gigerenzer's chapter "Where Do New Ideas Come From?" (chapter 3) offers further reasons for rejecting a sharp distinction between discovery and justification. He shows how the scientist's tools for justification may enter the context of discovery, informing scientific theories accordingly.

His examples of this "tools-to-theories heuristic," highly relevant to our general theme of creativity, concern the influence of statistical tools on the questions and presuppositions of psychologists. As he puts it, new ideas were discovered after experimental psychologists became familiar with new tools for data processing, rather than new data. But these new ideas then enabled the discovery of new data.

Various psychologists have suggested that the mind is an "intuitive statistician" of some kind. That is, the ordinary person's mental equipment includes much the same tools for thinking and/or perceiving as the researcher uses for the statistical analysis of experimental measurements. Gigerenzer examines the fate of a number of such suggestions, and shows that if the relevant statistical tools are already widely accepted by psychologists, such ideas may spread easily throughout the psychological community. If they are not, then the (premature) theorizing will seem unconvincing.

In short, measurement does not always come after the fact, but may come before it: it may help to define "the fact" itself. The experimental data are not simply given, but are generated in light of the data-analysis that will be used on them. What we count as "creativity" (or for that matter, as "intelligence") may depend on the methods we use to measure it.

It does not follow that measurement is necessarily misleading. A new form of measurement may enable us to clarify a previously vague, intuitive concept. All the central instances included under the intuitive concept may still be included, and their interrelations much clarified.

At the same time, the reasons for excluding the more problematic cases may be both evident and persuasive. In such a case, the measurement will have helped us to understand what the relevant phenomenon *is*, as well as how to compare different instances of it.

Examples of this "tool-to-theory" process at work can be seen in other chapters. For instance, the definition of creativity given in chapter 4 (and the psychological explanation suggested there) draws heavily on today's use of the computer as a tool for modeling the mind. Similarly, in chapters 7 and 8, the authors' commitment to statistical methods molds their operational definitions of creativity and other psychological concepts.

In my own chapter "What Is Creativity?" (chapter 4), I define and explain creativity in terms of the mapping, exploration, and transformation of structured conceptual spaces. A conceptual space is a style of thinking—in music, sculpture, choreography, chemistry, etc. It has various dimensions, limits, pathways, and levels. Moreover, it can be pervasively, and sometimes profoundly, altered in many different ways.

Conceptual spaces, and ways of exploring and transforming them, can in principle—and to some degree in practice—be modeled in computational terms. A computational theory of jazz improvisation, for example, or of line drawing, can help us to see clearly what is involved in the mapping and exploration of a given artistic style. It may also suggest ways in which that style might lead on to a different one.

The emphasis here is on the psychological theories concerned. The computer, as such, is irrelevant. Its importance is that it enables us to explore and test the implications of a complex psychological theory. Any lack in the creative powers of computer models should be attributed not to the computer, but to the theorist.

For instance, only a few of the programs discussed in chapter 4 can transform their conceptual spaces, as opposed to merely exploring them. It is difficult enough to define a thinking style clearly, and to specify ways of moving around within it. It is even more difficult to detail processes capable of changing the style in intelligible ways, and of distinguishing "valuable" transformations from nonsensical ones. But these are theoretical difficulties, not technological ones.

If we were able to say clearly what mental processes enable someone to think new thoughts, we could express (and test) those ideas computationally. Whether today's concepts and computer models—"classical," "connectionist," "self-organizing," "evolutionary"—would always suffice is, of course, another question.

Because of the importance of structure in the identification and evaluation of creativity, no simple metric can suffice to measure it. A measure of the structured complexity of a system, taking into account the "depth" of the relevant dimension(s), might in principle be possible. But no such measure exists at present. We can, however, compare different ideas in structural terms. A "grammar" for Frank Lloyd Wright's prairie houses, for instance, shows why designing a prairie house with two fireplaces is considerably "more creative" than adding an extra wing, or a balcony.

Structured conceptual spaces, and how to map them, are discussed also in chapter 5, "Creativity: Beyond the Darwinian Paradigm." But David Perkins uses the vocabulary of "Klondike spaces." The gold digger in the Klondike faces four problems. Gold is rare. Gold mines may be isolated. Leaving the current (nearly exhausted) source is risky. And gold may be absent across an entire plateau, so no one direction is obviously best. There is no question of the miner's always being abe to go straight to the best place. Even so, experience can help. A seasoned miner, who knows something of the local terrain, will probably have a better "nose" for finding gold than a tyro-prospector ignorant of the goldfields.

Perkins shows that scientists and inventors seeking new ideas face analogous problems. They typically appear to have a "Klondike map" of the relevant conceptual landscape. This internal (and largely unconscious) map enables them to guess whether the solution will be easy or difficult to find—and whether it is likely to require a "leap" to some far-flung peak in the conceptual landscape.

A creative system (society, mind, machine) may use such an informed sense of problem difficulty, in generating novelties that are relatively likely to be adaptive. So Perkins criticizes those psychologists who see human creativity as a Darwinian process of random generation and selective retention. Our individual and societal Klondike maps often guide us into the most promising areas. In other words, the Popperian notion that new ideas in science are always generated irrationally is mistaken. To be sure, justification is always needed: the prospector must check that the newly found area does indeed contain gold. But he need not, though sometimes he may, reach the unfamiliar area by a random walk.

Whereas chapters 4 and 5 are primarily concerned with how new ideas are generated in the mind, chapter 6 asks what sort of person is able to generate them. In "The Creators' Patterns," Howard Gardner outlines an extensive body of research on seven creative individuals of our own century: Einstein, Freud, Gandhi, T. S. Eliot, Stravinsky, Picasso, and Martha Graham. These individuals were chosen as exemplars of seven different types of intelligence, all of which human beings share but each of which may be especially well developed in some people and relatively weak in others.

Gardner's prime interest here is not in the differences between these types of intelligence, but in the similarities between the personalities of the seven creators. Is there some general profile of motivation and morals that characterizes the successful creator? Gardner concludes that there is.

The "exemplary creator" (an abstraction constructed by generalizing from various individual cases) comes from a family located outside the centers of social power and influence. The creator's family values education, without necessarily being educated. But the family is soon outgrown, and the young adult finds a group of peers (often in a city) who share the same interests. This social support is crucial, especially when the creator (typically after many years of committed apprenticeship) comes up with an idea so different from those currently approved that it is not easily understood, never mind accepted.

Self-confidence, stubbornness, and exceptionally hard work are then needed, to persevere with and to polish the new insight. Energy and commitment are essential, and the creator expects very high standards of self and of others. But these standards apply to the work done in the domain concerned. They do not normally include high moral standards: egotism, selfishness, and exploitation of others are common. Gardner reports that "a legacy of destruction and tragedy surrounds those who enter into the orbit of the creative individual." In a word, such individuals are "frankly, difficult."

Gardner remarks that highly successful creators retain more contact with their childhood, or even infancy, than other people do. This is not just a question of retaining relatively "infantile" thought processes. It also involves valuing specific childhood experiences long after they are normally forgotten.

His final point reinforces the positions argued in chapters 4 and 5. The creative person has two counteracting tendencies. One is to question every assumption, to reject the current styles of thinking. The other is to exhaust a domain, to explore it more systematically, more comprehensively, and more deeply than others have done before. In the terminology of chapter 4, the conceptual spaces are explored thoroughly before they are transformed. Thorough exploration is needed to locate the points, or the dimensions, at which a transformation would be interesting, even shocking. Evidently, however, putting these cognitive tendencies into practice requires some rather unattractive motivational qualities. The exemplary creator is not an exemplary person.

Gardner's biographical method, closely examining unique human beings (though attempting to derive generalizations from them), is eschewed by the authors of the last two papers. Neither Colin Martindale nor Hans Eysenck rely on open-ended interviews, diaries and letters, or personal anecdotes recounted by family and friends. Instead they use operational tests and statistical tools (like those discussed by Gigerenzer) to study creativity. But Eysenck, at least, asks many questions about what sorts of personality factors favor originality—and what he says is broadly consonant with Gardner's conclusions.

In chapter 7, entitled "How Can We Measure a Society's Creativity?", Martindale describes his work on a large corpus of English poetry, from Chaucer to modern times. His primary aim is to chart the creativity levels within this domain. In addition, he wants to see whether creativity levels correlate with other societal variables.

As his index of creativity, Martindale uses very simple measures of "primary process" thinking, such as concrete versus abstract vocabulary. These measures are intuitively plausible to the extent that one believes irrational, primary process thought to characterize creativity. Many psychologists, including Freud, have believed this. They are intuitively implausible, however, to the extent that they ignore what seems to be the most important thing of all: *what*, specifically, is being thought. As Martindale himself points out, his measures have nothing to do with the meaning of the poem, or with the rhetorical aim of the poet.

One might expect that these simple and meaningless indices could not possibly tell us anything interesting about poetic creativity. However, Martindale's statistical methodology shows that there have been fairly regular waves of stylistic variation through successive historical periods. By applying similarly simple—not to say crude—measures, similar waves can be seen in French poetry, in music, and in painting.

Some people's reaction to this approach is to scorn it as behaviorism gone berserk. They complain that to address a poem in this way is a travesty, a betrayal of the poet's aesthetic intent. But Martindale agrees: his statistical measures are not intended to capture the meaning of individual poems. They could not pick up a widespread change in the *content* of poetry, such as a concern with romantic love, the picaresque, or astronomy. Nor could they support Samuel Johnson's claim that "Only Donne would compare a good man to a telescope." If those are the aspects of poetic creativity with which one is concerned, Martindale's work is simply irrelevant.

The intriguing question remains. *Why*, when one considers successive bodies of contemporaneous poetry (and music, and painting), do these stylistic waves appear? Martindale suggests that when a style is introduced, its use is a relatively simple matter. As it becomes more familiar, it is pushed toward its limits—by means of increasingly complex and specific thought processes. When the switch is eventually made to a new style, the poet (musician, painter) can fall back on the relatively unspecific, uncritical images of primary process thinking. Martindale's emphasis on the gradual elaboration of poetic or musical styles is reminiscent of my own account, in terms of the increasingly complex mapping and exploration of conceptual spaces (chapter 4). But why should a transformation of the space bring primary process thinking in its wake? Why does a new style of writing poetry normally encourage poets, irrespective of content, to "regress" in this way?

Finally, in "The Measurement of Creativity" Eysenck reviews the psychometrics of creativity and its relations with many personal and motivational variables. Chapter 8 is a comprehensive and wide-ranging account of experimental work on many different aspects of creativity. As such, it cannot be summarized. But its main message can be simply stated: creativity *can* be measured, and the confluence of different measures (psychological and neurophysiological, for instance) makes scientific sense.

Just because something can be measured, it may not be worth measuring—and may not even exist. Suppose (to take an example suggested by Graham Richards) that a medieval psychologist had tried to measure *sanctity* by asking questions such as "Would you rather spend your Saturdays reading a holy book or going to a tournament?" This would not prove that sanctity is real. The existence of monkish behavior is entirely consistent with the falsity of religious claims about the theological base of sanctity properly so-called. Moreover, even if we were convinced that sanctity really exists, we would need to agree that the questionnaire is a valid index of it. The question about tournaments is intuitively acceptable (though in practice it might turn out to be unreliable). But "Do you give food to the traveling friars?" would only be helpful if the answer were negative. As for "Does your sister wear a wimple?", this would be utterly irrelevant.

With respect to the psychometrics of creativity, we need to accept that certain tests do indeed pick out what we are normally happy to call creative ideas. Once their validity has been thus agreed, and their reliability established, the tests can then be used as starting points in seeking further correlations—some of which may be unexpected or even counterintuitive.

Particular creative ideas often involve an unusual analogy, or a combination of dissimilar ideas. It is not surprising then that creativity is statistically associated with a general tendency to widen or overgeneralize conceptual categories. This tendency is characteristic of "psychoticism"—a common cognitive style, which includes "psychotics" at one end of the scale. It is perhaps more surprising that this cognitive tendency can be augmented or inhibited by specific psychotropic drugs, and that outline explanations can be suggested (in terms of neuronal function) of why this should be so.

Overinclusiveness (in the cognitive sense) correlates highly with such personality traits as being imaginative, unconventional, rebellious, individualistic, independent, autonomous, flexible, and intuitive. But it also correlates strongly with being conceited, cynical, disorderly, egotistical, hostile, outspoken, uninhibited, quarrelsome, aggressive, asocial, and—in the extreme—psychopathic. (Gardner's biographical evidence supports this generalization.) Eysenck suggests that creativity and contrariness, which do not seem to be essentially connected, may have evolved together because people who originate novel ideas need to be able to withstand the criticism of the conservative majority. (Again, Gardner's more informal discussion suggests the same thing.)

These chapters leave many questions unanswered, and many also unasked. But they do indicate the diverse intellectual demands that face us. We need to study psychology and history, individuals and groups, cognition and motivation. Much of our evidence will be informal, even intuitive; but we must express our ideas as clearly and test them as rigorously as we can. All this is required if we are to understand the rich complexities of creative thought.

Chapter 2

Making Up Discovery

Simon Schaffer

What kind of achievement does a scientific discovery represent? And what kind of achiever is a discoverer? "Discovery" and "achievement" have often been seen as intimately connected. Historians of the sciences have used "discoveries" as the benchmarks of progress. They have promoted a heroic model of discovery, in which such events are seen as exclusively mental processes exercised by figures of superior power. They have cultivated an accompanying picture of the discoverer, the isolated individual easily identified as the innovation's author. In this version, the work of discovery is suitable only for psychological analysis, and the subsequent endeavors to make a discovery convincing can be left to the attention of historians and philosophers. These pictures have their contemporary monuments and ceremonies, the reward systems of the sciences, and appealing histories that display the progress of the sciences as straightforwardly reliant on a succession of geniuses and breakthroughs. Such stories agree in categorizing discovery as certainly individual and recognizable. The influential philosopher Gilbert Ryle argued in his *The Concept of Mind* that "discovery" was an exemplary "achievement word" (like "checkmate,") for in using the term we must refer to the *results* of actions, rather than merely to the actions themselves. Ryle reckoned that "discovery" properly refers to a specific achievement, unambiguously situated in time, relying upon a previous set of appropriate activities (Ryle 1949: 149–151).

More recent studies of the process of discovery, however, have challenged this happy consensus. These studies have drawn our attention toward the intriguing relationship between the authorship of a discovery and its authorization as a discovery. The challenge can be illustrated by reconsideration of Ryle's claim. He notes that "discovery" is a label attributed to candidate actions after their performance. Retrospective judgment plays a crucial role in our use of this term. Furthermore, this judgment must be delivered by the "discoverer's" community. There are many examples of this process: in the history of psychology, for example, Gustav Fechner's program for a pan-psychic and antimaterialist cosmology, published in his remarkable visionary text *Zend-Avesta* (1851), was later systematically reinterpreted and reworked to provide the warrant for an experimental project in psychophysics (Boring 1961). The classic case is the so-called rediscovery of Mendel. Most historians have agreed that Mendel founded genetics in 1866, but that his work was overlooked and then rediscovered in 1900 by Correns, De Vries, and others. One chronicler of scientific discovery avers that Mendel's original paper was "essentially unread for three decades" and "entered the mainstream of biology after being rediscovered in 1900" (Barber 1961; Parkinson 1985; 365). But recent studies demonstrate that Mendel was not ignored, he was not concerned with genetics, and that his "rediscovery" in 1900 was a direct consequence of local controversies in Britain and Germany on issues such as biometrics and saltationism. The sociologist Augustine Brannigan puts the case like this: "the transformation in the status of Mendel's discoveries" shows that "events are discoveries not in virtue of how they appear in the mind, but how they are defined in and by a cultural criterion" (Brannigan 1981: 90).

This emphasis on the cultural criteria that define discoveries obviously poses problems for many conventional psychological approaches to the mental processes that allegedly characterize discovery in the sciences. Perhaps the most salient of these troubles is the source material on which a psychological account will rely. In his remarkable preface to Arthur Koestler's *The Act of Creation*, the psychologist Cyril Burt seemed to recognize that studying creativity "is not an issue that can be satisfactorily solved by the tools and techniques which present day psychologists commonly employ." Instead of mental testing and experimental research, Burt reckoned that "what is really needed is a systematic study carried out by one of those rare individuals who himself happens to possess this peculiar gift of creativity" (Koestler 1964: 16–17). However depressing the claim that only the truly creative can study creativity, Burt's remarks do pinpoint the fact that autobiography has played the primary role in the psychological analysis of innovation and discovery. When Koestler set out to show that creativity involved the process of bisociation, juxtaposing formerly unrelated concepts, his sources were typically memoirs produced by scientists whose discovering work had then been credited by their community: Newton and Franklin, Pasteur and Faraday, Maxwell and Einstein (Koestler 1964: 35, 677–702). Brannigan, in contrast, invites us to study the process of accreditation. Work that is not so credited is not a discovery. Psychologists who use these heroic autobiographies must assume the existence of, but often ignore, the cultural process of authorization.

An example of this problem is evident in Arieti's psychological study of scientific creativity. Arieti pushed a very similar story to that of Koestler: the truly creative scientist spots a hitherto unrecognized identity between two items, makes them into members of a new class, and then explores the properties of this new class (Arieti 1976: 270–271). But what defines a truly creative piece of science? Arieti conceded that not all scientific discoveries rely on creativity. He reckoned that many rely on mere exploration or technological invention, processes that for some reason he did not judge to be creative (Arieti 1976: 267–268). He limited himself to the depressingly familiar cases: Poincaré, Newton, Darwin, Galileo, Archimedes, and Einstein. He noted the problem that these episodes "seem almost like myths that have grown up around the memory of great men. These stories have the flavor of parables . . . that popular culture has created out of the ideas of these men." Unfortunately, Arieti did not explore the provocative implications of this suggestion about mythmaking. Instead, seeing no reason that these incidents could not have occurred as the parables suggest, he used them as his data (Arieti 1976: 279). But consider two of the more celebrated myths: Newton's apple, which allegedly prompted the discovery of the law of gravity, and Galileo's swinging lamp, which was supposed to have led to the discovery of the isochronism of the pendulum. Arieti ignored the circumstances in which these stories were produced or the history of the process by which isochronism and universal gravitation were established.

The principal source of the story about Galileo watching a swinging lamp in Pisa Cathedral in 1583 is his amanuensis Vincenzo Viviani, writing seventy five years later. Viviani's tale is riven with chronological errors. Galileo began exact pendulum experiments only in 1602. Viviani was prompted to tell a story about Galileo and pendulums because in the late 1650s he was engaged in a furious defense of Galileo's priority in developing the pendulum clock (Drake 1978: 20–21, 68–69, 419–420). The fortune of the tale of Newton and the apple is remarkably similar. The episode allegedly happened in the mid-1660s. Arieti used it to meditate on the difference between Newton's reaction to the fruit and that of a "regressed schizophrenic," who might instead have "thought that the moon could be eaten like an apple or sucked like a maternal breast." Fortunately, so the psychologist tells us, Newton instead creatively induced a new class of gravitating bodies. But the historical record reveals that until the mid-1680s Newton never developed a concept of universal gravitation and stayed firmly wedded to Cartesian and related models of ethereal perturbations of celestial motions. Only in 1684 did he finally invent the term "centripetal" force to describe the action pulling bodies toward their orbits' centers.

The compression of decades of episodic work into a single inspirational moment is utterly characteristic of these parables. The story of the apple was first told from the 1720s in the notes of Newton's disciples, and then institutionalized by his heir after 1797. Doubtless the immediate context of the story was the very violent fight surrounding the achievement, and priority, of Newton's mathematics that raged in the early eighteenth century. As the historian D. T. Whiteside sagely comments, "such are our icons of scientific worship" (Whiteside 1991: 17–19, 46). The continuing power of these icons may well be a topic for psychological inquiry, and the link between their production and the disciplinary defense of heroes' priority is suggestive. But they cannot be used as unproblematic material for the reconstruction of the working processes of scientific achievement.

So discovery starts to look less individual and specific, and more like a lengthy process of hard work and negotiation within a set of complex social networks. Discoveries become events judged significant by the scientific community, and discoverers the individuals those communities wish to recognize (Kuhn 1962). For example, William Bateson found it useful to "revive" Mendel in 1901 because he reckoned he could destroy biometric accounts of continuous variation using Mendel's work. In the 1930s Ronald Fisher baldly stated that "each generation has found in Mendel's paper only what it expected to find" (Brannigan 1981: 99–102; Darden 1977). Discoveries are made up in the course of making the disciplinary histories of specific scientific practices. The process of making up a discovery involves specifying its author, its location, and, most important, its content. This is why a consideration of the work of discovery is so valuable: it will tell us a great deal about how communities of inquirers organize themselves to mark what they count as success. Furthermore, this account of discovery within the functioning of social networks distracts our attention from the tedious debates about the distinction between discovery and invention, between sciences and arts. In what follows it is assumed that discovery and invention are cognate terms, referring to processes of construction and persuasion within the realms of prediction and control of our world.

The balance of this chapter is divided into four sections. The first develops the details of the discovery model that sees it as a label attributed to candidate events by authoritative communities. These attributions are retrospective, so the histories made up by such communities and turned into their canonical traditions are highly significant and productive, and should not be read at face value, nor dismissed as myths. The second section compares two other approaches—that of classical philosophy of science, which concentrates on the distinction between psychological inspiration and rational justification, and that of the psychology of creativity, which seeks to unravel the mental processes that the discoverer's mind is supposed to exhibit. It is argued that both epistemologists and psychologists have been disabled by the demarcation between inspiration and reason, notably because neither side seems able adequately to account for the processes by which discoveries are recognized as such. The third section summarizes and criticizes the orthodox sociological model of scientific discovery, which emphasizes the occurrence of multiple and simultaneous discoveries, and thence deduces the inevitability of scientific progress. Orthodox sociologists have been mistaken in their obsession with a deterministic account of scientific change. In the final section, three episodes of discovery in Britain in the 1840s are used to illustrate the view of discovery in cultural context. The episodes involve discoveries in paleontology, electromagnetism, and celestial mechanics. The chapter closes with some brief suggestions about the means by which the cultural model of discovery can be developed to allow a more general account of the sources of innovation.

Perspiration and Inspiration

In November 1878 Thomas Alva Edison wrote to his Paris agent about the progress of research on electric lighting. Edison reckoned that much more testing was necessary before the "discovery" of electric light could be announced to the world. He said that he needed a big, costly, new testing laboratory "so as to be able to meet and answer or obviate every objection before showing the light to the public or offering it for sale." Then he continued with a description of his own strategy:

> I have the right principle and am on the right track, but time, hard work and some good luck are necessary, too. It has been just so in all my inventions. The first step is an intuition, and comes with a burst, then difficulties arise—this thing gives out and then that—"Bugs"—as such little faults and difficulties are called—show themselves and months of intense watching, study and labor are requisite before commercial success—or failure— is reached. (Friedel and Israel 1987: 28–29)

Statements like these have been grist for many mills: psychologists concerned with the roots of creativity, historians concerned with the process of technical change, business analysts keen to derive methods and forms of training for future innovators, cognitive scientists looking for sequences of mental models. But we have good reason for suspicion. Hindsight does not have a good press, especially in histories of science and technology. Yet retrospection seems to be a constant feature of the stories of invention and discovery, especially those in the sciences. So how are we supposed to read the testimony left by the protagonists of achievement? Edison's caveat in this passage, the phrase "or failure," is crucial. The invention/discovery of electric light was part of long sequences of tentative, absurd, disastrous, and astonishing struggles. Edison was manager of the best private electro-technology laboratory in the world. He was master of key links with financiers and investors, publicists and technicians. Thomas Hughes has rightly judged that Edison's capacity as "systems builder," his ingenious management of extended networks of power, technique, and knowledge, hold the clue to his success as discoverer (Hughes 1983: chapter 2). He is not to be seen as the isolate his own memoirs represent. In fact, Edison used the term "caveats" for his series of research notes. His first "caveat" on electric light was drafted on 13 September 1878. In this note, Edison used schemes drawn from his successful telegraph work to design self-regulators for incandescent metal arcs. Only three days later, long before even these devices were working, a local newspaper announced "Edison's Newest Marvel. Sending Cheap Light, Heat and Power by Electricity." It is unsurprising, therefore, that his waspish assistant, Francis Jehl, would compare the "Wizard of Menlo Park" with P. T. Barnum, and describe him as "a sort of fetish for great masses of people that possess only a popular notion of an art." As Paul David has recently argued, the significance of the vast systems in which Edison plied his trade does not mean that "individuals have no real points of leverage from which to control the outcomes of such a macrocosmic, societal process." It does mean that "Innovation is perhaps less a product of uniquely creative individual attitudes . . . and more a matter of being pivotally situated during those comparatively brief passages of industrial history when the balance of collective choice can be tipped one way or another. Thomas Edison demonstrated this" (Friedel and Israel 1987: 13, 223; David 1992: 176).

The fetishism of discovery and invention is certainly an obstacle to its understanding. The heroic model suppresses the collective, communal features of assessment and judgment. It replaces temporally extended and complex processes involving the assemblage of material resources with an instantaneous "burst," as Edison put it. But, as Edison's splendidly exploitative and self-serving career illustrates, the public mythology of inspiration also does its work. It cannot simply be condemned, but must be explained. Edison's carefully crafted reminiscences closely match the generic "Lives of the Artists" so brilliantly analysed by Ernst Kris and Otto Kurz. In their 1934 study, *Die Legende vom Künstler*, the psychoanalyst Kris and the art historian Kurz laid out the standard and repetitive forms of the "artist's life." They point out that this genre is coextensive with the linkage of art works with authors, and they outline many recurrent features of the type: the innate genius discovered by a well-known master, inducted into the secrets of the trade, recognized by a cunning patron, inspired by an object of desire, and so on. Crucial to this series of mythic tropes is the concept of the "culture hero." The image of the culture hero became particularly important for historical literature. The origin of every artistic technique had to have an "inventor" (Kris and Kurz 1979: 21). Thus each art and technique acquired its genealogy through some founder, who was simultaneously divine and secular, autodidact and dynast. The means through which the image of culture hero solved these complex problems of legitimacy, by granting arts divine status while rendering them comprehensible and replicable, are as relevant to the sciences as the arts. Much recent work on discovery and invention in the sciences demonstrates that retrospection and celebration play key roles in the production of discovery. Because discoveries acquire their status as the result of subsequent work within the relevant community, the "fetishism" of discovery is therefore the consequence of the whole process through which change is analyzed, debated, and assessed. It is all too easy, after all, to demystify these images of the genius. It is better, however, to understand the function they play rather than to dismiss them as utterly illusory. A good way to understand, rather than satirize the heroic model is to relate it to our picture of the way disciplines acquire their *canons*, the sets of exemplary texts and authors that may be said to give the rule of behavior to the discipline. We should study the *invention* of tradition in company with its *demystification*. This applies with some force to recent work on scientific discovery, because, as has been emphasized, this work has concentrated on the ways in which so-called discovery stories get made up out of the collective memory of disciplinary groupings (Schaffer 1986).

It is by no means novel, of course, to suggest that retrospective assessment and disciplinary memory are central problems in the work of science. In his analysis of the standards of evaluation, the philosopher of science Imre Lakatos insisted that such evaluation could be undertaken only in comparisons between sets of theories, research programs pursued through extended time periods rather than between individual and ahistorically constructed theoretical sentences. Whatever the many defects of this account of evaluation, it did at least indicate the ways in which scientists make use of the track record of research programs in the course of their work (Lakatos 1970; Worrall 1982: 161–163; Zahar 1982). It is also rather familiar that retrospective stories play the significant role they do in our models of discovery. Following John Keegan's suggestive phrase, we could call such tales "General Staff Histories." Such a genre attributes decisive roles to certain individualized and prospective intentions located in the minds of the planners of action, construed solely with the benefit of hindsight. Retrospection becomes part of military science. Yet, as Keegan also shows, it is not enough merely to demystify the illusions of these accounts. We can also explore the functions performed by the apparent inevitability with which such stories are produced and read (Keegan 1978: 13–77).

In the history of science, the work of the patriarchal discoverers often needs considerable reinterpretation to make it look like a plausible source of current work in those fields. Mendel, again, is a good example, while that of the early X-ray crystallographers is another. Paul Forman has sensitively analyzed the founding "myth" of this enterprise, as presented in a series of anniversary celebrations of the practice of Roentgen scattering. He argues that in these stories, "an opinion which historically was beyond the fringe . . . becomes in the myth the dominant orthodox opinion in that science. The myth then has that 'widespread' opinion being overthrown by the mythicised event or discovery" (Forman 1969: 71). A similar set of maneuvers is at work even in the short term. Consider Newton's celebrated 1672 paper on his "crucial experiment" designed to demonstrate the heterogeneity of white light and of the link between refrangibility and color. The experiment had first been performed seven years earlier. Newton's description was highly idealized, ignoring most of the detailed protocols of the experiment. Ronald Laymon suggests that the crucial experiment Newton outlined could not have performed its persuasive role in sustaining the "discovery" if the details of the trial were considered, and only overthrew hostile views in its most idealized form. "General Staff Histories" of the debate then suppressed the process of idealization: "once a competition between theories has been decided and a winner chosen, the history of this competition very often is restricted to only the early stages of explicit deduction, where very idealised experimental descriptions are used" (Laymon 1978: 51, 76). This indicates one function for retrospection. Newton's crucial trial only worked in its most emblematic form. The forms it took at the early stages of the optical controversies were absent from official histories. This was how it achieved and retained its persuasive role. By extending and developing this aspect of memory in discovery stories, we can see how retrospection aids the production and reproduction of consensus, authority, and conviction inside scientific communities.

In their studies of these communities, sociologists and social historians of scientific knowledge have emphasized the local, situated character of scientific work. They have been increasingly skeptical of the grand narratives of progress and discovery. They have therefore used the canon as a soft target. Robert Boyle's program for organized experimentation is now represented as the proffered solution to the problems of the Restoration settlement of British government in the 1660s; Newtonian optics as a set of practices that required London-made prisms to work; "phlogiston" and "oxygène" as items whose distribution corresponded to the reproduction of specific instruments such as Priestley's eudiometers and Lavoisier's calorimeters (Shapin and Schaffer 1985; Schaffer 1989; Schaffer 1990). These stories are vulnerable to the following criticism: if concepts gain their meaning so locally, how do they get to work outside their context of production? A realist answer points to that which all possible settings have in common—the real world. A constructivist answer, however, stresses the work that the multiplication of contexts requires. The world must be changed to make local practices work elsewhere.

Here the approach of the biochemist and sociologist Ludwik Fleck is very suggestive. Fleck described science as a system of "thought collectives," recognizable sets of styles and methods that characterized specific fields and that became an integral part of scientists' culture. He used the phrase "directed perception" to describe the effect of enculturation of members in a thought style. The point of this analysis was to investigate discoveries by showing how novel claims become accepted facts for a particular group. Fleck mapped science along a spectrum from relatively esoteric to relatively exoteric constituencies. Along this spectrum he placed the specialist journals of proficient experts, the handbooks of defined disciplines, and the popular statements found in exoteric circles. We might naively judge that facts appear at the specialist end of the spectrum and travel ponderously downward through the handbooks to the popular level. Fleck challenged this picture. Disciplinary facts appeared in handbooks, situated between the immediacy of journals and the generality of the popular (Fleck 1979: 111–112). His important insight was that the popular zone is productive for the work of the esoteric zone, and not a simple consumer of the elite's deliverances. The move from the lab report to the universal knowledge claim will involve forging combinations of "exoteric knowledge, knowledge originating in other collectives, and strictly specialist knowledge." The insight matters because esoteric reports cannot effortlessly be put to use outside their context of production. To make a claim a fact, to make a discovery, it must fit the culture of the thought collective, and it must become "vivid" and "robust," that is, more popular, more exoteric. Claims in journals become well-known discoveries in handbooks through a complex process, deploying exoteric and esoteric elements. "Concepts originating in this way become dominant and binding on every expert." Discovered facts are the most, not the least, social of items (Fleck 1979: 113–119, 122).

Fleck's analysis of "tradition" was especially important for this argument. First, he indicated that the collectivization of novel claims as shared facts effectively erased the interests and senses of initial researchers' work. He gave the example of Lavoisier's notion of chemical element in contrast to that of modern chemistry. Lavoisier is now credited with the discovery of the law of conservation of mass, yet he introduced imponderables like light and caloric as elements. A century after Lavoisier, the great German chemist Wilhelm Ostwald viewed this apparent contradiction between the definition of the element and Lavoisier's notion of caloric or light as a "strange psychological phenomenon," the typical lack of complete vision of the heroic originator. "The ultimate step, which confirms a new idea and rejects old ones, is precisely the one which remains unnoticed and neglected by the creator of the new idea." Fleck attacked Ostwald's psychologism, replacing it with a sociological account: as the concept of chemical element became embodied in a set of familiar techniques and precepts, and embalmed in the chemical textbooks, the original setting in which Lavoisier worked became systematically distant from the new common sense of chemistry (Fleck 1979: 122–123). Second, therefore, Fleck emphasized that the traditional memory of the thought collective should be viewed by the analyst as a productive part of its disciplinary mechanism, not as an embarrassing myth. He made it a key part of the historian's task to study and explicate the functions of disciplinary histories and their public presentation (Fleck 1979: 144–145). This is an invitation that recent historians and sociologists of science have started to accept. Studies of popular declarations on scientific discoveries have progressed from the stage of cheerful endorsement, or mean-minded debunking, to a more considered account of the work of "scientists' accounts" as the reproduction of prized patterns of disciplinary behavior, as "systematic and functional," in Kuhn's felicitous phrase (Kuhn 1962).

The implication of these reflections is that discovery must take its place in an account of the way disciplinary practices build up their canons of heroes. As the sociopsychological studies of Kris and Kurz on the "image of the artist" indicate, there is no reason why this analysis should be limited to the natural sciences. Once we recognize the interpretative and social work involved in making a canon and keeping it sacred, we can project a better account of discovery stories. A historical program for the history of disciplinary discovery is likely to help us reformulate our account of the bearer of knowledge too.

The Man on the Clapham Omnibus

Thus far, we have considered the model of discovery as it has been studied by historians of science. But others, including scientists themselves, own this notion too. Here is a canonical discovery story. Koestler called it "the most important dream in history since Joseph's seven fat and seven lean cows" (Koestler 1964: 118). It was delivered by the chemist August Kekulé at the so-called Berlin Benzolfest held to commemorate the twenty-fifth anniversary of his publication of the structure of benzene:

> During my stay in London I resided for a considerable time in Clapham Road in the neighbourhood of the Common . . . One fine summer evening I was returning by the last omnibus. I fell into a reverie and lo, the atoms were gambolling before my eyes! Whenever hitherto these diminutive beings had appeared to me, they had always been in motion; but up to that time I had never been able to discern the nature of their motion. Now, however, I saw how, frequently, two smaller atoms united to form a pair; how a larger one embraced two smaller ones; how still larger ones kept hold of three or even four of the smaller; whilst the whole kept whirling in a giddy dance. I saw how the larger ones formed a chain, dragging the smaller ones after them, but only at the ends of the chain. I saw what our Past Master, Kopp, my highly honoured teacher and friend, has depicted with such charm in his "Molekular-welt," but I saw it long before him. The cry of the conductor: "Clapham Road," awakened me from my dreaming; but I spent a part of the night in putting on paper at least sketches of these dream forms. This was the origin of structure theory. (Japp 1898: 100)

The man on the Clapham omnibus becomes a hero. The bus conductor, here playing the role of Coleridge's equally celebrated "Person from Porlock," intervenes just in time to compel the visionary to put his reveries on paper, and thus make up the truth. August Kekulé's celebrated reminiscence, delivered in a lecture of 1890 about events that had supposedly happened thirty-five years earlier, has often been analyzed as an exemplary discovery story. Paul McReynolds comments that, inspired by Kekulé's narrative, "recent scholarship has strongly emphasized the prominent role that metaphors and analogies have played in scientific creativity" (McReynolds 1990: 136). And since such discoveries are taken to be the essence of intellectual achievement at its highest pitch, any analysis of a passage such as this will promise a more general account of how the mind can innovate in episodes of breakthrough. Eduard Farber urged that this unique moment contained all the essential details of the real discovery process (Farber 1966). Koestler detected schizophrenic qualities in Kekulé's "hallucinatory flights," while G. E. Hein pointed out the significance of the chemist's training in structural thinking in his early work as an architect (Koestler 1964: 170–171; Hein 1966). There was a consensus that in episodes like these we see the mind at work; that scientific discovery is just such an individualized, localized event; and that its mystery is very much part of its appeal.

More recently, however, analysts have begun to reinterpret these reveries' significance, and have begun to point to their place in a sequence of reasoning processes within the prolonged history of chemical doctrine between Faraday and Ostwald. Kekulé described reveries about giddily dancing atoms that he experienced in 1855 and about circling snakes in 1862, the latter allegedly promoting his formulation of a ring model for the benzene molecule. Margaret Boden perceptively stresses Kekulé's "chemical expertise" as a precondition of the significance of his reveries and notes that his benzene model was confirmed "only after much argument." She also points out that Kekulé's model of carbon bonding in benzene rings, while taken as dominant in the later nineteenth century, is not now the model chemists use (Boden 1990: 50–58). Rather similarly, Howard Gruber points at the *process* rather than the moment of this discovery, and agrees that Kekulé's vision "must be seen as inserted in historical time . . . On that time-scale there was a highly social process of collaboration, controversy and dialogue" (Gruber 1981: 49). Terms such as "collaboration" hold the clue. Discovery comes to be seen as a process susceptible to sociological, historical, and psychological inquiry. Lamb and Easton, in their influential study of the phenomenon of multiple discoveries, insist that the reveries display structures of inference that must not be so compressed as to make of discovery an "occult, creative process" (Lamb and Easton 1984: 32).

The demystification of discovery as reverie is welcome for analysis of the conditions of achievement. The error that Lamb and Easton damn as occultism helps sustain an allegedly self-evident distinction between the so-called context of discovery and the context of justification, that is, between the psychological processes of innovation and the logical work through which innovation is adjudicated. On this showing, dreams are for psychologists, reasons are for philosophers. The distinction is attributed to Hans Reichenbach, who argued in 1938 that epistemology is only concerned with the latter. Reichenbach's notorious distinction is to be understood as a job description for philosophers of science. "It would be a vain attempt to construct a theory of knowledge which is at the same time logically complete and in strict correspondence with the psychological processes of thought," he wrote. "Epistemology thus considers a logical substitute rather than real processes" (Reichenbach 1938: 5). The effects of this exercise in beating the bounds have been profound. The central traditions of Anglophonic philosophy of science have agreed with this definition of their task. Siegel has recently declared that "while Kekulé's discovery of the benzene ring in his sleep may be of great interest for a variety of psychological investigations, all such investigations belong to the context of discovery. The evaluative task—the substantiation of the correctness of the proposed model of the benzene molecule—is *the only concern* that can properly be called epistemological. It alone is appropriate to the context of justification" (Siegel 1980: 300).

We must not mistake the import of these claims. They all tend to force the epistemologist further away from the historical course of scientific action. After all, the production of parables of discovery is certainly connected with the acceptance of these events as discoveries. Siegel's response is that this only makes the process of discovery relevant to the "context of *decision*," to the reasons why scientists actually do adopt new theories; but, Siegel insists, "what we are after in the context of justification . . . is an account that enlightens us as to whether these reasons are *good* reasons" (Siegel 1980: 310). Like Siegel, the philosopher of science Larry Laudan has also stressed the distinction between stages of discovery, pursuit, decision, and justification. Significantly, he made these stages temporally successive moments in the process of science. Scientists discover, then they elaborate, and last they try to justify their work (Laudan 1977: 108–114). Like many of his colleagues, Laudan has intervened in debates on the existence of a "logic of discovery," that is, the existence of a rational account of the discovery process. He rightly states that this debate only makes sense if "discovery" is construed "rather narrowly as concerned with 'the eureka moment,' i.e. the time when a new idea or conception first dawns" (Laudan 1980: 174). McMullin concurs that discovery must be accounted as "the initial creative formulation, prior to the question of explicit assessment" (Nickles 1978: 28).

These divisions between assessment and creativity have their most obvious effect not only in the withdrawal of epistemologists from the process of discovery, but also in the way psychologists describe innovation. Siegel announces that philosophers cannot account for the processes by which innovations are historically produced, while Boden wisely cautions that psychologists cannot provide any account of why particular claims are historically innovative as such. She reckons that the psychological task is the explanation of novelty "with respect to the individual mind" (Boden 1990: 32–34). So this division of labor leaves unanswered the problem of the history of discovery. Look again at Kekulé's dream stories. Their importance in the psychological literature cannot be overstated. Boden points out that "had Kekulé never mentioned his phantom snakes . . . historians of science would never have discovered them" (Boden 1990: 231). At the same time, we may add, had the chemical community not credited, and then publicly honored, Kekulé's model of benzene, then psychologists would not be interested in his "phantoms." Here is the puzzle of retrospection in making up discovery. Psychologists studying scientific discovery are only likely to investigate claims that are later credited.

Kekulé's claims, seen from this perspective, have a very intriguing role. In his historical study of Kekulé's work on benzene structure, Alan Rocke demonstrates how retrospection works. In 1858 Kekulé published a cryptic reference to the "denser" arrangement of carbon atoms in aromatic compounds. But in a paper on aromatics two years later he made no reference to any kind of ring model for benzene isomers and compounds. According to his Benzolfest reminiscence, the reverie about snakes happened after all this, in early 1862. In his first public account of benzene structure, delivered in January 1865, however, he claimed that in his 1858 paper "I did indeed make it appear that I had a completely formed idea" of the benzene structure. So on this showing the model was "completely formed" before the reverie took place (Rocke 1985: 364–365, 367–368; Wotiz and Rudofsky 1984: 721). It is not important whether Kekulé's claim of 1865 is to be preferred to his claim about the reverie made in 1890. What matters is the varying and constructive role played by public memory and long drawn out, collective scientific work.

The benzene story provides other examples of this process. The benzene model was only published after lengthy collaborative work in Kekulé's fine new chemistry laboratory at Ghent and after other chemists began to publish on the topic in the early 1860s. When he did go public for the first time in the January 1865 paper, Kekulé made little of the ring structure and its implication for the positional explanation of the isomerism of benzene substitutes. He did not stress these points, now seen as so crucial, until a paper delivered in May of that year. Even then, as Rocke shows, Kekulé judged the ring to be made up of six *hydrogen* atoms, not carbons as is now thought. The carbon model was only announced in 1866, by Adolf Claus, and then retrospectively attributed to Kekulé ever after (Rocke 1985: 369–371). It is reasonable to ask when the cyclohexatriene model was discovered. The answer depends entirely on what we require of that model. If all we require is that some kind of ring structure for aromatics be described, then Kekulé's originality is in question. If we require something more specific, for example, that there be carbon atoms at the points of the ring, then once again it was Claus and not Kekulé who first announced this. The decision that Kekulé was the true and only begetter of the cyclohexatriene model—and thus the psychologists' decision that his reveries connected with this model are worth studying—is entirely dependent on a complex, lengthy, and collective process of debate inside the European chemical community. Contemporaries recognized this: the relationship between Kekulé's status as authoritative chemical teacher and inspirational discoverer of the benzene ring was much discussed well before he first publicly described his reveries. Certainly Kekulé's dreams had already become a standing joke among German chemists by the 1880s, and featured in a mocking paper on monkeys catching each other by their tails in a spoof publication of 1886 (Wotiz and Rudofsky 1984: 722–723). And at the Benzolfest in 1890, as Ramsay and Rocke emphasize, Kekulé presented his reveries not to simply advertize the role of his own inspirations, but rather to highlight the rational, lengthy, and complex process through which scientific work of any kind comes to be judged as a significant discovery (Ramsay and Rocke 1984: 1094).

It would be unjustifiable and pessimistic to dismiss the 1890 speech from serious consideration, whether historical or psychological. But analysts need to understand what is to be discovered here. The Benzolfest speech did a great deal of disciplinary work. By 1890 Kekulé was "a scientific fossil," the organizers of the Benzolfest set out to make him "a superhuman genius" and the celebration was designed to defend the status of chemistry at a time of major crisis for that science in Germany (Schiemenz 1993). Kekulé's address acted as a counterblast against what were seen as overempirical tendencies in late nineteenth-century scientific methodology. Recall Ostwald's exactly contemporary account, cited earlier, of what he called the "strange psychology" characteristic of heroic discoveries in chemistry (Fleck 1979: 122–123). Kekulé helped raise the status of imagination and deduction in scientific inquiry. His account needs firmly to be placed in the setting of fin-de-siècle debates inside the disciplines of philosophy and psychology. It should not be treated as an innocent account produced in ignorance of the then existing theories of creativity and innovation (Japp 1898: 138; Rocke 1985: 379–380). This is a plea for a reflexive account of the history of psychological and philosophical models of creativity and discovery, and a recognition that these models help innovative communities judge and manage their own discoveries. Debates on the logic and the psychology of discovery have their own history. Laudan has cobbled together a conjectural version of this history. Once upon a time, philosophers such as Bacon and Descartes, Locke and Leibniz all believed that there were rules for discovery. Inquirers could be trained to make discoveries. According to Laudan, they believed this because they believed that true science was infallible knowledge, and so the only way such knowledge could be justified would be by analzying how it was made (Laudan 1980: 176–178). But then, roughly halfway through the nineteenth century, it came to be accepted that science could speak about unobservable entities and was not restricted to empirical generalizations. Electromagnetism and thermodynamics are good examples of sciences that do this. So, too, was Kekulé's version of organic chemistry. Once this had happened, philosophers began to demand less than infallibility from their sciences, and so they gave up looking for a set of rules for aspiring discoverers to follow. At roughly the same time, we may notice, the concept of the scientific genius appeared: that amazing figure whose very lack of discipline allowed great discoveries to be made and then exploited by the mundane and plodding savants (Lauden 1980: 182).

We do not have to accept Laudan's story in all its details. But he is right to point out that until the early Victorian period there was a widespread faith in the existence of teachable rules for making discovery. This claim characterized Enlightenment accounts of the methods of natural philosophy. Joseph Priestley, for one, held that natural philosophers could and should be trained to make discoveries, and argued in his *History of Electricity* (1767) that "the interests of science have suffered by the excessive admiration and wonder with which several first rate philosophers are considered . . . and an opinion of the great equality of mankind in point of genius would be of real service in the present age" (Priestley 1775; II 167–169). And Laudan is also right to argue that nineteenth-century philosophies first subverted and then abandoned this faith. Thus William Whewell declared in front of the British Association for the Advancement of Science in 1833 that "we cannot create, we cannot even direct, the powers of discovery." He reckoned that a hierarchy should be created dividing superior geniuses, who made discoveries, from humbler but well-trained scientists who would follow up and exploit "discoveries which might otherwise expire with the great geniuses who produced them" (Whewell 1833; Whewell 1857: II 368–370). No doubt the division we have been contemplating, between the tasks of psychology and those of epistemology, is also sustained by this Whewellian distinction. It remains disabling to demarcate a rationalist philosophy that adjudicates upon the standards scientists use and a psychology that is forbidden to stray beyond impenetrable moments of illumination. An epistemic distinction between justification, on the one hand, and discovery, decision, and choice of the other, renders that epistemology irrelevant to the explanation of achievement. It also creates major problems for a psychological program that must rely on, but is forbidden to analyze, the ways in which historically significant innovations are judged to be such. We must stop telling stories about discovery that privilege the dreamer on the Clapham omnibus, whose mental life is fit only for psychological processing, and the cool philosopher, who alone will let us know whether we were right to believe the dreamer's visions.

In Search of the Source

As an alternative to this great divide, social scientists have been increasingly concerned with general discovery models that neither lapse into mysticism nor confine themselves to purely evaluative questions. It turns out that the search for discovery methods has not lost its appeal. Quite the reverse: we are witnessing a revival of projects that promise to identify the sources of creativity. We should recall, however, that psychological talk can often be used not to explain discovery, but to explain it away. Here is the Victorian explorer Richard Burton on his rival John Speke:

> We had scarcely breakfasted before [Speke] announced to me the startling fact that he had discovered the sources of the White Nile. It was an inspiration, perhaps: the moment he sighted the [Lake], he felt at once no doubt but that the "Lake at his feet gave birth to the interesting river which had been the subject of

so much speculation, and the object of so many explorers." The fortunate discoverer's convictions were strong, his reasons were weak—and probably his sources of the Nile grew in his mind as his Mountains of the Moon had grown under his hand . . . By a tacit agreement it was, therefore, avoided, and I should never have resumed it had my companion not stultified the results of the expedition by putting forth a claim which no geographer can admit and which is at the same time so weak and flimsy that no geographer has yet taken the trouble to contradict it. (Burton 1860: II 204–209)

In his controversy with Speke about the discovery of the source of the Nile, Burton uses the term "inspiration" in just the opposite sense to that of Kekulé. Burton's insights into Speke's psyche are designed not to credit but to demolish the discovery story. Psychologists have neglected autobiographies of reverie where the reverie did not turn out to be creditworthy. What would (and did) justify the term "discovery" here was the subsequent work of the Royal Geographical Society and the British Association. In the fatal contests between Burton, Speke, Grant, and Baker, the very term "source" changed its meaning. Protagonists variously reckoned that waterfalls, lakes, or springs would count as "the source of the Nile," and they disagreed about whether the label could be justly attached simultaneously to two, or even five, different places. Ingenious shifts retrospectively redefine the character, place, and content of such discoveries. In their fights, protagonists use their own languages of psychology and of sociology: they point to "inspirations" and "corroborations" in equal measure.

The use of psychological analysis to discredit a discovery is at least as intriguing as its use to explain one. In discreditation, a rather different form of psychological vocabulary will be used. Where psychologists of creativity give high value to the individual, to the capacities of bisociation or of creative analogizing, psychologists of delusion will often draw attention toward dogmatic conviction, and thence to issues such as cognitive dissonance. In other words, as Burton's hostile remarks about Speke remind us, the psychologies that are devoted to demolishing a discovery claim will link the claimant with a wider, collective milieu—hence Burton's remarks about Speke's awareness of the interest of "many explorers." Indeed, historians of science have often lapsed into this notion of crowd psychology to deal with otherwise apparently pathological scientific work. A fine example is the episode of 1903–6 during which the French physicist René-Prosper Blondlot and many of his colleagues produced and experimented with a new form of waves called N rays. These rays were produced by a range of incandescent bodies, metals under strain, and, eventually, by animal muscles and human bodies. The best historical account of this debate, that of Mary Jo Nye, explains the apparent success of Blondlot's group in terms of the crowd psychology of early twentieth-century French science: its interests in spiritualism, its fierce national and local pride, and the tight networks of influence and patronage that dominated career patterns at the time (Nye 1980).

It is not immediately clear why the term "psychology" is especially appropriate here. As Nye demonstrates, the N ray episode can be accounted for in terms of conventional social and historical features of scientific debate. The interests at work were also involved in research conducted in prewar France that did not suffer the fate of N rays, such as Becquerel's work on uranium or Curie's on radium. Perhaps psychopathological talk seems necessary because of a certain historical embarrassment about the course of these events. Blondlot's findings were indeed replicated by several other scientists. N rays were so robust that the psychologist Gustave Le Bon claimed priority in their discovery—another intriguing link between this episode and crowd psychology, a science Le Bon helped invent. In a well-known but extremely dubious story, Blondlot's trials were finally demolished when the American physicist Robert Wood visited his laboratory and tricked Blondlot into reporting the presence of N rays even when Wood had covertly removed significant bits of the setup. As Malcolm Ashmore has recently argued in a critical analysis of Wood's strategies, this story of trickery and delusion itself appears in many contradictory versions and in the service of many widely varying philosophies. Social psychology could just as easily be used to explain why Wood's tricks worked as to explain why N rays were ever credible. Why, after all, should a visiting American trickster have been able to destabilize a well-attested laboratory trial? Ashmore comments that here "physics loses out to social psychology; an unreplicated phenomenon [Wood's action] defeats a well replicated phenomenon [Blondlot's N rays]" (Ashmore 1993: 90). Just as psychologists of creativity study the reveries of scientists who do eventually turn out to be creditworthy, psychologists of delusion study the reveries of those who are, later on, judged to have failed. This distinction merely reinforces an asymmetry between the splendors of success and the embarrassments of failure. Such asymmetries are certainly part of the stuff of scientists' judgments when controversies about discoveries are settled. They cannot easily be used, however, to explain how scientists behave during the course of these controversies.

Historians of science have only recently learned to cease their embarrassment about controversies and see them as crucial sites for investigating how scientists work. In controversies, the conventions and assumptions of normal conduct are brought forth for examination. What must invisibly have underlain this conduct now becomes visible. Contests about discovery are excellent examples of this, because in such "priority disputes" the conventions of authorship and authority are most lucidly disputed and constructed. In this sense, priority guides us to the source of discovery—not because we might be concerned with the adjudication of such priority disputes ourselves (though much historical ink has been spilled on such a pointless end), but because the practices that help make up discovery are the practices through which such disputes are resolved. But this is a novel claim, and does not fit well with what has been taken to be the common concern of much sociology of science of the past. Received models of discovery and priority in the sciences have hitherto been obsessed by the twin phenomena of *priority disputes* and *multiple discoveries*. Sociologists have often seen the former as pathological because of the prevalence of the latter. Since multiples are apparently so common, it is absurd, allegedly, for scientists to worry about their priority to the extent they do. Thus in 1957 Robert Merton urged that priority disputes were to be seen as deviations from proper conduct.

> Then begins the familiar deterioration of standards. Reinforced by the group loyalties and often by chauvinism, the controversy gains force, mutual recriminations of plagiary abound, and there develops an atmosphere of thorough-going hostility and mutual distrust. (Merton 1962: 475)

An entire research program in the sociology of science has concentrated on the relationship between the pathology of priority disputes and the ubiquity of multiples. The program had two aims: the correction of errant science, and the insistence that no purely individualist or psychological model of discovery would work. In 1922 the sociologists Ogburn and Thomas listed almost 150 independent multiple discoveries, such as logarithms (by Bürgi, Napier, and Briggs), the nebular hypothesis (by Kant and Laplace), photography (by Daguerre and Fox Talbot), or telegraphy (by Henry, Morse, Cooke, and Wheatstone). They did not distinguish between science and technics. They did concede that "the contribution of one person in some cases is more complete than that of another" (Ogburn and Thomas 1922: 93). They concluded, however, that given the wide distribution of multiples, cultural preparation and technical development were the most important determinants of progress and invention. Merton agreed. In his study of multiple discoveries he attacked the "fallacy of the lone man of science," and claimed that "all scientific discoveries are in principle multiples including those that on the surface appear to be singletons" (Merton 1973: 356). In a satisfying Enlightenment tone, he declared that "once the right path is followed, discoveries in limitless number will arise from the growing stock of knowledge" (Merton 1973: 346). This claim has been influentially endorsed by several sociological studies. In his study, *The Scientific Community,* Hagstrom used anthropological models of gift-giving to understand the occurrence of priority conflicts, and gave Merton's model of universal multiples provisional support (Hagstrom 1965: 12–23). Some forms of epistemological realism, of course, would have no problem with the claim that discoveries have an inevitable quality, since the structure of the world is pregiven. But we should note that the Mertonian claim is much stronger. The pattern of multiple discovery as the result of deterministic social factors explains not only the convergence of discovery but also its timing. At each stage of the zeitgeist, it is claimed, a given set of discoveries will be there to be made. Both psychologism and epistemic realism are to be denied through this account.

The most recent articulation of this model is that of Lamb and Easton. In their important work, *Multiple Discovery,* they argue that multiples govern scientific progress. While denying the realism that would explain convergence as a result of a shared external world, they do describe their approach as "evolutionary realism," because they claim that the direction of scientific development is independent of individual initiative: "science awaits no individual and discoveries emerge and develop in a favorable environment, often in defiance of the strictures of authoritative personalities, restrictive methodologies and canons of rationality" (Lamb and Easton 1984: 24). They go further than did the Mertonians in their challenge to notions of mentalism and genius. Merton had seen outstanding innovators as a simple accelerating device: "The individual of scientific genius is the functional equivalent of a considerable array of other scientists of varying degrees of talent" (Merton 1973: 366). Lamb and Easton respond that individual productivity is an unworkable account of innovative change, since what is in question is the recognition and responsiveness of science to change. Instead, they place all the explanatory weight on the impersonal forces of evolution: "It is not the genius who creates the paradigm, but the paradigm that creates the genius who gives expression to it" (Lamb and Easton 1984: 125). If not genius, then what is this evolutionary force? For these analysts, the list of factors that drive scientific evolution is rather familiar. These include material forces and instrumentation: the discovery of X rays was inevitable (and inevitably multiple) once many late-nineteenth-century workers were using discharge tubes. They also include the level of scientific ideas (here Darwin's use of political economy is often cited) and the preparedness of culture to accept change (Lamb and Easton 1984: 185–195).

These sociological accounts are, in fact, relatively banal. No doubt this gives them some appeal. Even historians not known for their sympathy to a sociological approach have been moved by the story about the prevalence of multiples. Thus, for example, in his detailed account of the notorious priority dispute between Newton and Leibniz, A. R. Hall endorses Merton's analysis of convergence and simultaneity. Hall also enriches the account by pointing to specific features in Baroque natural philosophical culture that may well have prompted the prevalence both of multiples and of priority fights: there were few conventions governing the behavior of the republic of letters; personal honor was associated with original authorship; the progress of learning was not seen as inevitable but as contingent on inspiration and high status (Hall 1980: 6, 255). Like Merton, too, Hall finds priority fights of this intensity a cause of embarrassment: "to examine the last years of the calculus dispute does not increase one's admiration for some of the greatest of mankind . . . It is no surprise to find the dispute concluding amid the futility of offensive wagers, and childish abuse. Who could care?" (Hall 1980: 232). However, at the end of his analysis Hall registers a caution that is of immense significance for all revisionist studies of these questions of multiple discovery. He asks: "did Newton and Leibniz discover the same thing?" This is the nub of the issue. It does indeed, as Hall puts it, open the Pandora's box of the problem of discovery (Hall 1980: 257–259). For this question completely subverts the premise of the Mertonian program. To ask about the *identity* of discoveries is to shift our attention from the allegedly self-evident progress and convergence of science toward the work through which discoveries are authored and authorized. This is an extremely desirable shift. To understand the sources of achievement, we need to understand the means culture uses to assign credit and authority.

Moved by these considerations, more recent studies of the discovery process have rightly abandoned the Mertonian approach. Hostility to the emphasis on zeitgeist has produced some strange bedfellows. Dean Keith Simonton, for example, has recently urged a thoroughgoing psychological account of innovation, focusing on the trial-and-error process of mental reasoning through which new mental models can be developed by individual investigators. It is very much in his interests, therefore, to reject the interpretation of multiples that makes them count against psychologism. So he points out that this stress on zeitgeist overrates the significance of multiple discovery: "multiples" often conceal wide differences in character; discoverers of "multiples" often know of each others' work; the rediscovery of some earlier and neglected work, as in the Mendel case, demonstrates that the milieu cannot account for the origination of the discovery; finally, the Mertonian model treats sufficient conditions for a discovery as though they were necessities (Simonton 1988: 135–148). Simonton is not prepared to give up the story of multiples, however, for he is able to show that they can in fact be generated stochastically, given the right mix of psychological features (Simonton 1988: 149–176). His argument that in discovering work "chance permutations are selectively retained, articulated and disseminated" is less compelling than his critique, however. For the basic claim remains crucial: discovery is at least as much a judgmental process in culture as it is the intrinsic property of some isolated mind.

A recent study by Brannigan and Wanner conclusively demonstrates that the canonical lists of multiples developed by Ogburn, Thomas, and Merton are simply unsound. The problems Simonton identifies, especially the feature of science's history through which discoveries are stipulated as such retrospectively in culture, is well attested (Brannigan and Wanner 1983). Brannigan argues that "all of the judgments and social processes which go into the production of a list of multiples are effaced by the simple serial identification of the discoveries and their claimants" (Brannigan 1981: 152). Recent studies of the Leibniz-Newton controversy, of the discovery of oxygen, and of the early twentieth-century investigation of conditioned responses all show that in controversy actors fight to stipulate relations of identity and difference. In the 1710s, it was crucial for the Newtonian group in London to argue that Leibnizian calculus differed in no significant respect from their master's fluxional techniques. They could show that the Hanoverian court philosopher was incompetent and unworthy of employ in Britain. In the 1730s, when the Newtonians were assaulted by Bishop Berkeley as irreligious, it suited the Newtonians' purposes to argue that the Bishop's criticisms certainly applied to Leibnizian infinitesimals, but that fluxions were good and proper terms in a rational, Anglican mathesis (Shapin 1981; Cantor 1984). Similarly, a catalogue of scientific breakthroughs tells us that in 1774 "Priestley isolates and in a sense discovers oxygen. The oxygen is not recognised as such by Priestley but is interpreted as 'dephlogisticated air'" (Parkinson 1985: 194). But Priestley's "dephlogisticated air" and Lavoisier's "gaz oxygène" fitted into radically different networks, cosmologies, and practices. A perspective that emphasizes the articulation of the meanings of terms in systems of technique is useful here. Priestley made his concept "phlogiston" work via its embodiment in specific instruments and routines, especially the "eudiometer," which measured the phlogiston content of air samples. And phlogiston linked together aerial and moral virtue. The meanings and implications of all these practices were different in Lavoisier's Paris. There, calorimetry rendered the new chemistry sensible and feasible. These two systems were by no means incommensurable, in the Kuhnian sense. It was possible for rational negotiation to proceed between them. But this negotiation involved the persistent definition and redefinition of the significance of terms and practices in local settings. No global account of the "multiple discovery of oxygen" is possible here save through the retrospection of official nineteenth-century historiography of chemistry (Schaffer 1990).

The almost exactly contemporary work on what are now called conditioned responses by Ivan Pavlov and Edwin Twitmyer provides another example of the negotiated sense of discoveries' identity. As Deborah Coon has shown in her study of this work, the 1904 announcement by the Pennsylvania psychologist Edwin Twitmyer of trials of "a new and unusual reflex arc" in stimulating subjects' knee jerks was almost completely ignored by American psychologists, even though it now seems to coincide almost exactly with Pavlov's work on the conditioning of alimentary processes. Coon shows how the immense resources of Pavlov's laboratory helped establish the significance of his work in comparison with that in Philadelphia. She also demonstrates that for Twitmyer himself the work on psychically elicited reflexes had a very different significance from that developed in the 1910s by Pavlov and then by the early behaviorists. William James's influential defense of dualism was an important means through which all such trials on association would be interpreted, and delimited, in prewar American psychological debates. Pavlov's eponymous success, therefore, cannot be accounted as an invisible multiple discovery, but instead as the result of an intriguing change in the culture of the American psychological community (Coon 1982). These reflexions on the practical work through which discoveries are made up should, at last, lay to rest the ghost of multiple discoveries and displace this research site by the more promising one of the authorization and attribution of innovation and change.

The Ends of Discovery

This inquiry into authorization and attribution does not mean that we should give up the search for a more general account of the sources of discovery. The emphasis on the ways discoveries are made up provides real opportunities for the development of models of innovative behavior. It might be fruitful to consider such a model in a specific setting. We would predict that at periods when new social forms are being developed within the sciences, and when, consequently, new accounts of authority and discovery are in the course of construction, debates about priority and innovation would be most fraught. We have seen that the so-called second scientific revolution of the early nineteenth century was such a period, especially with respect to the philosophy of discovery. For it was at this period that the search for a method of discovery was given up, and when, as Whewell observed, the discoverers' elite was now to be distinguished from pedestrian inquirers. Teaching laboratories and research institutions, new disciplines, new rallies of active cultivators of the sciences, and new forms of relation between science and its audiences all emerged. So at this conjecture, too, historians have been able to locate new forms of practice in the allocation of credit and meaning in discoveries. Three celebrated discoveries made in Britain in the 1840s will be considered to show how contemporary ends were satisfied in the course of innovative work. These are the discovery of dinosaurs, of the effect of electromagnetism on light, and of the planet Neptune. Each case presents the characteristic troubles of multiples and priority. Did William Buckland or Gideon Mantell first discover dinosaurs? Did John Herschel anticipate Michael Faraday's detection of the rotation of the plane of polarized light in strong electromagnetic fields? Did the mathematicians Urbain Leverrier and John Couch Adams, or even some humble astronomical observer, really discover the new planet? We will see that their contemporaries' attempts to answer these questions lead us to contemplate the cultural conventions by which the communities of the new sciences plied their trade, and the ends they made their sciences serve.

The discovery of dinosaurs has played a canonical role in stories of multiple discovery and the inevitability of scientific advance. Lamb and Easton treat the work of Buckland and Mantell as an obvious multiple: in 1818 Buckland located "what were later classified as megalosaurus bones" at Stonesfield, while at Tilgate quarry in 1822 Mantell and his wife uncovered a set of fossil teeth, to be baptized "Iguanodon" in 1824. Lamb and Easton reckon that this case sits uneasily with Kuhn's notion of sudden revolution in a crisis, since no great anomaly was recognized here. But they do treat the event as inevitable: "This gradual *intellectual* shift explains why the remains of dinosaurs were found in such large numbers within the space of two decades, after lying peacefully in the earth for several millennia" (Lamb and Easton 1984: 104–105, my stress). Other historians of paleontology agree: in a hagiographic study of the episode, Delair and Sarjeant comment that "inevitably, as the tempo of geological investigation increased around the beginning of the nineteenth century, several further discoveries of dinosaur bones were made before their true nature came to be perceived" (Delair and Sarjeant 1975: 10). But what was "discovered" here? and what is the sense of this term before recognition of "their true nature"? Delair and Sarjeant themselves provide a long list of of prediscovery locations of what we would now judge to be dinosaurs, stretching back to at least the seventeenth century. And Lamb and Easton, who attribute the crucial "intellectual" shift to Cuvier's theory of extinctions, nevertheless acknowledge that the great French paleontologist denied that Mantell's fossils were ancient. Clearly a more sensitive account of early Victorian paleontological culture is required here.

Cuvier and his allies, such as the eminent anatomist Richard Owen, play a key role in the story as the adjudicators of nature's contents and the definers of paleontology's ends. They provide the tribunal before which the facts must be tested. Buckland told Cuvier of his Stonesfield finds by 1820. At this stage, he reckoned they must belong to some reptile, or "fossil lizard." During 1821, he also located "whale-like" bones on the Isle of Wight, and in 1822 he published his Stonesfield find. At the same time, Mantell circulated notice of his Tilgate find. Fellows of the Geological Society reckoned it was piscine, or mammalian. Cuvier, the master anatomist, judged it was a rhinoceros, and, alongside Buckland, told Mantell not to publish. The finds dropped from the news until 1824. Then Mantell, unhappy with the expert assessment of the Tilgate fossils, collaborated with a group at the Hunterian Museum and urged the similarity of these teeth to those of iguanas. His friend Conybeare baptized the fossil "Iguanodon." Cuvier now conceded that this was "a new animal, a herbivorous reptile." At the same period, Buckland gave a significant speech at the Geological Society, in which he at last publicized the name "Megalosaurus" for the Stonesfield bones, a name also coined with Conybeare. In passing, he also mentioned his Isle of Wight find, making much of the similiarity between this and Mantell's "Iguanodon." Does this make Buckland the discoverer of the Iguanodon? Delair and Wilson judge not: "since he did not appreciate their significance until after Mantell's work, the latter was indeed the true discoverer of Iguanodon" (Delair and Sarjeant 1975: 21). This was also what contemporaries judged: when Mantell arranged the presentation of his fossils at the Royal Society of 1825, he was immediately elected a Fellow, and quite rapidly a very large number of other remains were all assimilated under this Iguanodon type.

We see, therefore, that by the late 1820s a "lizard-paradigm" has emerged in British paleontology (Desmond 1979: 227). Under the heading "Megalosaurus" and "Iguanodon," a large quantity of fossil material is organized around the pattern types of very large lizards, perhaps as great as seventy feet in length. Notice that these classes bear little relation to subsequent, or indeed our own, paleontology. Bones from throughout Britain were fitted into these classes. Delair and Wilson note that "Mantell did not realize their novel character and attributed all to Iguanodon" (Delair and Sarjeant 1975: 24). So it is clear that their phrases "recognition of their significance" and "perception of their true nature" are inappropriate here. The expressions do no explanatory work: they add nothing to the Royal Society's actual decision of 1825. What has happened is a collective process, negotiated within the authoritative institutions of early Victorian paleontology—Cuvier's Museum, the Hunterian, the Geological Society, the Royal Society—as to the significance of these finds. We should also note that we remain a long way from "dinosaurs." So Lamb and Easton's conjecture that Cuvier's "intellectual shift" was responsible for the appearance of dinosaurs is wrong: it was responsible for the formation of the "lizard paradigm" of the 1830s.

In a masterly analysis, Adrian Desmond has fully explicated the transformation of the 1830s lizard paradigm into the dinosaur model of the 1840s. Richard Owen is the protagonist, and Desmond stresses the ends he wished to make the fossils serve. The principal end in Owen's strategy was the destruction of French materialist transformism, a target he shared with Cuvier. Both anatomists rejected the morally subversive and theologically dubious doctrine of permanent progressive and continuous evolution. So Owen set out to make the "fossil lizards" into noble and ecologically dominant "dinosaurs," a very different animal. If our contemporary lizards were the dwarfish successors of these once dominant beasts, then transformists' claims for permanent and smooth progress in nature's history would be destroyed. So in 1841, using the prestigious platform of the British Association, Owen declared that "the Megalosaurs and Iguanodons rejoicing in these most perfect modifications of the Reptilian type must have played the most conspicuous parts that this world has ever witnessed in oviparous and coldblooded creatures." He dropped the fossil lizards' size from Buckland's 70 feet to 30 feet by giving them an upright pose and changing the "lizard paradigm" size estimation method. "Dinosaurs" were made up as quadrupeds of almost mammalian aspect, plausible monarchs of a former earth. In this form they were introduced to the Victorian public and their monarch at Crystal Palace in 1854 (Desmond 1979: 225–230). Hence the Victorian "dinosaur." The moral of this story is straightforward: Owen changed the local practices and global models of the earlier paleontologists. He wielded his authority in Victorian culture to do so, and his end was avowedly moral. The "true significance" of the Tilgate bones was a resource to be made up and fought for. This account does not mini- mize—indeed it relies upon—scientists' creativity. But it stresses the cultural and practical ends which that creativity serves.

These ends, we've seen, are articulated in the conventions of con- temporary culture. Owen's dinosaurs were not designed by fiat. Using Fleck's analysis, outlined earlier, we can say that the facts of these dinosaurs were constructed in the zones between popular culture and specialist technique, where the skilled anatomies of the Hunterian Museum could be allied with the crowds at the Crystal Palace. "De- signing the dinosaur" meant producing a tradition, in which Buck- land's fossil lizards were now to be seen as "anticipations" of the truth, and where Gideon Mantell could now be seen as the dinosaurs' discoverer. We can understand the discoveries of the 1840s, therefore, by looking very carefully at the cultural landscape and cultural heroes of the period. In *The Mill on the Floss*, George Eliot described the epoch's conventions and role models:

> Good society has its claret and its velvet carpets, its dinner-
> engagements six weeks deep, its opera and its fairy ballrooms;
> rides off its ennui on thoroughbred horses, lounges at the club,
> has to keep clear of crinoline vortices, gets its science done by
> Faraday, and its religion by the superior clergy who are to be met
> in the best houses. . . .

By the 1840s, Faraday had been canonized as The Discoverer. The label was embalmed in the very title of John Tyndall's hagiography of the Victorian sage. Tyndall would then extend this "Faraday model" to understand other luminaries, such as Edison: "such minds resemble a liquid on the point of crystallization, stirred by a hint, crystals of constructive thought immediately shoot through them" (Friedel and Israel 1987: 223). According to Whewell, Faraday's discoveries in elec- trolysis were "the greatest event which has ever happened in the history of chemistry," an "epoch" through which Whewell was living (Faraday 1971: 297). The discovery of electromagnetism was similarly credited. Herschel echoed Whewell in 1846, insisting that electro- magnetism "affords the second instance which science has witnessed of the complete *concilience* [sic] into one of two separate and previously independent sciences" (Gooding 1985: 233). The career of electro- magnetism would thus be the proving ground for several rival theories of excellent science and its discovery. During the years after Faraday's development of electromagnetic induction in summer and autumn 1831, he rapidly acquired heroic status: Whewell heard Faraday's triumphant introduction of the discovery at the Royal Society in 1834, while the Duke of Somerset wrote to Charles Babbage in 1835 that "the story of Faraday is just one that is sure to make a great noise. There is something romantic and quite affecting in such a conjunction of poverty and passion for science . . . he comes out as the Hero of chemistry" (Heyck 1982: 56). Whewell, for one, wanted to make sure that this romantic story had a moral that suited his purposes. He evocatively described his own survey of the sciences' past to Herschel as "a history of all the physical sciences . . . from Tubal Cain to Faraday" (Todhunter 1876: II 248–249). The mythic role of the Royal Institution professor was an essential element in Herschel's and in Whewell's dealings with him, as for many other contemporaries. As a culture hero, in the sense defined by Kris and Kurz, Faraday became the patriarchal founder of his science, a Victorian Tubal Cain, and his discoveries within it an indispensable resource.

Faraday's announcements of the effect of electromagnetism on light in autumn 1845 played just this role. The "magneto-optical effect" was eventually absorbed into the official tradition of Victorian electromagnetism. It was given a standard reading and a common interpretation. We find this reading, most notably, in Clerk Maxwell's 1873 *Treatise on Electricity and Magnetism*, the textbook of Cambridge physics: Faraday "was acquainted with the method of studying the strains produced in transparent solids by means of polarized light" and "varied these experiments in many ways," so "he succeeded in establishing a relation between light and magnetism." "We shall take Faraday's discovery as our starting point for further investigation into the nature of magnetism" (Maxwell 1891: II 452). Now this canonization effaces the culture in which Faraday's own work was initially performed, and it necessarily suppresses the plasticity of interpretations of that work. In order to make up Faraday's discovery, Maxwell rewrote its history. The research of autumn 1845 stands inside lengthy series of negotiations and collaborations within the electromagnetic networks of early Victorian Britain. These include government-commissioned investigations, conducted at the Royal Institution, on the qualities of heavy glass with a view to improve British optical production; even earlier research, pursued at the London Institution in the 1820s, when investigators such as Herschel, Peter Barlow, Babbage, Davy, and their colleagues all worked hard on relations between light, electricity, and magnetism; and, significantly, the dynamical research of William Thomson, whose address at the British Association in summer 1845 was the immediate and decisive stimulus for Faraday's renewed trials that autumn (James 1985; Gooding 1985; Smith and Wise 1989: 256–257). Thomson used his own collaboration with Faraday to build up ether models of field strain. Despite its fundamental role in the local articulation of the magneto-optic effect in the 1840s and 1850s, Maxwell wrote this "ether dypsomania" out of the history of Faraday's discoveries in his story of the 1870s (Smith and Wise 1989: 260). Equally important was the way in which the concerns of the "London electromagnetic network" simply vanished from the record.

This intriguing disappearing act can be followed through the responses to Faraday's announcement by Herschel and by Whewell. Faraday performed his trials of autumn 1845 in deep secrecy, communicating only with Thomson and forbidding visits to his lab. He released news of his magneto-optical work to Whewell privately in November 1845: "I am sure that when *you* have *this discovery you will understand and appreciate it.*" According to Whewell, the science of electromagnetism was to be defined by its establishment of the fundamental idea of polarity. But Faraday and Thomson would use this work precisely to destroy the polar interpretation of the field (Faraday 1971: 466). So Whewell complained of "the overcharged importance of Faraday's view of his recent discoveries." Clarification of the fundamental idea needed to interpret the magneto-optic experiments required "a clear mathematical head," a theoretical skill that Whewell believed Faraday conspicuously lacked. Whewell asked Herschel whether he might help: "have you seen or repeated Faraday's experiments; and can you get any theoretical hold of them?" (Todhunter 1876: II 334–335). Whewell had to find ways of saving his fundamental idea: an ideal opportunity emerged in a lecture at Faraday's own institution. Making polarity the explanation of magneto-optics demanded Whewell's best rhetoric: "New ideas in science gradually and slowly become clearer and clearer . . . Polarity is a new idea which is not yet clear." Whewell made up a canonical tradition for electromagnetism, and showed a large chart listing the polarities Faraday had identified. But the entry corresponding to magneto-optics and polarization was filled in with a "?" Whewell cleverly placed Faraday's work in its connection with other sciences, with electrochemistry and optics, with crystallography and the wave theory of heat. The challenge that Faraday's recent work seemed to pose to the fundamental idea did not diminish its value as an organizing principle whose meaning was in the course of emergence. But this was a visionary conclusion. Whewell never printed such a chart in his *Philosophy*: he found no map on which to place the work of the Royal Institution's laboratory nor a language with which to describe it.

When Whewell asked Herschel for help, his demand was timely. Herschel was himself engaged in a very fraught exchange with Faraday on just this topic. Herschel told Faraday that back in 1823, at a gathering of the London electromagnetic network, he had already tried this same magneto-optic experiment. At the end of a demonstration of a big new battery at the London Institution, Herschel had then tried to see if light's polarization plane would turn along the axis of a copper coil. "The effect was *nil*." Assuming that Faraday's 1845 trials were in all other respects the same as his own of 1823, Herschel had to explain away his failure. He cited the exhaustion of the battery and the dimensions of the wire. This meant that Faraday counted as the discoverer of magneto-optic rotation. "He who proves, discovers," Herschel wrote (Gooding 1985: 234). As David Gooding perceptively notes in his detailed study of the episode, at this stage Herschel interpreted Faraday's experiments as a routine improvement on his own. But this interpretation was unstable. Discoveries have no fixed meaning. For during winter 1845–46 Herschel learned that, thanks to Thomson's prompting, Faraday had not done more or less what had been tried in the 1820s; he'd done something very different. He had used strong magnetic fields and put dense glass in the field. So now Herschel tried out a new version of the story: the reason the 1823 trial failed was not because of a weak battery, but because of a theoretically significant factor: "a *medium* it appears is necessary." The contrast between 1823 and 1845 showed that Herschel was right to argue that rotations only happen in dense media. If he'd used glass in 1823 he would have discovered rotations. Faraday was sceptical of this view, since he reckoned rotations would happen in a vacuum. But his 1845 trials simply didn't prove this (Gooding 1985: 239). We see that the nature and meaning of discovery varies and that retrospection and judgment are decisive. When traditional stories are constructed to make sense of the discoveries of the past, the practices that generated key phenomena are effaced, and the phenomena themselves only survive in the most idealized form. Thus in autumn 1845, Herschel and Faraday agreed that Faraday had discovered magneto-optic rotations and that Herschel simply lacked good instruments. The weakened battery mattered. In spring 1846 Herschel reckoned that he had proved that these rotations needed dense media, and Faraday accepted that he had more work to do to show they didn't. The weakened battery was forgotten. Gooding sums up: "the identity of an experiment—its importance and significance—is not fixed: it is plastic" (Gooding 1989: 70).

The treatment of Faraday's work by its author, by Herschel, Whewell, Thomson, and Maxwell, shows this plasticity at work. Different features of a candidate set of performances—in this case, polarity, battery strength, strains in the ether, glass density—will be emphasized by different actors with different ends in view. And this is not simply a question of hermeneutic skill; it is a matter of the practical features of the work of discovery with the instruments that culture provides. Our analysis of the sources of discovery must attend to the culture of the research communities in which work is pursued, and to the traditions those communities make up for themselves.

These aspects of communality and canonization are excellently illustrated in our final case of 1840s discovery: the Neptune episode. The narrative of this planet's discovery has all the satisfying features of high tragedy mixed with low farce. At the start of the 1840s, the perturbations of Uranus from its predicted path had become a central concern for the research schools of celestial mechanics. In Britain, this research school was centered in Cambridge's mathematical culture; in France, in the mathematicians of the Academy of Sciences. The key theoretical technology of this program was perturbation theory, and this theory would allow the estimation of the position and motion of a disturbing body beyond Uranus. This was certainly not the only conceivable account: other astronomers postulated ether resistance or the breakdown of gravity at Uranian distances. But such accounts were banned from celestial mechanics (Grosser 1962: 46–49). So in September 1845 the wrangler John Couch Adams handed the director of the university's observatory, Challis, elements of the perturbing body, and passed them on to the Astronomer Royal and Cambridge graduate George Airy the next month. The following summer, the French analyst Urbain Leverrier began work on the problem. In the same month, June 1846, Airy told Whewell of Adams's and Leverrier's work. On Airy's prompting, Challis now began a search, hoping to find a moving star where Adams predicted. In August, Leverrier published complete elements of the body, and, on the suggestion of the amateur astronomer Hind, Challis changed his search method to the one Leverrier recommended, a search for a planetary disc. On 23 September 1846, using Leverrier's method, the Berlin astronomer J. G. Galle found a plausible candidate object; Challis observed it from Cambridge just six nights later (Grosser 1962: 102–117; Smith 1989: 403–407).

Inevitably, given the practical culture of 1840s astronomy, attribution of the planet's discovery was very troubled. In autumn 1846, just months after his remark to Faraday that "he who proves, discovers," Herschel reckoned that "Neptune ought to have been born an Englishman and a Cambridge man every inch of him." The implication was that the new planet should be recruited to the cause of celestial mechanics, not that of observational astronomy. The Royal Society initially judged otherwise: with criticism of Airy's delay and Challis's incompetence ringing throughout Britain, they awarded the palm to

Leverrier. Two years later, a similar award was given Adams, almost entirely due to Airy's prompting (Grosser 1962: 118–138; Smith 1989: 414–417). The tale plays an exemplary role in all models of discovery. It raises the pair of problems we've seen connected to all discovery stories: the question of the inevitability of multiple discoveries; and the question of the mental habits of the successful discoverer. First, the problem of multiples. The Mertonian program judges this a classic multiple. The discovery of the extra-Uranian planet, it is urged, was obviously inevitable given the state of astronomical technique. Lamb and Easton even allege, absurdly, that Adams's work "was not published largely because of the prevailing distrust of mathematics in England" (Lamb and Easton 1984: 79). But we have already noted, in the cases of dinosaurs and of magneto-optics, that the "identity" of alleged multiples is a matter of negotiation within research communities. So here, Adams's predicted path for the planet was very different from that of Leverrier. The judgment that they made "the same" prediction was a question to be settled by the astronomical community (Simonton 1988: 138). Even more intriguingly, the orbit of the planet after autumn 1846 deviated markedly from either prediction. The American astronomers Peirce and Walker reckoned that "Neptune is not the planet whose orbit was calculated by Leverrier and Adams, but a different one which happened to be in the same neighbourhood" (Pannekoek 1953: 134). In America, this critique was influential: there, Neptune was neither Cantabrigian nor Parisian. The attack mounted by American astronomers on the boasts of European scientists were used as part of a campaign to stress the autonomy and worth of the scientific enterprise of the New World (Smith 1989: 419; Hubbell and Smith 1992). The new planet was thus made to serve many purposes, and the data that described it could not command universal assent. The case well illustrates the way in which cultural resources make up discoveries and their authors.

A similar reflection applies to the problem of discoverers' success and the existence of a logic or a psychology of discovery. The proponents of celestial mechanics could have abandoned the inverse-square law given the challenge Uranus posed. But they didn't, and instead hypothesized a perturbing planet. Doesn't this show that loyalty to a research program and its methods is the essence of successful discovery? Philosophers such as N. R. Hanson have certainly reckoned so (Hanson 1958: 204). But Leverrier used just the same technique to predict the existence of a planet, Vulcan, between the Sun and Mercury, in order to explain the precession of the latter's perihelion. The prediction prompted a lengthy search, whose futility was only to be demonstrated after Einstein's work of the 1910s (Brannigan 1981: 31).

The search for discovery's source cannot rely on stipulations of good method. Nor, for reasons we have already rehearsed, are we likely to get much help from a psychological approach that would treat the "discoverer of Neptune" as possessed of a creative mentality, while viewing the "visionary of Vulcan" as a deluded dogmatist, even though both the discoverer and the visionary were the same man. We rely, descriptively, on the cultural resources that help make up these events, and we note that among these resources are the contemporary accounts of philosophy and psychology available to the community of the time. A recent study by Robert Smith elucidates the relation between the Cambridge philosophy of discovery of the 1840s and the Neptune events there. Smith shows that the Cambridge network that dominated celestial mechanics at the time reckoned that Cambridge was the right site for the new planet's discovery. They did so because of their Whewellian conception of discoverers' status as the intellectual elite. Hence Herschel's chauvinism, Airy's otherwise inexplicable delays and secrecy, and the energy with which Adams's claims were (successfully) urged against the French rivals and American heretics. The character of Neptune in Victorian celestial mechanics relied on these resources and these models (Smith 1989: 421).

In this triad of discovery episodes, we have adopted a thoroughgoing descriptivism. We have sought to map the maneuvers and techniques that resulted in the stabilization of a discovery and a discoverer. We face the typical problem, discussed above, of the localism of the sociology of knowledge. How is such local agreement ever rendered more general? The peril is real but avoidable. Historical models can be constructed that allow us to understand the common features of such episodes and the ways in which local techniques are made to work elsewhere. Here are two suggestions for further research on this basis:

1. We have stressed the significance of the radical changes in scientific formation in the 1840s. Among these, we can single out the appearance of "research schools," organized and formal systems of research training and inquiry. These were centered in teaching labs, observatories, museums, and hospitals. The research schools allow us to understand, in each case, how the local resolution of discovery was rendered general, and where the great division between discoverers and technicians was created. Attribution of discovery celebrates exemplary practices. Owen's comparative anatomy, Faraday's experimental electromagnetism, and Adams's celestial mechanics were all such examples. Just to the extent that these practices could be embodied in training programs and then rendered general, so these men were judged discoverers and their discoveries displayed in the text-

books of new disciplines. Faraday's privacy, for example, was an initial obstacle to the production of consensus around his work. When commemorated in the training regimes at Maxwell's Cambridge, and not until then, Faraday became the discoverer of a phenomenon whose implications were standardized in the dynamical theory of the electromagnetic field. So a good site for further research will be the emergence and structure of these training regimes and research schools. Work by historians such as Geison and Morrell is fundamental here. In his brilliant study of the success of Liebig's chemistry teaching lab and the failure of that of Thomas Thomson in the early nineteenth century, Morrell is able to give a provisional list of the features that make such regimes work: a charismatic director of established reputation launches research around a well-defined problem in an expanding field; the regime can promise fast training, rapid publication, and good career prospects; links with support staff should be robust and reliable (Morrell 1972). Geison developed this account into a general set of models of research schools' success (Geison 1981). With the collective and cultural focus on discovery, this approach is a promising one, for it draws our attention toward the cultures that promote innovation and the ways these changes are recognized and defined.

2. The significance of support staffs in research schools indicates a second area for inquiry. Between 1830 and 1870, and especially in the period of the Great Exhibition (1851) and subsequent Crystal Palace displays, the very term "scientific instrument" began to acquire its various special senses (Warner 1990: 86–88). Since the attribution of discovery is a marking out and celebration of exemplary practices, we can follow these practices as they become embodied in robust and mobile pieces of equipment. Recall how Owen wrecked the earlier "lizard paradigm" method of estimating animal size, by substituting simple scaling with a complex method of counting vertebrae. The dinosaur discovery was also the authentication of this method. Similarly, the "triumph" of celestial mechanics, through which Leverrier "found a planet at the bottom of his inkwell," helped make perturbation theory the central technique in which Cambridge mathematicians were to be trained and examined. It became part of what Andrew Warwick calls the "theoretical technology" of Cambridge mathematicians, just as Adams became their cultural hero (Warwick 1992: 631–634). This suggests that a project on the sources of innovation and discovery should study the close collaborations between researchers, instrument makers, technicians, and distributors, for these collaborations are the sources of innovations' varying meanings. The strength of links between support staffs and researchers sustains the standardization of their cultural practices.

We see this very clearly in the work of Howard Becker on innovation and routine in art worlds, and the recent studies by Steven Shapin on lab technicians in the seventeenth century (Shapin 1988). Becker and Shapin point to the significance of the labor relations of sites of production; the instruments and techniques used; and, as Becker puts it, the claim that in major innovations "people experience them as a choice among alternative institutional arrangements and working companions rather than as an inventive and creative leap." It follows that "changes in art occur through changes in worlds. Innovations last when participants make them the basis of a new mode of co-operation, or incorporate a change into their ongoing co-operative activities. Innovations begin as, and continue to incorporate, changes in an artistic vision or idea. But their success depends on the degree to which their proponents can mobilize the support of others" (Becker 1982: 298, 309–310). Instruments and the work patterns in which they are implicated help make up discoveries: they provide the resources with which discovery work is defined. And they also help propagate the discoveries, for to share a cultural hero is a key part of belonging to the same cultural group. Studying research and training institutions, support staffs, and instrumentation may well advance our understanding of the way in which changes in arts—and sciences—are really changes in worlds.

Acknowledgments

I thank Margaret Boden, Rob Iliffe, Nick Jardine, Steve Shapin, and Andy Warwick for their generous help.

References

Arieti, S. 1976. *Creativity: The Magic Synthesis.* New York: Basic Books.

Ashmore, M. 1993. "The Theatre of the Blind." *Social Studies of Science* 23: 67–106.

Barber, B. 1961. "Resistance by Scientists to Scientific Discovery." *Science* 134: 596–602.

Barnes, B. 1982. *T. S. Kuhn and Social Science.* London: Macmillan.

Becker, H. 1982. *Art Worlds.* Los Angeles: University of California Press.

Boden, M. 1977. *Artificial Intelligence and Natural Man.* Brighton: Harvester.

Boden, M. 1990. *The Creative Mind: Myths and Mechanisms.* London: Weidenfeld and Nicolson.

Boring, E. G. 1961. "Fechner: Inadvertent Founder of Psychophysics." *Psychometrika* 26: 3–8.

Brannigan, A. 1981. *The Social Basis of Scientific Discoveries.* Cambridge: Cambridge University Press.

Brannigan, A., and R. A. Wanner. 1983. "Historical Distribution of Multiple Discoveries and Theories of Scientific Change." *Social Studies of Science* 13: 417–435.

Burton, R. F. 1860. *The Lake Regions of Central Africa,* 2 vols. London.

Cantor, G. N. 1984. "Berkeley's *The Analyst* Revisited." *Isis* 75: 668–683.

Coon, D. J. 1982. "Eponymy, Obscurity, Twitmyer and Pavlov." *Journal of the History of the Behavioral Sciences* 18: 255–262.

Darden, L. 1977. "William Bateson and the Promise of Mendelism." *Journal of the History of Biology* 10: 87–106.

David, P. A. 1992. "Heroes, Herds and Hysteresis in Technological History: Thomas Edison and the 'Battle of the Systems' Reconsidered." *Industrial and Corporate Change* 1: 129–180.

Delair, J. B., and W. A. S. Sarjeant. 1975. "The Earliest Discoveries of Dinosaurs." *Isis* 66: 5–25.

Desmond, A. J. 1979. "Designing the Dinosaur: Richard Owen's Response to Robert Edmond Grant." *Isis* 70: 224–234.

Drake, S. 1978. *Galileo at Work.* Chicago: University of Chicago Press.

Faraday, M. 1971. *Selected Letters,* ed. L. P. Williams. Cambridge: Cambridge University Press.

Farber, E. 1966. "Dreams and Visions in a Century of Chemistry." *Advances in Chemistry* 56: 129–139.

Fleck, L. 1989. *Genesis and Development of a Scientific Fact.* Chicago: University of Chicago Press.

Forman, P. 1969. "The Discovery of the Diffraction of X rays by Crystals: A Critique of the Myths." *Archive for History of the Exact Sciences* 6: 38–71.

Freidel, R., and P. Israel. 1987. *Edison's Electric Light.* New Brunswick: Rutgers.

Geison, G. L. 1981. "Scientific Change, Emerging Specialties and Research Schools." *History of Science* 19: 20–40.

Gooding, D. 1985. "He who Proves, Discovers: Herschel, Pepys and the Faraday Effect." *Notes and Records of the Royal Society* 39: 224–244.

Gooding, D. 1989. "History in the Laboratory." In F. James, ed., *The Development of the Laboratory.* London: Macmillan, 63–82.

Grosser, M. L. 1962. *The Discovery of Neptune.* Cambridge, MA: Harvard University Press.

Gruber, H. E. 1981. "On the Relation between 'Aha Experiences' and the Construction of Ideas," *History of Science* 19: 41–59.

Hagstrom, W. O. 1965. *The Scientific Community.* New York: Basic Books.

Hall, A. R. 1980. *Philosophers at War: The Quarrel between Newton and Leibniz.* Cambridge: Cambridge University Press.

Hanson, N. R. 1958. *Patterns of Discovery.* Cambridge: Cambridge University Press.

Hein, G. E. 1966. "Kekulé and the Architecture of Models." *Advances in Chemistry* 56: 1–12.

Heyck, T. W. 1982. *The Transformation of Intellectual Life in Victorian England* London: Croom Helm.

Hubbell, J. G., and R. W. Smith. 1992. "Neptune in America: Negotiating a Discovery." *Journal for the History of Astronomy* 23: 261–292.

Hughes, T. P. 1983. *Networks of Power.* Baltimore: Johns Hopkins University Press.

James, F. A. J. L. 1985. "The Optical Mode of Investigation: Faraday on Matter and Light." In F. James and D. Gooding, eds., *Faraday Rediscovered.* London: Macmillan, 137–162.

Japp, F. R. 1898. "Kekulé Memorial Lecture." *Journal of the Chemical Society* 73: 97–138.

Keegan, J. 1978. *The Face of Battle.* Harmondsworth: Penguin.

Koestler, A. 1964. *The Act of Creation.* London: Hutchinson.

Kris, E., and O. Kurz. 1979. *Legend, Myth and Magic in the Image of the Artist.* New Haven: Yale University Press.

Kuhn, T. S. 1962. "Historical Structure of Scientific Discoveries." *Science* 136: 760–764.

Lakatos, I. 1970. "Falsification and the Methodology of Scientific Research Programmes." In I. Lakatos and A. Musgrave, eds., *Criticism and the Growth of Knowledge*. Cambridge: Cambridge University Press, 91–195.

Lamb, D., and S. M. Easton. 1984. *Multiple Discovery: The Pattern of Scientific Progress*. Amersham: Avebury Press.

Laudan, L. 1977. *Progress and Its Problems*. Los Angeles: University of California Press.

Laudan, L. 1980. "Why Was the Logic of Scientific Discovery Abandoned?" In T. Nickles, ed., *Scientific Discovery, Logic and Rationality*. Dordrecht: Reidel, 173–183.

Laymon, R. 1978. "Newton's *Experimentum Crucis* and the Logic of Idealization and Theory Refutation." *Studies in History and Philosophy of Science* 9: 51–77.

McReynolds, P. "Motives and Metaphors: A Study in Scientific Creativity." In David E. Leary, ed., *Metaphors in the History of Psychology*. Cambridge: Cambridge University Press, 133–172.

Maxwell, J. C. 1891. *A Treatise on Electricity and Magnetism*, 2 vols., 3rd ed. Oxford: Clarendon.

Merton, R. K. 1962. "Priorities in Scientific Discovery." In B. Barber and W. Hirsch, eds., *The Sociology of Science*. New York: Free Press.

Merton, R. K. 1973. *The Sociology of Science*. Chicago: University of Chicago Press.

Morrell, J. B. 1972. "The Chemist Breeders: The Research Schools of Liebig and Thomas Thomson." *Ambix* 19: 1–46.

Nickles, T., ed. 1978. *Scientific Discovery: Case Studies*. Dordrecht: Reidel.

Nye, M. J. 1980. "N-rays: an Episode in the History and Psychology of Science." *Historical Studies in Physical Science* 11: 126–156.

Ogburn, W. F., and D. S. Thomas. 1922. "Are Innovations Inevitable?" *Political Science Quarterly* 37: 83–98.

Olby, R. 1979. "Mendel no Mendelian?" *History of Science* 17: 53–72.

Pannekoek, A. 1953. "The Discovery of Neptune." *Centaurus* 3: 126–137.

Parkinson, C. L. 1985. *Breakthroughs: A Chronology of Great Achievements in Science and Mathematics*. London: Mansell.

Priestley, J. 1775. *History of Electricity*, 3rd ed. London.

Ramsay, O. B., and A. J. Rocke. 1984. "Kekulé's Dreams: Separating the Fiction from the Fact." *Chemistry in Britain* 20: 1093–1094.

Reichenbach, H. 1938. *Experience and Prediction*. Chicago: University of Chicago Press.

Rocke, A. J. 1983. "Subatomic Speculations and the Origin of Structure Theory." *Ambix* 30: 1–18.

Rocke, A. J. 1985. "Hypothesis and Experiment in the Early Development of Kekulé's Benzene Theory." *Annals of Science* 42: 355–381.

Rudofsky, S. F., and J. H. Wotiz. 1988. "Psychologists and the Dream Accounts of August Kekulé." *Ambix* 35: 31–38.

Ryle, G. 1949. *The Concept of Mind*. London: Hutchinson.

Schaffer, S. 1986. "Scientific Discoveries and the End of Natural Philosophy." *Social Studies of Science* 16: 387–420.

Schaffer, S. 1989. "Glass Works." In D. Gooding et al., eds., *The Uses of Experiment*. Cambridge: Cambridge University Press, 67–104.

Schaffer, S. 1990. "Measuring Virtue: Eudiometry, Enlightenment and Pneumatic Medicine." In A. Cunningham and R. K. French, eds., *The Medical Enlightenment of the Eighteenth Century*. Cambridge: Cambridge University Press, 281–318.

Schaffer, S. 1990a. "Genius in Romantic Natural Philosophy." In A. Cunningham and N. Jardine, eds., *Romanticism and the Sciences*. Cambridge: Cambridge University Press, 82–98.

Schiemenz, G. 1993. "A Heretical Look at the Benzolfest." *British Journal for the History of Science* 26: 195–205.

Shapin, S. 1981. "Of Gods and Kings: Natural Philosophy and Politics in the Leibniz-Clarke Disputes." *Isis* 72: 187–215.

Shapin, S. 1988. "The House of Experiment in Seventeenth-Century England." *Isis* 79: 373–404.

Shapin, S., and S. Schaffer. 1985. *Leviathan and the Air Pump*. Princeton: Princeton University Press.

Siegel, H. 1980. "Justification, Discovery and the Naturalizing of Epistemology." *Philosophy of Science* 47: 297–321.

Simonton, D. K. 1988. *Scientific Genius: A Psychology of Science*. Cambridge: Cambridge University Press.

Smith, R. 1989. "The Cambridge Network in Action: The Discovery of Neptune." *Isis* 80: 395–422.

Smith, C., and M. N. Wise. 1989. *Energy and Empire: A Biographical Study of Lord Kelvin*. Cambridge: Cambridge University Press.

Todhunter, I. 1876. *William Whewell: An Account of His Writings*. London: Macmillan.

Warner, D. J. 1990. "What Is a Scientific Instrument, When Did It Become One and Why?" *British Journal for the History of Science* 23: 83–93.

Warwick, A. 1992. "Cambridge Mathematics and Cavendish Physics." *Studies in History and Philosophy of Science* 23: 625–656.

Whewell, W. 1833. "Address." *Report of the Third Annual Meeting of the British Association*. London, 1834.

Whewell, W. 1857. *Philosophy of the Inductive Sciences*, 3rd ed. London: Parker.

Whiteside, D. T. 1991. "The Prehistory of the *Principia* from 1664 to 1686." *Notes and Records of the Royal Society* 45: 11–61.

Worrall, J. 1982. "The Pressure of Light: The Strange Case of the Vacillating Crucial Experiment." *Studies in History and Philosophy of Science* 13: 133–171.

Wotiz, J. H., and S. Rudofsky. 1984. "Kekulé's Dreams: Fact or Fiction." *Chemistry in Britain* 20: 720–723.

Zahar, E. 1982. "Logic of Discovery or Psychology of Invention?" *British Journal for the Philosophy of Science* 34: 243–261.

Chapter 3

Where Do New Ideas Come From?

Gerd Gigerenzer

In 1928, Karl Popper submitted a dissertation on the psychology of thinking, in which he defended the pluralism of Karl Bühler's psychological research methods, including introspection, against Moritz Schlick's physical reductionism. Bühler and Schlick were his doctoral advisors. Popper (1979, p. 106) later asserted that he was so embarrassed by his dissertation that he never looked at it again. This dissertation marked the end of Popper's brief fascination with the psychology of research and thinking. A few years later, in his *Logik der Forschung* (1935), he had already eliminated the psychology of research as a genuine topic from his philosophy of science. Popper denied the very existence of the object named in the (strangely translated) English title of his book, *The Logic of Scientific Discovery* (1959):

> The question of how it happens that a new idea occurs to a man—whether it is a musical theme, a dramatic conflict, or a scientific theory—may be of great interest to empirical psychology; but it is irrelevant to the logical analysis of scientific knowledge. . . . Accordingly, I shall distinguish sharply between the process of conceiving a new idea, and the methods and results of examining it logically. As to the task of the logic of knowledge—in contradistinction to the psychology of knowledge—I shall proceed on the assumption that it consists solely in investigating the methods employed in those systematic tests to which every new idea must be subjected if it is to be seriously entertained. . . . My view of the matter, for what it is worth, is that there is no such thing as a logical method of having new ideas, or a logical reconstruction of this process. My view may be expressed by saying that every discovery contains "an irrational element", or "a creative intuition", in Bergson's sense. (pp. 31–32)

Many of Popper's contemporaries came to associate discovery with irrationality and lucky guesses, romanticized as fundamentally mysterious. New ideas somehow emerge in dreams, rainstorms, beds, and the like. In contrast, justification of new ideas came to be associated with logic, mathematics, and statistics. Popper bequeathed the study of discovery to psychology and sociology, perhaps because of his deep, postdissertation distaste for these fields "riddled with fashions, and with uncontrolled dogmas." His critique of Thomas Kuhn betrayed a similar sentiment: "the idea of turning for enlightenment concerning the aims of science, and its possible progress, to sociology or to psychology (or, as Pearce Williams recommends, to the history of science) is surprising and disappointing" (Popper 1970, pp. 57–58).

Popper's sharp and asymmetrical distinction between the contexts of discovery and justification (either discovery isn't worthy of serious study, or those who study it aren't worthy of serious attention) has provoked a literature of protest in science studies, protests that insist upon the relevance of discovery to justification. In this paper, I take issue with Popper's distinction from the opposite side: I shall argue that in modern psychology, and quite plausibly in other disciplines, justification influences discovery.

My thesis is that scientists' tools for justification provide new metaphors and concepts for their theories. In what follows I will present a case study of how theories of mind were discovered after experimental psychologists became familiar with new tools for data processing, and not, as one might expect, with new data. New tools, I would like to argue, tend to be used by scientists as a source of new ideas—a heuristic of discovery that I have called the *tools-to-theories heuristic* (Gigerenzer 1991).

The related point that experimental practice has a life of its own, emphasizing instruments, techniques, and skills, has been recently put forward against the theory-dominated view of science. Gooding, Pinch, and Schaffer introduced their *Uses of Experiments* (1989) with the claim that experiments are "more interesting and significant than the received stories about science imply" (p. xiv). Hacking (1983, p. 150) advocated a back-to-Bacon movement, emphasizing that measurements and experiments do not always test theories, and that observation can precede theory. According to Gooding (1989, p. 192), "What experimenters actually *did* in order to construct observable, publicly accessible phenomena will sometimes influence how they *thought* about the outcomes of their experiments."

My thesis is twofold: (1) *Discovery:* New tools for justification can motivate new metaphors and concepts, once they are entrenched in the professional routine of a given scientist. (2) *Acceptance:* Once the new tool-laden metaphors and concepts have been proposed by an individual scientist (or group), they are more likely to be accepted in the general scientific community if its members share the professional routine that motivated the new metaphors and concepts.

I will restrict my analysis to one important laboratory practice, the statistical analysis of experimental measurements. I will begin with a discussion of Egon Brunswik's probabilistic functionalism, the first case known to me where a new statistical tool compelled its user to perceive the mind as an *intuitive statistician,* using the same tools as the researcher. Brunswik epitomizes the case of discovery without acceptance. Afterward, I will analyze cases of discovery with broad acceptance.

Probabilistic Functionalism

In 1927, one year earlier than Popper, Egon Brunswik (1903–1955) submitted his dissertation to the University of Vienna, indeed to the same advisors, Bühler and Schlick. Like Popper, Brunswik attempted to resolve the conflicting ideas of the two. Bühler asserted that in order to study language, thinking, and other cognitive functions, it is necessary to study all of three aspects, *Erleben* (the world of inner experience), *Benehmen* (the world of behavior, physical and physiological), and *Gebilde des objektiven Geistes* (the objective world of written documents etc., which anticipates Popper's "third world"). Schlick, in contrast, insisted that all of psychology must be reducible to physical concepts. While Popper sided with Bühler in his dissertation, Brunswik tried to strike a compromise between the incompatible theoretical positions of his mentors. Given their differences, this was no small task. Bühler, for instance, concluded from his research that the relationship between the object-world and perception (*Erleben*) is fundamentally ambiguous. The same color is perceived differently if placed against backgrounds varying in color. Similarly, words do not have fixed meanings. Particular meanings at any given time, he said, can only be inferred from the sentence or narrative in which a word is embedded. In contrast, Schlick and members of the Vienna Circle contended that scientific language not only should but could be reduced to a neutral observational language; that is, to invariant sense-data referents. They maintained that each scientific term must have one and only one sense datum (or one set) as a referent. For Brunswik, a participant of both Bühler's famous Wednesday and Schlick's Thursday discussion groups, these contradictory positions triggered an intellectual crisis (Leary 1987).

Brunswik sided with Bühler on the issue of ambiguous cues. But overall he was looking for some compromise, which he found in Hans Reichenbach's argument that all human knowledge is probabilistic.

Brunswik's experimental work can only be fully understood against this background. The important point here is that in the late 1930s, Brunswik changed his techniques for measuring *perceptual constancies*, that is, measuring the degree to which perception approximates or, as Brunswik preferred to say, "achieves" the physical world when background and context are varied. Originally, Brunswik's experimental research was in Bühler's tradition. Typically, he would ask subjects to judge one target variable (e.g., the size of a coin, the area of a rectangle), while systematically varying one or more context variables (such as the value of the coin, the shape of the rectangle). Brunswik found perceptual constancy to be consistently less than perfect, for example, the size of a coin was overestimated if its face value was large (Brunswik 1934). This fits nicely with Helmholtz's notion that perception is unconscious inference. Because all proximal information (such as the size of the retinal image of a coin) is ambiguous with respect to the coin's actual size, perception necessarily relies on further cues (such as value) which have come to be associated by experience with the intended variable (the size, in this case). The degree to which perception achieves the variable intended, that is, the degree of perceptual constancy, was measured by what later became called the *Brunswik ratio* (a function of the difference between judgment and actual physical size).

In 1937, Brunswik accepted a position at Berkeley, and started to use the tools of the English statistical tradition of Francis Galton and Karl Pearson. He replaced the Brunswik ratio with correlation and regression statistics. Perceptual achievement, that is, the degree of correspondence between perceptual judgment and physical size, was now measured in terms of the correlation between the two, and measurements were taken in a natural environment where context variables floated freely. This contrasted sharply with his earlier work in which he systematically varied only one or a few context variables, while keeping all others constant. Similarly, the degree to which a person utilizes a cue (such as the value of a coin) when making a judgment about the intended variable (such as the size of a coin), was measured by a correlation. So was the ecological validity of cues, the degree to which a cue is indeed a reliable indicator of a target variable. This resulted in a new experimental practice—the representative design—that had not been used before to analyze perceptual achievement (Brunswik 1940, 1955). The goal of this enterprise, which he termed *probabilistic functionalism*, was to determine to what degree an organism is adapted to a world that it only perceives through uncertain cues.

After Brunswik started to use the new statistical tools in the late 1930s, he began to think of an organism in new terms, namely as an *intuitive statistician* (Gigerenzer 1987). In the same way that the Brunswikian researcher measures achievement, the perceptual system was supposed to unconsciously calculate correlations and regressions to infer the structure of the world from ambiguous cues. Not only was Brunswik the first to use these tools for analyzing perception in terms of achievement, cue utilization, and ecological validity, he was also the first to propose the analogy between statistical tool and mind.

Brunswik's ideas received much attention at the time, only to be generally rejected. Why? Correlation and regression statistics had become Brunswik's indispensable tools, but these were not the indispensable tools of his colleagues from the experimental community. Even worse: correlation and regression, as opposed to techniques of isolation and control, were the indispensable tools of the experimenters' rival community, "correlational" or "differential" psychologists, who studied individual differences in intelligence and personality. The schism between the "Holy Roman Empire" of correlational psychology and the "Tight Little Island" of experimental psychology, as Cronbach (1957) put it, had been repeatedly taken up in presidential addresses before the American Psychological Association (Cronbach 1957; Dashiell 1939). The lack of esteem on both sides has been well documented (Thorndike 1954). Brunswik could not persuade his colleagues of the experimental community to accept the statistical tools of the rival community as a model of how the mind works. Ernest Hilgard, one of the leading experimenters at the time, did not mince words in his discussion and rejection of Brunswik's ideas: "Correlation is an instrument of the devil" (Hilgard 1955, p. 228).

Lack of acceptance went hand in hand with lack of understanding. In his time, Brunswik's program and his analogy between statistical tool and mind were generally incomprehensible to his colleagues (Gigerenzer 1987). In the German-speaking world that Brunswik had left, no equivalent divide between rival communities with competing methodological imperatives existed. In America, Brunswik saw his idea of an organism as an intuitive statistician fall into the chasm between the two established communities. As Edwin Boring, the dean of the history of psychology, put it, "Brunswik was a brilliant man who wasted his life" (cited in Hammond 1980, p. 9). In 1955, after a series of articles appeared criticizing his probabilistic functionalism and bristling with incomprehension, Egon Brunswik committed suicide. He never lived to see the spectacular success of his idea of the mind as an intuitive statistician that was to come. Ironically, the success was borne on the shoulders of the tools against which Brunswik had fought in vain: the experimental and statistical tools of Sir Ronald A. Fisher.

New Tools: The Inference Revolution

Two decades after Brunswik had changed his investigative practice, almost all experimental psychologists had, with the exception of a few dissidents, adopted new tools of experimentation and statistical inference. The direction of change was not Brunswikian, it was Fisherian. David Murray and I have called this revolution in research practice the "inference revolution" (Gigerenzer and Murray 1987), because it established statistical inference as the sine qua non of scientific method in psychology.

Textbooks after the inference revolution of the 1950s have been consistently silent on the radical change in research practice that occurred at that time. Yet there is an intriguing story to be told here. The nineteenth century knew at least three major types of psychological experimentation, exemplified by Wilhelm Wundt's experimental psychology (including introspection) in Leipzig, Francis Galton's anthropometry in London, and Charcot's experimental hypnosis in Paris (Danziger 1990). Among the experimental practices added to this list in the first half of the twentieth century were the demonstrational experiment as used in Gestalt psychology, the two types of Brunswikian experiments described above, and the treatment group experiment that flourished in the 1920s and 1930s in the United States. The inference revolution eliminated all this pluralism and institutionalized one kind of practice, the randomized treatment group experiment, as the only authoritative method of psychological research in the United States. A decade or two later, this streamlining wave overran European psychology as well, although with less force.

There are two keys to understanding what happened and why. First, psychologists' marketing of their methods to the education industry in the United States; second, R.A. Fisher's doctrine that experiment and statistics are two sides of the same coin. Regarding the first, professors in the United States in the first half of this century felt a much stronger pressure to legitimatize their activity as practically useful than did their German colleagues (Danziger 1990). The U.S. educational system was the major consumer for marketable methods. Questions that educational administrators had to answer, such as whether a new curriculum would result in better average achievement in a classroom, could not be answered by the Wundtian experiment. In a Wundtian experiment, a single person—always a highly trained and experienced observer such as Wundt himself—was investigated by means of systematic introspection and controlled experimentation. Wundt aimed to explore the causal laws of the mind. In contrast, the educational administrator focused on *average achievement* rather than on *causal mechanisms* of the mind, and the subjects under observation were a flock of pupils rather than professors and Ph.D.'s. The Wundtian experiment proved practically useless as a marketable method and was soon replaced by the treatment group experiment, which was more amenable to practical application. A treatment group experiment used two (or more) groups of subjects (such as two classrooms). One group, the treatment group, received, say, a new instructional method. The other group, the control group, received the old instructional method. By comparing the difference between the averages in each group against some measure of random variation, a statistical decision could be made concerning the superior instructional method.

Danziger (1990) has documented the rise of studying group averages and the fall of single-case experiments such as the Wundtian paradigm. For instance, in the *American Journal of Psychology*, a journal of basic research, the percentage of empirical studies reporting group data only rose from 25% in 1914–16 to 35%, 55%, and 80% in 1924–26, 1934–36, and 1949–51, respectively. If the assertion that marketable methods fueled the rise of the treatment group experiment is correct, then these figures should have skyrocketed earlier in the applied journals. This is indeed the case. For instance, in the *Journal of Applied Research* and the *Journal of Educational Psychology*, the percentage of empirical studies reporting group data exclusively was already 77% and 75%, respectively, in 1914–16, and rose above 90% in the 1930s. The new research practice spread from the applied fields to basic research.

The second key for understanding the inference revolution is Fisher's (1935) doctrine that experiment and statistics must be understood as a single, integrated whole. Key features of the statistical model, such as repetition, independence, and randomization, had to be incorporated into the experimental design. Fisherian statistics—more precisely, significance testing—fit the new treatment group experiment as if it were tailor-made for it. The use of many subjects instead of one or two corresponded to the principles of repetition and independence, and the analysis of group averages seemed to be the natural domain of significance testing. The treatment group experiment only lacked the element of randomization, which could easily be added. Psychologists now owned a powerful, marketable experimental method and an equally powerful technique of statistical inference: the "method of science," as it was (mistakenly) called in their textbooks and journals.

Randomized experiments and statistical inference were such a perfect match that they virtually ruled out all competitors. To Brunswik's chagrin, statistics became tied to the principles of experimental control and isolation, rather than to the analysis of achievement in natural environments. Statistical inference, in particular Fisher's significance testing, later merged with Neyman-Pearson hypotheses testing, and became institutionalized in textbooks, university curricula, and editorials of the major journals. By the early 1950s, half of the psychology departments of leading universities in the United States had already made inferential statistics a requirement in their graduate programs (Rucci and Tweney 1980). By 1955, more than 80% of the empirical articles in four leading journals used Fisherian significance testing (Sterling 1959). Editors demanded significance testing in prospective articles, and used the level of significance as a measure of the quality of research (e.g., Melton 1962). Students could no longer get Ph.D.'s and researchers could no longer publish articles without playing with the new tools.

The overwhelming force of that inference revolution was reflected in the difficulties encountered by the small group of dissidents. Consistent with the marketing-methods thesis, which implies that new tools spread from applied fields into basic research, the main resistance came from some of the most distinguished researchers. B. F. Skinner, for example, ordered his fellow behaviorists to follow him rather than Fisher. The statisticians "have taught statistics in lieu of scientific method" (Skinner 1972, p. 319). Despite being at the height of his career at the time, Skinner and his followers were forced to found a new journal in 1958, the *Journal of the Experimental Analysis of Behavior*, in order to be able to continue publishing experimental data on one or a few pigeons, without group averages and statistical inference. This resistance was not unique to behaviorists, nor to researchers with as little statistical training as Skinner. R. Duncan Luce, one of the foremost mathematical and statistical psychologists of our time, also reports that a major reason that he and his colleagues founded the *Journal of Mathematical Psychology* in 1964 was to escape the editors' pressure to perform the same ritualized methods of statistical testing in a mindless and nondiscriminating manner (Luce 1989).

The inference revolution has reinforced the *inductivist* philosophy in psychological research. In Fisher's (1935) words: "Inductive inference is the only process known to us by which essentially new knowledge comes into the world" (p. 7). And he equated inductive inference with disproving null hypotheses by means of significance testing. I have always wondered why there seems to have been so little exchange between the logical positivists proclaiming the inductive approach to science, such as Carnap and Reichenbach, and the English statistical school of Fisher and others, whose methods could actually make the program work. Despite the lack of internal contact, Fisher's and Popper's programs have often been portrayed as similar. The major reason being that Fisher's system entails the same asymmetry as Popper's, namely that a hypothesis can never be proved, only disproved (whatever the latter means in statistical testing). (Of course, this reading of Popper's method as disproving null hypotheses does not do justice to the Popperian program of setting up a bold theory and trying to falsify it.) The textbooks' success in presenting scientific method as a monolithic truth, by merging Popper with Fisher, and Fisher with Neyman and Pearson and other statistical approaches, allowed experimental psychology in the United States to define itself as a predominantly inductivist enterprise. As we shall see, the inductive bias has reappeared in the tool-laden theories of mind.

New Ideas: The Cognitive Revolution

The cognitive revolution of the 1960s did more than overthrow behaviorism in the United States and rehabilitate earlier mentalist concepts. It has redefined the mental per se. One source of the discontinuity was new tools, statistics and computers, that suggested new ideas about the mind. In earlier work, I have already traced in some detail the transformation of the mind as a function of the tools-to-theories heuristic (Gigerenzer 1988, 1991, 1992; Gigerenzer and Murray 1987). The following two examples are drawn from that work.

Causal Reasoning: Mind as Statistician
David Hume's dictum was that causal relations cannot be legitimately inferred from observation alone. The mind does, however, infer them. What kind of causal relations does the mind perceive willy-nilly? By what mechanisms is phenomenal causality forced upon us? Before the inference revolution, several European psychologists had addressed these and related questions. Albert Michotte ([1946]1963) analyzed how certain temporal-spatial relations between visual objects, such as moving dots, produced phenomenal causality. The Gestalt psychologists, in particular Karl Duncker ([1935]1945), analyzed conditions of phenomenal causality beyond spatial and temporal contiguity, such as correspondence of form and material. Jean Piaget (1930) worked on the development of causal reasoning in children.

After the inference revolution in the United States, Harold H. Kelley (1967, 1973), from the University of California, Los Angeles, discovered a new idea. He proposed in his *attribution theory* that the long-sought laws of causal reasoning are in fact the familiar tools of the behavioral scientists: R.A. Fisher's analysis of variance (ANOVA).

> The assumption is that the man in the street, the naive psychologist, uses a naive version of the method used in science. Undoubtedly, his naive version is a poor replica of the scientific one—incomplete, subject to bias, ready to proceed on incomplete evidence, and so on. Nevertheless, it has certain general properties in common with the analysis of variance as we behavioral scientists use it. (Kelley 1973, p. 109)

Kelley assumed that when attributing a cause to an effect, the mind calculates an analysis of variance with three independent variables, which he called person, entity, and circumstances (time and modality). These are classes of possible causes. For instance, in a study by McArthur (1972), subjects were given the following information:

> Paul is enthralled by a painting he sees at the art museum. Hardly anyone who sees the painting is enthralled by it. Paul is also enthralled by almost every other painting. In the past, Paul has almost always been enthralled by the same painting. (p. 110)

Subjects were asked what caused the effect (being enthralled by the painting). Is the cause located in Paul (person), the painting (entity), the particular circumstances (time), or some interaction of these factors? The information provided to the mind's supposed intuitive ANOVA specified the covariation of the three independent variables—person, entity, and circumstances—with the dependent variable, the observed behavior. In the above example, the data given is that others disagree with Paul, which is called *low consensus;* that Paul responds equally to all paintings, which is called *low distinctiveness;* and that Paul is consistent over time, which is called *high consistency.* From such information Kelley concluded that the mind calculates causal inferences similar to the way social scientists do, by calculating F-ratios (after *F*isher), the ratio of between-conditions variance to error variance.

> The first criterion (distinctiveness) seems to correspond to the numerator or between-condition term in the usual F-ratio and the last three criteria (consistency over time, modality, and persons) correspond to the error or within-condition term. As a measure, then, of a person's state of information regarding a

given entity, the theory suggests an analogue of the F-ratio in which the degree of differentiation between the various entities is compared with the stability of attribution (based on the consistencies and consensus) with respect to the given entry. (Kelley 1967, p. 198)

In the above example, distinctiveness is low (small variance across paintings), consensus is low (high variance across persons), and consistency is high (small variance over time). Therefore, the F-value is low for entity and circumstances (time), but high ("significant") for person, and the subject should perceive the cause in the person.

By the time Kelley publicized his analogy between the analysis of variance and causal reasoning, almost all articles in the major experimental journals used techniques of statistical inference, and in about 70% of these cases, ANOVA was used as a tool for statistical inference and for justifying causal claims (Edgington 1974). The theory of the ANOVA-mind was quickly accepted by Kelley's colleagues from the experimental social community, and causal attribution became one of their central research topics. Kelley and Michaela (1980) could report more than 900 references in one decade. Unlike Brunswik's intuitive statistician, Kelley's intuitive statistician used the tools of his experimental community, not those of a competing one.

Let us now look at some "fingerprints" of the tool, to show how radically the vision of the Fisherian mind has changed understanding of and research on causal reasoning.

1. *Kinds of causal reasoning.* The work of Michotte reflects the Aristotelian conception of four kinds of causes—formal, final, material, and efficient cause. Piaget (1930) even distinguished seventeen kinds of causal relations in children's thought. By analogy with the tool, the Fisherian mind focused on only one kind of cause, the very cause that ANOVA promises to identify (similar to Aristotle's material cause).

2. *Nature of causal reasoning.* According to Michotte and the Gestalt theorist, causal perception is direct, spontaneous, and needs no inference—this is largely due to laws inherent in the perceptual field. ANOVA, however, is used in psychology as a tool for inductive inferences from data to hypotheses. Consequently, the causal reasoning of the ANOVA-mind proceeds by inductive inference, from data to the potential causes as hypotheses. Causal reasoning became data-driven induction.

3. *How to study causal reasoning?* ANOVA needs repetitions or numbers as data, in order to estimate variances. Consequently, to investigate causal reasoning, subjects were presented with

information about the frequency of events (see above), which played little role in Piaget's, Michotte's, and Duncker's work. Finally, the experimental tests of hypotheses concerning the ANOVA-mind (e.g., Do consensus and distinctiveness information have the same impact on causal inference?) were also performed by ANOVA. This circularity is a direct consequence of the tools-to-theories heuristic employed by Kelley, and had Brunswik succeeded, the same circularity would apply.

Practical Context versus Mathematical Structure
The reader might object that this case study does not illustrate how features of the practical context of justification projected onto features of the mind. It might equally well illustrate that psychologists were quick in realizing that a mathematical structure (such as ANOVA) emulates precisely how the mind really works. Some of my experimental colleagues have criticized my analysis using this and similar arguments (Jungermann and Wiedemann 1989; Schulz 1989). It is not easy to convince someone who believes that today's theory of X fits exactly how X is, that such a splendid theory might mirror something in addition to reality pure and simple.

Two points will demonstrate that the tools-to-theories heuristic cannot be used to defend a spurious neo-Platonism. The first concerns the existence of different *methodological preferences* between research communities—an issue relevant in Kelley's as well as in Brunswik's case. Analysis of variance was institutionalized in experimental psychology, whereas correlation and factor analysis were the indispensable methods of differential psychology. I conjecture that there is no a priori reason why analysis of variance should be a more appropriate model of causal attribution than factor analysis. Both tools have been used in their respective communities to identify causal relations. Kelley repeatedly credited the German emigrant Fritz Heider for having motivated his theory of causal attribution. Yet Heider (1958, pp. 123, 297) had talked about an implicit "factor analysis," albeit metaphorically. In truth, Kelley did not follow Heider, nor did he extend Heider's factor analysis metaphor. Heider, like Brunswik, came from a German-speaking background, where no comparable schism between two communities with different methodological imperatives existed. Although perhaps inspired by Heider, Kelley's theory of mind incorporated the statistical tools familiar to him and his colleagues in the U.S. experimental community.

The second point involves the distinction between the mathematics and the application of a statistical tool. An institutionalized routine of justification has two components: mathematics and a shared understanding of its application. The application of a tool is generally underdetermined by the mathematics. For instance, nothing in the mathematics of a significance test (as an analysis of variance) instructs the experimenter to use the test to reject hypotheses or to reject data (so-called outliers). Researchers must find means to solve both problems: they must get rid of bad hypotheses and bad data.

Experimental psychologists have used significance tests exclusively for testing hypotheses, and not for testing data. This approach is perceived as consistent with both Fisher's and Popper's emphasis on rejecting hypotheses. Researchers, in contrast, have handled dubious data informally, relying on judgment rather than statistics. Statistical texts for psychologists are uniformly silent on the problem of faulty data. When calculating an analysis of variance, experimenters trust the data (the error is taken care of by the error term in the F-ratio) and mistrust the hypotheses. By analogy, the mind was alleged to use the tool in the same way: trusting the information given (the data), and testing hypotheses.

In other disciplines and in other periods, significance tests were used to test data, not hypotheses. In early nineteenth-century astronomy, for instance, significance tests were standard practice (Swijtink 1987). Astronomers, however, used significance tests to reject bad data (outliers), trusting, at least provisionally, in their hypotheses (such as the hypothesis of a normal distribution of observations). As a thought experiment, assume that the astronomers' practice rather than the current practice had been institutionalized during the inference revolution. If some researcher had argued that the mind itself used the new tools, then causal reasoning would have been perceived as theory-driven rather than data-driven. Both in Kelley's real case and in our thought experiment, the mathematics attributed to the mind are the same. But in each case, the mind calculates for a different purpose. In our thought experiment, the mind would use the mathematics for the same purpose as the astronomer: to select between good and bad (or reliable and false) observation and information—on the basis of some at least provisionally accepted causal hypothesis.

Kelley's analogy between tool and mind stimulated a research program of gargantuan proportions in the 1970s and 1980s (Fisch and Daniel 1982). In the United States, causal attribution became one of the central research topics in social psychology, even to the point of defining the discipline. Fisher's claim that experimental design and statistical analysis are inseparable and indispensable to scientists had been projected onto the mind. Attribution is a "lay version of experimental design and analysis" (Jones and McGillis 1976, p. 411). Variants of the homunculus statistician were proposed. Ajzen and Fishbein (1975), for instance, argued that the homunculus is a Bayesian rather than a Fisherian. Last but not least, the analogy between tool and mind helped to support the individualism inherent in most of social psychology in the United States. Justified by the analogy, research could focus on the individual mind rather than on social interaction. In designing experiments and calculating statistical tests, social interactions did not seem to play a substantial role for the experimenter, nor did they seem pertinent to the mind's causal reasoning.

I will now provide a second case study, from an area that seems to be completely independent of experimental social psychology.

Sensory Detection and Discrimination: Mind as Statistician
One of the most fundamental concepts in the experimental psychology of the nineteenth century and the first half of the twentieth century was that of a sensory "threshold." Since Herbart (1816), detection of a stimulus (Is there a sound or not?) and discrimination between two stimuli (Which coin is heavier?) have been explained using the threshold metaphor. Detection occurs only if the effect a stimulus has on the nervous system exceeds a certain threshold value, the "absolute threshold." Detecting a difference (discrimination) between two stimuli occurs if the excitation from one stimulus exceeds that of the other by an amount greater than a "differential threshold." Fechner (1860) had used differential thresholds (also called "just noticeable differences") to construct a scale of sensation intensity. He defined the intensity of sensation as the number of differential thresholds, from the absolute threshold to the sensation being measured. Fechner assumed that thresholds were fixed, otherwise they could not be used to calibrate a yardstick of sensation. To Titchener (1905), the differential thresholds were his sought-after elements of the mind (he counted about 44,000 such elements). The central role of the threshold concept in psychophysics and beyond is surveyed in Gigerenzer and Murray (1987).

After the inference revolution, the psychophysics of thresholds was revolutionized by the metaphor of the mind as a statistician. W. P. Tanner and J. A. Swets suggested that the process of detecting a stimulus or discriminating between two stimuli is analogous to deciding between two statistical hypotheses (Swets 1964; Tanner and Swets 1954). Their *theory of signal detectability (TSD)* posited that the mind "decides" whether there is a stimulus or only noise, just as a statistician of the Neyman-Pearson school decides between two hypotheses. In Neyman-Pearson hypotheses testing, two sampling distributions (hypotheses H_0 and H_1) and a decision criterion are defined. The data observed is transformed into a likelihood ratio, and compared with the decision criterion (which is also a likelihood ratio). Depending on which side of the criterion the data fall, the decision "reject H_0 and accept H_1," or vice versa, is made. In straight analogy, the theory of signal detectability explains how the mind detects a weak "signal" against a background of "noise." The mind calculates two sampling distributions for "noise" and "signal plus noise" based on previous experience, and then sets its decision criterion accordingly. Just as a statistician of the Neyman-Pearson school sets the decision criterion according to cost-benefit considerations (the relative costs of Type I and Type II errors), mental detection and discrimination are assumed to depend on similar cost-benefit considerations (the two possible decision errors are now called "misses" and "false alarms"). The sensory input is transduced into a language that allows the brain to calculate its likelihood ratio, and depending on which side of the criterion the ratio falls, the subject says "no, there is no signal" or "yes, there is a signal." Tanner and his colleagues, like Kelley and Brunswik, made their analogy between mind and statistical tool explicit. Tanner (1965) referred to his new view of the mind as a "Neyman-Pearson" detector, and, in unpublished work, his flow-charts included a homunculus statistician performing the unconscious statistics of the brain (Gigerenzer and Murray 1987, pp. 49–53).

The new analogy between mind and statistical tool was so forceful that it toppled the century-old concept of fixed thresholds, radically changing our understanding of the nature of detection and discrimination. Here, for illustration, are three fingerprints of the tool:

1. *Nature of detection and discrimination.* The concept of a threshold came to be replaced by the twin notions of observer's attitude and observer's sensitivity. Just as in Neyman-Pearson statistics, the subjective element (e.g., cost-benefit considerations that define the decision criterion) is distinguished from a mathematical element, so did detection and discrimination come to be understood as involving two analogous elements: attitudes such as cost-benefit considerations, and sensory processes.

2. *New research questions.* The new analogy made new questions thinkable. For instance, what conditions cause changes in the mind's decision criterion? Experiments were conducted on vision and hearing that suggested that the mind adjusts the decision criterion as a function of factors such as monetary payoffs and instructions concerning the relative danger of misses and false alarms (e.g., Green and Swets 1966; Swets 1964). These experiments empirically contradicted the notion of fixed thresholds.

Seen from the new perspective, earlier research had confounded sensory and nonsensory processes in the "threshold"
explanation.

3. *New kind of data.* In Fechner's classical *method of right and wrong
cases,* a threshold was defined as that physical value corresponding to a specified percentage of correct "greater" judgments. The
data generated were those percentages of correct "greater" judgments (i.e., the percentage of "right cases," which is the complement of the percentage of wrong cases, because they add up
to 100%). Similarly, in L. L. Thurstone's (1927) influential *law of
comparative judgment,* the data generated were the percentages of
right cases. In the modern language of signal detectability, the
traditional data in psychophysics were the hit rate, and its
complement, the percentage of misses. A statistician of the
Neyman-Pearson school, however, deals with two kinds of
errors, Type I (false alarm) and Type II (misses). Consequently,
the new analogy between mind and statistician made the
eneration and analysis of both kinds of errors indispensable,
a practice that was not common before in the study of sensory
processes.

The theory of signal detectability recast psychophysics in the image
of techniques introduced by the inference revolution. It was quickly
generalized to other cognitive processes, including memory (Wickelgreen and Norman 1966; Murdock 1982) and eyewitness testimony
(Birnbaum 1983).

As in the case of Kelley's causal attribution theory, the new idea did
not originate from incomprehensible mysteries of creativity or, as
Popper (1959, p. 278) once declared, from guesses "guided by the
unscientific." Quite the contrary, it originated from what experimental
psychologists used to call, following Fisher's rhetoric, the "method of
science" (e.g., Kelley 1973, p. 109). Nor did the new idea originate
from new data, pace the inductivist view held by so many experimental scientists. The situation was the opposite of inductivism. *The new
analogy between mind and tool in fact contradicted the available data of one
of the longest research traditions in psychology.* In their first exposition of
the theory of signal detectability, Tanner and Swets (1954) explicitly
admitted that their new theory "appears to be inconsistent with the
large quantity of existing data on this subject" (p. 401). The incom-
patibility of the new theory with the old data did not prevent its broad
acceptance. As I have discussed, the theory of signal detectability
relied on conceptual tools that changed the kind of data generated in
experiments on vision and hearing. The old data became as obsolete

as the old theory. The new tool created a new theory, and along with the new theory, a new kind of data.

The Mind as Intuitive Statistician

These two case studies illustrate the profound change new tools of justification can work upon theory. In the 1960s, 1970s, and 1980s a broad range of cognitive processes were redefined through the analogy with statistical inference, including pattern recognition, adaptive memory, problem solving, and information processing (for an analysis of the conceptual change, see Gigerenzer 1991; Gigerenzer and Murray 1987). The spectrum of tool-laden theories ranges from largely metaphorical analogies to more or less precise replicas of the statistical tools. Usually the view of the mind as an intuitive statistician is linked to the metaphor of the mind as an intuitive scientist. The two metaphors are often used by psychologists as interchangeable, despite the fact that scientists—such as physicists, chemists, and molecular biologists—rarely if ever use the statistical tools institutionalized in psychology.

The English perceptual psychologist R. L. Gregory, for instance, a major contemporary proponent of the Helmholtzian tradition, is referring to the methods of science when he says that "perception is similar to science itself" (Gregory 1980, p. 63):

> The cognitive strategy carried out by brains is not so like what physics *describes* as it is like the *methods* of physics. More specifically, it is surely scientific *method* which is the best paradigm we have of how data can be used for discovering the nature of things and predicting from past experience—by building and selecting predictive hypotheses. (Gregory 1974, pp. xxvii–xxviii)

What is the method of science that the brain uses? Gregory (1974, p. 525) refers to Fisher's dictum that inductive inference is the only way to get new knowledge about the world. Consequently, Gregory refers to the mind as an "induction machine" or "betting machine" that uses the (new) tools of the experimental community in psychology. Gregory asks why perceptual forms are stable even if visual information is ambiguous. His answer is not surprising: "We may account for the stability of perceptual forms by suggesting that there is something akin to statistical significance which must be exceeded by the rival interpretation and the rival hypothesis before they are allowed to supersede the present perceptual hypothesis" (p. 528). Gregory's "induction machine" is an eclectic statistician who uses Fisherian significance testing as well as Neyman-Pearson and Bayesian statistics, without clearly distinguishing between these various tools. This eclectic mind mirrors the eclectic teaching of statistics, which conflates competing views into one, apparently uncontroversial, monolithic tool.

One reason for the psychologists' rather parochial view of the matter seems to be that their statistical textbooks, echoing Fisher's rhetoric, teach that statistical inference coupled with Fisher's experimental design is the method of science.

The examples of discovery I have dealt with here are modest compared with the canonical literature in the history of science concerning the ideas of a Copernicus or a Darwin. Nevertheless, in the narrower context of recent cognitive psychology, the theories I have discussed, as well as others based on the analogy between mind and statistics not dealt with here, count among the most influential. In this more prosaic context of discovery, the tools-to-theories heuristic can account for a range of significant theoretical innovations.

Conclusions

These case studies draw attention to a neglected source of new ideas: scientists' tools. The present thesis explicates discovery in terms of the tools-to-theories heuristic, and acceptance in terms of the reputation, familiarity, and credibility of a tool in a given scientific community. I will conclude with a discussion of a few general implications.

Institutionalized Rituals of Scientific Justification

The mechanical, routinized methods (as opposed to the logical analysis) of justification have met with little interest from philosophers of science (Nickles 1989). I believe that the institutionalization of statistical inference in psychology and beyond—in parts of empirical sociology, education, medicine, archaeology, biology, and most of the social sciences—provides a key example for such rituals of justification. From the several models of experimentation and statistical inference available in the statistical literature, psychologists forged one methodological imperative during the inference revolution. Some of the social reasons for this selection process, such as generating marketable methods, have been pointed out above (see also Danziger 1990). It is worth noting that textbooks used to teach statistics to psychologists are rarely written by statisticians. For the most part, psychologists received their training from statistical textbooks written by psychologists who virtually never discuss extant competing statistical theories. Instead, these textbooks usually present an anonymous and incoherent mishmash of Fisher's significance testing and Neyman-Pearson hypotheses testing, billed as *the* method of justification. Having been taught that statistics is statistics is statistics, the community came to be persuaded of the tool's universal applicability and credibility (Gigerenzer et al 1989).

I was trained as an experimental psychologist and was taught this monolithic methodological imperative. I have been taught that statistical significance defines when an effect is "real" and a difference is a "fact." Thereby I entered a world of statistical illusions, which are not accidental, but necessary to sustain the authority and power of the tool. Examples of these illusions can be found in textbooks and editorials, and range from confusing a result that is "statistically significant" with a result that is replicable, real, reliable, or significant in terms of its effect size, to the equally deluded belief that there is one and only one best method of statistical inference (Gigerenzer 1993). Mechanical use of statistics—as opposed to statistical thinking—and statistical illusions, however, were the prices experimenters were willing to pay for the authority gained by an institutionalized tool that seems synonymous with scientific method itself.

From Institutionalized Tools to Compelling Theories
Under the heading "Realising Nature," Gooding, Pinch, and Schaffer (1989) begin with the observation: "Experimental strategies are epistemologically compelling when they rely on methods and assumptions which are not themselves being challenged by the audience to which they are addressed" (p. 13). On my account, this observation can be extended to the origins and acceptance of theories as well. Theories become epistemologically compelling when they are modeled after methods and practices that are sacrosanct to the audience being addressed. Generally, the tools-to-theories heuristic can explain how the institutionalized practice of justification leads to the discovery of corresponding metaphors of mind and, at the same time, forms the basis of their acceptance. In the case studies, I gave a few examples of features of the institutionalized tools and their standard use, such as the inductivist ethos and the illusion that there is only one statistics, that have left clear traces in the new theories advanced (see Gigerenzer 1991).

Which Comes First, Discovery or Justification?
There seems to be an obvious answer to this question. First, an idea has to be discovered, and then methods of justification enter the scene to test the new idea. In the debate on whether discovery is a genuine topic for understanding science, for instance, both sides in the debate have construed the issue to be whether the earlier stage of discovery

should be added to the later stage of justification (Nickles 1980). In contrast, I have described a situation in which methods of justification come first, and discovery follows. Here the context of justification explains the context of discovery.

References

Ajzen, L., and Fishbein, M. 1975. "A Bayesian Analysis of Attribution Processes." *Psychological Bulletin* 82: 261–277.

Birnbaum, M. H. 1983. "Base Rates in Bayesian Inference: Signal Detection Analysis of the Cab Problem." *American Journal of Psychology* 96: 85–94.

Brunswik, E. 1927. *Strukturmonismus und Physik*. Unpublished doctoral dissertation, University of Vienna.

Brunswik, E. 1934. *Wahrnehmung und Gegenstandswelt: Grundlegung einer Psychologie vom Gegenstand her*. Leipzig: Deuticke.

Brunswik, E. 1940. "Thing Constancy as Measured by Correlation Coefficients." *Psychological Review* 47: 69–78.

Brunswik, E. 1955. "Representative Design and Probability Theory in a Functional Psychology." *Psychological Review* 62: 193–217.

Cronbach, L. J. 1957. "The Two Disciplines of Scientific Psychology." *American Psychologist* 12: 671–684.

Danziger, K. 1980. "The History of Introspection Reconsidered." *Journal of the History of the Behavioral Sciences* 16: 241–262.

Danziger, K. 1990. *Constructing the Subject: Historical Origins of Psychological Research*. Cambridge: Cambridge University Press.

Dashiell, J. F. 1939. "Some Rapprochements in Contemporary Psychology." *Psychological Bulletin* 36: 1–24.

Duncker, K. 1945. "On Problem Solving." *Psychological Monographs* 58 (5, whole no. 270) (original work published 1935).

Edgington, E. S. 1974. "A New Tabulation of Statistical Procedures Used in APA Journals." *American Psychologist* 29: 25–26.

Fechner, G. T. 1860. *Elemente der Psychophysik* (2 vols). Leipzig: Breitkopf & Härtel. English translation of Vol. 1 only: G. T. Fechner, *Elements of Psychophysics* (H. E. Adler, trans.). New York: Holt, Rinehart & Winston, 1966.

Fisch, R., and Daniel, H. D. 1982. "Research and Publication Trends in Experimental Social Psychology: 1971–1980. A Thematic Analysis of the Journal of Experimental Social Psychology, and the Zeitschrift für Sozialpsychologie." *European Journal of Social Psychology* 12: 335–412.

Fisher, R. A. 1935. *The Design of Experiments*. Edinburgh: Oliver & Boyd.

Gigerenzer, G. 1987. "Survival of the Fittest Probabilist: Brunswik, Thurstone, and the Two Disciplines of Psychology." In L. Krüger, G. Gigerenzer, and M. S. Morgan, eds., *The Probabilistic Revolution: Vol. 2. Ideas in the Sciences* (pp. 49–72). Cambridge, MA: MIT Press.

Gigerenzer, G. 1988. "Woher kommen Theorien über kognitive Prozesse?" *Psychologische Rundschau* 39: 91–100.

Gigerenzer, G. 1991. "From Tools to Theories: A Heuristic of Discovery in Cognitive Psychology." *Psychological Review* 98: 254–267.

Gigerenzer, G. 1992. "Discovery in Cognitive Psychology: New Tools Inspire New Theories." *Science in Context* 5: 329–350.

Gigerenzer, G. 1993. "The Superego, the Ego, and the Id in Statistical Reasoning." In G. Keren and C. Lewis, eds., *A Handbook for Data Analysis in the Behavioral Sciences: Methodological Issues.* Hillsdale, NJ: Erlbaum.

Gigerenzer, G., and Murray, D. J. 1987. *Cognition as Intuitive Statistics.* Hillsdale, NJ: Erlbaum.

Gigerenzer, G., Swijtink, Z., Porter, T., Daston, L., Beatty, J., and Krüger, L. 1989. *The Empire of Chance: How Probability Changed Science and Everyday Life.* Cambridge: Cambridge University Press.

Gooding, D. 1989. "'Magnetic Curves' and the Magnetic Field: Experimentation and Representation in the History of a Theory." In D. Gooding, T. Pinch, and S. Schaffer, eds., *The Uses of Experiment. Studies in the Natural Sciences.* Cambridge: Cambridge University Press

Gooding, D., Pinch, T., and Schaffer, S. 1989 (eds.). *The Uses of Experiment. Studies in the Natural Sciences.* Cambridge: Cambridge University Press.

Green, D. M., and Swets, J. A. 1966. *Signal Detection Theory and Psychophysics.* New York: Wiley.

Gregory, R. L. 1974. *Concepts and Mechanisms of Perception.* New York: Scribner.

Gregory, R. L. 1980. "The confounded eye." In R. L. Gregory and E. H. Gombrich, eds., *Illusion in Nature and Art.* New York: Scribner.

Hacking, I. 1983. *Representing and Intervening.* Cambridge: Cambridge University Press.

Hammond, K. R. 1980. "Introduction to Brunswikian Theory and Methods." *New Directions for Methodology of Social and Behavioral Science* 3: 1–11.

Heider, F. 1958. *The Psychology of Interpersonal Relations.* New York: Wiley.

Herbart, J. F. 1816. *Lehrbuch zur Psychologie.* Hamburg and Leipzig: G. Hartenstein (2nd ed., 1834), translated by M. K. Smith, as J. F. Herbart, *A Text-book in Psychology.* New York: Appleton.

Hilgard, E. R. 1955. "Discussion of Probabilistic Functionalism." *Psychological Review* 62: 226–228.

Jones, E. E., and McGillis, D. 1976. "Correspondent Inferences and the Attribution Cube: A Comparative Reappraisal." In J. H. Harvey, W. J. Ickes, and R. F. Kidd, eds., *New Directions in Attribution Research* (Vol. 1, pp. 389–420). Hillsdale, NJ: Erlbaum.

Jungermann, H., and Wiedemann, P. 1989. "Wer hat Angst vor Tversky Kahneman? Gigerenzers Interpretation eine kognitive Illusion?" *Psychologische Rundschau* 39: 217–222.

Kelley, H. H. 1967. "Attribution Theory in Social Psychology. In D. Levine, ed., *Nebraska Symposium on Motivation* (Vol. 15). Lincoln: University of Nebraska Press.

Kelley, H. H. 1973. "The Process of Causal Attribution." *American Psychologist* 28: 107–128.

Kelley, H. H., and Michaela,. I. L. 1980. "Attribution Theory and Research." *Annual Review of Psychology* 31: 457–501.

Leary, D. E. 1987. "From Act Psychology to Probabilistic Functionalism: The Place of Egon Brunswik in the History of Psychology." In M. G. Ash and W. R. Woodward, eds., *Psychology in Twentieth-Century Thought and Society* (pp. 115–142). Cambridge: Cambridge University Press.

Luce, R. D. 1989. "Autobiography." In G. Lindzey, ed., *Psychology in Autobiography,* Vol. 8. Stanford: Stanford University Press.

McArthur, L. A. 1972. "The How and What of Why: Some Determinants and Consequences of Causal Attribution." *Journal of Personality and Social Psychology* 22: 171–193.

Melton, A. W. 1962. "Editorial." *Journal of Experimental Psychology* 64: 553–557.

Michotte, A. 1963. *The Perception of Causality*. London: Methuen. (Original work published 1946.)

Murdock, B. B., Jr. 1982. "A Theory for the Storage and Retrieval of Item and Associative Information." *Psychological Review* 89: 609–626.

Nickles, T. 1980. "Introductory Essay: Scientific Discovery and the Future of Philosophy of Science." In T. Nickles, ed., *Scientific Discovery, Logic, and Rationality* (pp. 1–59). Dordrecht, The Netherlands: Reidel.

Nickles, T. 1989. "Justification and Experiment." In D. Gooding, T. Pinch and S. Schaffer, eds., *The Uses of Experiment. Studies in the Natural Sciences*. Cambridge: Cambridge University Press.

Piaget, J. 1930. *The Child's Conception of Causality*. London: Kegan Paul.

Popper, K. 1928. *Zur Methodenfrage der Denkpsychologie*. Unpublished doctoral dissertation, University of Vienna.

Popper, K. 1959. *The Logic of Scientific Discovery*. New York: Basic Books. (Original work published 1935.)

Popper, K. 1970. "Normal Science and Its Dangers." In I. Lakatos and A. Musgrave, eds., *Criticism and the Growth of Knowledge*. Cambridge: Cambridge University Press.

Popper, K. 1979. *Ausgangspunkte. Meine intellektuelle Entwicklung*. Hamburg: Hofmann & Campe.

Rucci, A. J., and Tweney, R. D. 1980. "Analysis of Variance and the 'Second Discipline' of Scientific Psychology: A Historical Account." *Psychological Bulletin* 87: 166–184.

Schulz, U. 1989. "Bemerkungen zu 'Woher kommen Theorien über kognitive Prozesse?' von Gerd Gigerenzer." *Psychologische Rundschau* 39: 222–223.

Skinner, B. F. 1972. *Cumulative Record*. New York: Appleton Century Crofts.

Sterling, T. D. 1959. "Publication Decisions and Their Possible Effects on Inferences Drawn from tests of Significance—or Vice Versa." *Journal of the American Statistical Association* 54: 30–34.

Swets, J. A. 1964. "Is There a Sensory Threshold?" In J. A. Swets, ed., *Signal Detection and Recognition by Human Observers*. New York: Wiley.

Swijtink, Z. G. 1987. "The Objectification of Observation: Measurement and Statistical Methods in the Nineteenth century." In L. Krüger, L. J. Daston, and M. Heidelberger, eds., *The Probabilistic Revolution: Vol. 1. Ideas in History* (pp. 261–285). Cambridge, MA: MIT Press.

Tanner, W. P., Jr. 1965. *Statistical Decision Processes in Detection and Recognition* (Technical Report). Ann Arbor: University of Michigan, Sensory Intelligence Laboratory, Department of Psychology.

Tanner, W. P., Jr., and Swets, J. A. 1954. "A Decision-Making Theory of Visual Detection." *Psychological Review* 61: 401–409.

Thorndike, R. L. 1954. "The Psychological Value Systems of Psychologists." *American Psychologist* 9: 787–789.

Thurstone, L. L. 1927. "A Law of Comparative Judgment." *Psychological Review* 34: 273–286.

Titchener, E. B. 1905. *Experimental Psychology: A Manual of Laboratory Practice*. Vol. 2, Part, 2. New York: Macmillan.

Wickelgreen, W. A., and Norman, D. A. 1966. "Strength Models and Serial Position in Short-Term Recognition Memory." *Journal of Mathematical Psychology* 3: 316–347.

Chapter 4

What Is Creativity?

Margaret A. Boden

The Definition of Creativity

Creativity is a puzzle, a paradox, some say a mystery. Inventors, scientists, and artists rarely know how their original ideas arise. They mention intuition, but cannot say how it works. Most psychologists cannot tell us much about it, either. What's more, many people assume that there will never be a scientific theory of creativity—for how could science possibly explain fundamental novelties? As if all this were not daunting enough, the apparent unpredictability of creativity seems to outlaw any systematic explanation, whether scientific or historical.

Why does creativity seem so mysterious? To be sure, artists and scientists typically have their creative ideas unexpectedly, with little if any conscious awareness of how they arose. But the same applies to much of our vision, language, and commonsense reasoning. Psychology includes many theories about unconscious processes. Creativity is mysterious for another reason: the very concept is seemingly paradoxical.

If we take seriously the dictionary definition of creation, "to bring into being or form out of nothing," creativity seems to be not only beyond any scientific understanding, but even impossible. It is hardly surprising, then, that some people have "explained" it in terms of divine inspiration, and many others in terms of some romantic intuition, or insight. From the psychologist's point of view, however, "intuition" is the name not of an answer, but of a question. How does intuition work?

People of a scientific cast of mind, anxious to avoid romanticism and obscurantism, generally define creativity in terms of "novel combinations of old ideas." Accordingly, the surprise caused by a "creative" idea is said to be due to the improbability of the combination. Many psychometric tests designed to measure creativity work on this principle.

The novel combinations must be valuable in some way, because to call an idea creative is to say that it is not only new, but interesting.

(What is "interesting" in a given domain is studied, for instance, by literary critics, historians of art and technology, and philosophers of science.) However, combination theorists typically omit value from their definition of creativity. Perhaps they (mistakenly) take it for granted that unusual combinations are always interesting; and perhaps psychometricians make implicit value judgments when scoring the novel combinations produced by their experimental subjects. But since positive evaluation is part of the meaning of "creative," it should be mentioned explicitly.

Also, combination theorists typically fail to explain how it was possible for the novel combination to come about. They take it for granted, for instance, that we can associate similar ideas and recognize more distant analogies, without asking just how such feats are possible. But in many of the cases that are acclaimed in the history books, it is the recognition of the novel analogy that is so surprising. A psychological theory of creativity needs to explain how analogical thinking works.

These two cavils aside, what is wrong with the combination theory? Many ideas—concepts, theories, instruments, paintings, poems, music—that we regard as creative are indeed based on unusual combinations. For instance, part of the appeal of the Lennon-McCartney arrangement of *Yesterday* was their use of a cello, something normally associated with music of a very different kind; this combination had never happened before. Similarly, the appeal of Heath-Robinson machines lies in the unexpected uses of everyday objects. Again, poets often delight us by juxtaposing seemingly unrelated concepts. For creative ideas such as these, a combination theory (supplemented by a psychological explanation of analogy) would go a long way, and might even suffice.

Many creative ideas, however, are surprising in a deeper way. They concern novel ideas that not only *did not* happen before, but that—in a sense to be clarified below—*could not* have happened before.

Before considering just what this "could not" means, we must distinguish two senses of *creativity*. One is psychological (let us call it P-creativity), the other historical (H-creativity). A valuable idea is P-creative if the person in whose mind it arises could not have had it before; it does not matter how many times other people have already had the same idea. By contrast, a valuable idea is H-creative if it is P-creative *and* no one else, in all human history, has ever had it before.

H-creativity is something about which we are often mistaken. Historians of science and art are constantly discovering cases in which other people, even in other periods, have had an idea popularly attributed to some national or international hero. Even assuming that the idea was valued at the time by the individual concerned, and by some relevant social group, our knowledge of it is largely accidental. Whether an idea survives, whether it is lost for a while and resurfaces later, and whether historians at a given point in time happen to have evidence of it, depend on a wide variety of unrelated factors. These include fashion, rivalries, illness, trade patterns, economics, war, flood, and fire.

It follows that there can be no systematic explanation of H-creativity, no theory that explains *all and only* H-creative ideas. Certainly, there can be no *psychological* explanation of this historical category. But all H-creative ideas, by definition, are P-creative too. So a psychological explanation of P-creativity would include H-creative ideas as well.

Even a psychological explanation of creativity is hostage to the essential element of value. Even a cliché (which may be P-novel to a particular person) can be valued, if it expresses some useful truth; but not all P-novel ideas will be regarded by us (or by the person originating them) as worth having. So a psychologist might sometimes say, "Certainly, little Ms. Jane Gray could not have had that particular idea before—but it's not worth having, anyway. You can't call it *creative!*" (Likewise, a historian might say, "Yes, Lady Jane Gray did have that idea before anyone else did—but so what? It's worthless, so you can't call her *creative!*".) Such value judgments are to some extent culture-relative, since what is valued by one person or social group may or may not be valued—praised, preserved, promoted—by another (Brannigan 1981).

However, our concern is with the origin of creative ideas, not their valuation (the context of discovery, not of justification). Admittedly, criteria of valuation sometimes enter into the originating process itself, so the distinction is more analytical than psychological. But our prime focus is on how creative ideas can arise in people's minds.

What does it mean to say that an idea "could not" have arisen before? Unless we know that, we cannot make sense of P-creativity (or H-creativity either), for we cannot distinguish radical novelties from mere "first-time" newness.

An example of a novelty that clearly *could* have happened before is a newly generated sentence, such as "The pineapples are in the bathroom cabinet, next to the oil paints that belonged to Machiavelli." I have never thought of that sentence before, and almost certainly no one else has either.

The linguist Noam Chomsky remarked on this capacity of language speakers to generate first-time novelties endlessly, and he called language "creative" accordingly. His stress on the infinite fecundity of language was correct, and highly relevant to our topic. But the word "creative" was ill-chosen. Novel though the sentence about Machiavelli's oil paints is, there is a clear sense in which it *could* have occurred before. For it can be generated by the same rules that can generate other English sentences. Any competent speaker of English could have produced that sentence long ago—and so could a computer, provided with English vocabulary and grammatical rules. To come up with a new sentence, in general, is not to do something P-creative.

The "coulds" in the previous paragraph are computational "coulds." In other words, they concern the set of structures (in this case, English sentences) described and/or produced by one and the same set of generative rules (in this case, English grammar).

There are many sorts of generative system: English grammar is like a mathematical equation, a rhyming schema for sonnets, the rules of chess or tonal harmony, or a computer program. Each of these can (timelessly) describe a certain set of possible structures. And each might be used, at one time or another, in actually producing those structures.

Sometimes we want to know whether a particular structure could, in principle, be described by a specific schema, or set of abstract rules. Is "49" a square number? Is 3,591,471 a prime? Is this a sonnet, and is that a sonata? Is that painting in the Impressionist style? Is that building in the "prairie house" style? Could that geometrical theorem be proved by Euclid's methods? Is that word string a sentence? Is a benzene ring a molecular structure that is describable by early nineteenth-century chemistry (before Friedrich von Kekulé's famous fireside daydream of 1865)? To ask *whether an idea is creative or not* (as opposed to how it came about) is to ask this sort of question.

But whenever a particular structure is produced in practice, we can also ask what generative processes actually went on in its production. Did a particular geometer prove a particular theorem in this way, or in that? Was the sonata composed by following a textbook on sonata form? Did the architect, consciously or unconsciously, design the house by bearing certain formal principles in mind? Did Kekulé rely on the then-familiar principles of chemistry to generate his seminal idea of the benzene ring, and if not how did he come up with it? To ask how an idea (creative or otherwise) *actually arose* is to ask this type of question.

We can now distinguish first-time novelty from radical originality. A merely novel idea is one that can be described and/or produced by the same set of generative rules as are other, familiar, ideas. A genuinely original or radically creative idea is one that cannot. It follows that the ascription of creativity always involves tacit or explicit reference to some specific generative system.

It follows, too, that constraints—far from being opposed to creativity—make creativity possible. To throw away all constraints would be to destroy the capacity for creative thinking. Random processes alone, if they happen to produce anything interesting at all, can result only in first-time curiosities, not radical surprises. (This is not to deny that, in the context of background constraints, randomness can sometimes contribute to creativity [Boden 1990, ch.9].)

Exploring and Transforming Conceptual Spaces

The definition of creativity given above implies that, with respect to the usual mental processing in the relevant domain (chemistry, poetry, music, etc.), a creative idea is not just improbable, but *impossible*. How could it arise, then, if not by magic? And how can one impossible idea be more surprising, more creative, than another? If the act of creation is not mere combination, or what Arthur Koestler (1964) called "the bisociation of unrelated matrices," what is it? How can creativity possibly happen?

To understand this, we need the notion of a conceptual space. (This idea is used metaphorically here; later, we shall see how conceptual spaces can be described in specific, rigorous, and explicit terms.) The dimensions of a conceptual space are the organizing principles that unify and give structure to a given domain of thinking. In other words, it is the generative system that underlies that domain and defines a certain range of possibilities: chess moves, or molecular structures, or jazz melodies.

The limits, contours, pathways, and structure of a conceptual space can be mapped by mental representations of it. Such mental maps can be used (not necessarily consciously) to explore—and to change—the spaces concerned.

Conceptual spaces can be explored in various ways. Some exploration merely shows us something about the nature of the relevant conceptual space that we had not explicitly noticed before. When Dickens described Scrooge as "a squeezing, wrenching, grasping, scraping, clutching, covetous old sinner," he was exploring the space of English grammar. He was reminding the reader (and himself) that the rules of grammar allow us to use any number of adjectives before a noun. Usually, we use only two or three; but we may, if we wish, use seven (or more). That possibility already existed, although its existence may not have been realized by the reader.

Some exploration, by contrast, shows us the limits of the space, and perhaps identifies points at which changes could be made in one dimension or another. One modest example occurred at the Mad Tea-Party:

> "It's always six o'clock now," the Hatter said mournfully.
> A bright idea came into Alice's head. "Is that the reason so many tea-things are put out here?" she asked.
> "Yes, that's it," said the Hatter with a sigh: "it's always tea-time, and we've no time to wash the things between whiles."
> "Then you keep moving round, I suppose?" said Alice.
> "Exactly so," said the Hatter: "as the things get used up."
> "But what happens when you come to the beginning again?" Alice ventured to ask.

As usual in Wonderland, Alice got no sensible reply (the March Hare interrupted, saying, "Suppose we change the subject"). But her question was a good one. She had noticed that the conceptual space of the Mad Tea-Party involved a repetitive procedure (moving from one place setting to the next), which eventually would reach a point where something new would have to happen. That "something" could be many different things. When there were no clean things left on the tea table, the moving around might stop permanently, and the creatures would go hungry; or it might stop temporarily, while the clock was ignored and the washing up was done; or the creatures might drop their previous qualms about hygiene, and go on using the unwashed plates, which would get dirtier with every cycle; or they might bend down to pick some grass and quickly wipe the dishes with it . . . . The March Hare's interruption prevented Alice from finding out which (if any) of these were chosen. The point, however, is that she had identified a specific limitation of this space, and had asked what could be done to overcome it.

To overcome a limitation in a conceptual space, one must change it in some way. One may also change it, of course, without yet having come up against its limits. A small change (a "tweak") in a relatively superficial dimension of a conceptual space is like opening a door to an unvisited room in an existing house. A large change (a "transformation"), especially in a relatively fundamental dimension, is more like the instantaneous construction of a new house, of a kind fundamentally different from (albeit related to) the first. Most of the changes to tea-party behavior suggested above would be small, allowing the tea party to continue but in a slightly modified form. The first, however, might destroy the space, if the participants starved to death.

A complex example of structural exploration and change can be found in the development of post-Renaissance Western music. This music is based on the generative system known as tonal harmony.

From its origins to the end of the nineteenth century, the harmonic dimensions of this space were continually tweaked to open up the possibilities (the rooms) implicit in it from the start. Finally, a major transformation generated the deeply unfamiliar (yet closely related) space of atonality.

Each piece of tonal music has a "home key," from which it starts, from which (at first) it did not stray, and in which it must finish. Reminders and reinforcements of the home key were provided, for instance, by fragments of scales decorating the melody, or by chords and arpeggios within the accompaniment. As time passed, the range of possible home keys became increasingly well defined. Johann Sebastian Bach's "Forty-Eight," for example, was a set of preludes and fugues specifically designed to explore—and clarify—the tonal range of the well-tempered keys.

But traveling along the path of the home key alone became insufficiently challenging. Modulations between keys were then allowed, within the body of the composition. At first, only a small number of modulations (perhaps only one, followed by its "cancellation") were tolerated, between strictly limited pairs of harmonically related keys. Over the years, however, the modulations became increasingly daring, and increasingly frequent—until in the late nineteenth century there might be many modulations within a single bar, not one of which would have appeared in early tonal music. The range of harmonic relations implicit in the system of tonality gradually became apparent. Harmonies that would have been unacceptable to the early musicians, who focused on the most central or obvious dimensions of the conceptual space, became commonplace.

Moreover, the notion of the home key was undermined. With so many, and so daring, modulations within the piece, a "home key" could be identified not from the body of the piece, but only from its beginning and end. Inevitably, someone (it happened to be Arnold Schoenberg) eventually suggested that the convention of the home key be dropped altogether, because it no longer made sense in terms of constraining the composition as a whole. (Significantly, Schoenberg suggested various new constraints to structure his music making: using every note in the chromatic scale, for instance.)

Another example of extended exploration, this time with an explicit map to guide it, was the scientific activity spawned by Mendeleyev's periodic table. This table, produced in the 1860s for an introductory chemistry textbook, arranged the elements in rows and columns according to their observable properties and behavior. All the elements within a given column were in this sense "similar." But Mendeleyev left gaps in the table, predicting that unknown elements would eventually be found with the properties appropriate to these gaps (no known element being appropriate).

Sure enough, in 1879 a new element (scandium) was discovered whose properties were what Mendeleyev had predicted. Later, more elements were discovered to fill the other gaps in the table. And later still, the table (based on observable properties) was found to map onto a classification in terms of atomic number. This classification explained why the elements behaved in the systematic ways noted by Mendeleyev.

These examples show that exploration often leads to novel ideas. Indeed, it often leads to ideas, such as new forms of harmonic modulation, that are normally called creative. In that sense, then, conceptual exploration is a form of creativity. However, exploring a conceptual space is one thing: transforming it is another. What is it to transform such a space?

One example has been mentioned already: Schoenberg's dropping the home-key constraint to create the space of atonal music. Dropping a constraint is a general heuristic, or method, for transforming conceptual spaces. The deeper the generative role of the constraint in the system concerned, the greater the transformation of the space.

Non-Euclidean geometry, for instance, resulted from dropping Euclid's fifth axiom, about parallel lines meeting at infinity. (One of the mathematicians responsible was Lobachevsky, immortalized not only in encyclopedias of mathematics but also in the songs of Tom Lehrer.) This transformation was made "playfully," as a prelude to exploring a geometrical space somewhat different from Euclid's. Only much later did it turn out to be useful in physics.

Another very general way of transforming conceptual spaces is to "consider the negative": that is, to negate a constraint. (Negating a constraint is not the same as dropping it. Suppose someone gets bored with eating only red sweets: to choose *any nonred sweet* is different from choosing *any sweet, whatever its color*.)

One well-known instance of constraint negation concerns Kekulé's discovery of the benzene ring. He described it like this:

> I turned my chair to the fire and dozed. Again the atoms were gambolling before my eyes. . . . [My mental eye] could distinguish larger structures, of manifold conformation; long rows, sometimes more closely fitted together; all twining and twisting in snakelike motion. But look! What was that? One of the snakes had seized hold of its own tail, and the form whirled mockingly before my eyes. As if by a flash of lightning I awoke."

This vision was the origin of his hunch that the benzene molecule might be a ring, a hunch that turned out to be correct.

Prior to this experience, Kekulé had assumed that all organic molecules are based on strings of carbon atoms (he had produced the string theory some years earlier). But for benzene, the valencies of the constituent atoms did not fit.

We can understand how it was possible for him to pass from strings to rings, as plausible chemical structures, if we assume three things (for each of which there is independent psychological evidence). First, that snakes and molecules were already associated in his thinking. Second, that the topological distinction between open and closed curves was present in his mind. And third, that the "consider the negative" heuristic was present also. Taken together, these three factors could transform "string" into "ring."

A string molecule is what topologists call an open curve. Topology is a form of geometry that studies not size or shape, but neighbor relations. An open curve has at least one end point (with a neighbor on only one side), whereas a closed curve does not. An ant crawling along an open curve can never visit the same point twice, but on a closed curve it will eventually return to its starting point. These curves need not be curvy in shape. A circle, a triangle, and a hexagon are all closed curves; a straight line, an arc, and a sine wave are all open curves.

If one considers the negative of an open curve, one gets a closed curve. Moreover, a snake biting its tail is *a closed curve that one had expected to be open.* For that reason, it is surprising, even arresting ("But look! What was that?"). Kekulé might have had a similar reaction if he had been out on a country walk and happened to see a snake with its tail in its mouth. But there is no reason to think that he would have been stopped in his tracks by seeing a Victorian child's hoop. A hoop is a hoop, is a hoop: no topological surprises there. (No topological surprises in a snaky sine wave, either: so two intertwined snakes would not have interested Kekulé, though they might have stopped Francis Crick dead in his tracks, a century later.)

Finally, the change from open curves to closed ones is a topological change, which by definition will alter neighbor relations. And Kekulé was an expert chemist, who knew very well that the behavior of a molecule depends not only on what the constituent atoms are, but also on how they are juxtaposed. A change in atomic neighbor relations is very likely to have some chemical significance. So it is understandable that he had a hunch that this tail-biting snake molecule might contain the answer to his problem.

Plausible though this talk of conceptual spaces may be, it is—thus far—largely metaphorical. I have claimed that in calling an idea creative one should specify the particular set of generative principles with respect to which it is impossible. But I have not said how the (largely tacit) knowledge of literary critics, musicologists, and historians of art and science might be explicitly expressed within a psychological theory of creativity. How can this be done? And, the putative structures having been made explicit, how can we be sure that the mental processes specified by the psychologist really are powerful enough to generate such-and-such ideas from such-and-such structures? This is where computational psychology can help us.

The Relevance of Computational Psychology

Computational psychology draws many of its theoretical concepts from artificial intelligence, or AI. Artificial intelligence studies the nature of intelligence in general, and its method is to try to enable computers to do the sorts of things that minds can do: seeing, speaking, storytelling, and logical or analogical thinking.

But how can computers have anything to do with creativity? The very idea, it may seem, is absurd. The first person to denounce this apparent absurdity was Ada, Lady Lovelace, the friend and collaborator of Charles Babbage. She realized that Babbage's "Analytical Engine"—in essence, a design for a digital computer—could in principle "compose elaborate and scientific pieces of music of any degree of complexity or extent." But she insisted that the creativity involved in any elaborate pieces of music emanating from the Analytical Engine would have to be credited not to the engine, but to the engineer. As she put it, "The Analytical Engine has no pretensions whatever to *originate* anything. It can do [only] *whatever we know how to order it* to perform."

If Lady Lovelace's remark means merely that *a computer can do only what its program enables it to do,* it is correct—and, from the point of view of theoretical psychology, helpful and important. It means, for instance, that if a program manages to play a Chopin waltz expressively, or to improvise modern jazz, then the musical structures and procedures (the generative structures) in that program *must* be capable of producing those examples of musical expression or improvisation. (It does not follow that human musicians do it in the same way: perhaps there is reason to suspect that they do not. But the program specifies, in detail, *one* way in which such things can be done. Alternative theories, involving different musical structures or psychological processes, should ideally be expressed at a comparable level of detail.)

But if Lady Lovelace's remark is intended as an argument denying any interesting link between computers and creativity, it is too quick and too simple. We must distinguish four different questions, which are often confused with each other. I call them Lovelace questions, because many people would respond to them (with a dismissive "No!") by using the argument cited above.

The first Lovelace question is whether computational concepts can help us understand how *human* creativity is possible. The second is whether computers (now or in the future) could ever do things that at least *appear to be* creative. The third is whether a computer could ever *appear to recognize* creativity—in poems written by human poets, for instance, or in its own novel ideas about science or mathematics. And the fourth is whether computers themselves could ever *really* be creative (as opposed to merely producing apparently creative performance, whose originality is wholly due to the human programmer).

Our prime interest is in the first Lovelace question, which focuses on the creativity of human beings. The next two Lovelace questions are psychologically interesting insofar as they throw light on the first. For our purposes, the fourth Lovelace question can be ignored. It is not a scientific question, as the others are, but in part a philosophical worry about "meaning" and in part a disguised request for a moral-political decision (Boden 1990, ch. 11).

The answers I shall propose to the first three questions are, respectively: *Yes, definitely; Yes, up to a point;* and *Yes, necessarily (for any program that appears to be creative).* In short, computational ideas can help us to understand how human creativity is possible. This does not mean that creativity is predictable, nor even that an original idea can be explained in every detail after it has appeared. But we can draw on computational ideas in understanding in scientific terms how "intuition" works.

The psychology of creativity can benefit from AI and computer science *precisely because*—as Lady Lovelace pointed out—a computer can do only what its program enables it to do. On the one hand, computational concepts, and their disciplined expression in programming terms, help us to specify generative principles clearly. On the other hand, computer modeling helps us to see, in practice, what a particular generative system *can* and *cannot* do.

The results may be surprising, for the generative potential of a program is not always obvious: the computer may do things we did not know we had "ordered it" to perform. And, all too often, it may fail to do things that we fondly believed we had allowed for in our instructions. So expressing a psychological theory as a program to be run on a computer is an excellent way of testing its clarity, its coherence, and its generative potential.

In the discussion so far, I have relied on some computational concepts, such as *generative system* and *heuristic*. I have not had to explain these concepts by reference to computer programs, for they were introduced into our language long before the invention of computers, by people studying the nature and psychology of mathematical proof.

For psychological purposes, however, it can be helpful to ask how specific heuristics might play a role in a functioning computer. For what they do in that artificial context can be clearly understood, and so may help us to clarify what could (and what could not) be going on in human thought. Similarly, a consideration of actual AI programs can help us to understand more clearly how conceptual spaces can be identified, constructed, explored, or transformed. Even if a program falls far short of the comparable human reality (which is usually the case), its failings can lead, in true Popperian fashion, to progress in the psychological theory concerned.

Conceptual Spaces in the Visual Arts

Many human artists use computers as tools, to help them create things they could not have created otherwise. A graphics artist, for instance, may get new ideas from computer graphics, and so-called computer music may use sounds that no orchestra could produce. Most of these examples, however, are not pertinent here.

The relevant cases are those where the new ideas are made possible by a systematic analysis of the artistic genre concerned. Most relevant of all, for our purposes, are those (few) computer programs that produce aesthetically valuable creations themselves or which, in their attempts to do so, throw light on the psychological processes underlying human art. The conceptual spaces involved may be highly complex, and the computational power of a computer will then be needed to show just what spatial forms the (programmed) genre can or cannot generate.

Some conceptual spaces involved in spatial design have been mapped as algorithms simple enough to be followed "by hand," at least if the highest levels of potential complexity are ignored (Stiny and Gips 1978; Stiny 1991). Architects and environmental planners, for instance, have used "spatial grammars" to generate new "sentences," novel spatial structures that are intuitively acceptable instances of the genre concerned. Previously unseen examples of Palladian villas, Mughul gardens, and Frank Lloyd Wright's "prairie houses" have been designed accordingly (Stiny and Mitchell 1978,

1980; Koning and Eizenberg 1981). The decorative arts have received similar attentions: traditional Chinese lattice designs have been described by a computer algorithm, which generates the seemingly irregular patterns called "ice rays" as well as the more obviously regular forms (Stiny 1977).

The ice ray example shows that a rigorous analysis of a conceptual space can uncover hidden regularities, and so increase—not merely codify—our aesthetic understanding of the style. The same applies to the analytical work on prairie houses. The architectural grammarians who developed this analysis point out that a renowned expert on Lloyd Wright's buildings had been unable to explicate the notion of *balance* in prairie-style houses: he had described it as "occult." Their analysis has uncovered the principles of spatial balance involved. It shows which aspects are relatively fundamental (like Euclid's axioms in geometry, or *NP* and *VP* in syntax), and how certain features are constrained by others.

In the genre of prairie houses, the origin of the generative design (the first "axiom") is the fireplace. The majority of these houses have only one fireplace. Occasionally, however, Lloyd Wright replaced the single hearth by several fireplaces. Because of the pivotal role of the fireplace in this particular style, this number variation generates "a veritable prairie village of distinct but interacting prairie-style designs," all within a single building (Koning and Eizenberg, p. 322).

The aesthetic styles of Palladian villas, Mughul gardens, prairie houses, and Chinese lattices are all relatively austere. So perhaps it is not surprising that "grammatical" analyses of them can be found. Nor is it surprising that these analyses can often be followed by hand: an architect can design a prairie house, using the relevant grammar, without ever using a computer. What of more "free" aesthetic styles, and art objects inspired by natural forms rather than by geometrical shapes?

Consider line drawings of human figures, for example. Some computational work done by Harold Cohen—already a well-known professional painter when he started working with computers—is pertinent here. Over the past two decades, Cohen has written a series of programs that produce pleasing, and unpredictable, line drawings (McCorduck 1991). I have one in my office, and on several occasions a visitor has spontaneously remarked, "I like that drawing! Who did it?" (see figure 4.1). These drawings have been exhibited at the Tate and other major art galleries around the world, and not just for their curiosity value.

Each of Cohen's programs explores a certain style of line drawing and a certain subject matter. The program may draw acrobats with

Figure 4.1
(Reprinted by permission of Harold Cohen.)

large beach balls, for instance, or human figures in the profuse vegetation of a jungle. (As yet, Cohen has not written a coloring program that satisfies him; meanwhile, he sometimes colors his programs' drawings by hand.)

Much as human artists have to know about the things they are depicting, so each of Cohen's programs needs an internal model of its subject matter. This model is not a physical object, like the articulated wooden dolls found in artists' studios, but a generative system: what one might call a "body grammar." It is a set of abstract rules that specify, for instance, not only the anatomy of the human body (two arms, two legs), but also how the various body parts appear from various points of view. An acrobat's arm pointing at the viewer will be foreshortened; a flexed arm will have a bulging biceps; and an arm lying behind another acrobat's body will be invisible.

The program can draw acrobats with only one arm visible (because of occlusion), but it cannot draw one-armed acrobats. Its model of the human body does not allow for the possibility of there being one-armed people. They are, one might say, unimaginable. If, as a matter of fact, the program has never produced a picture showing an acrobat's right wrist occluding another acrobat's left eye, that is a mere accident of its processing history: it *could* have done so at any time. But the fact that it has never drawn a one-armed acrobat has a deeper explanation: such drawings are, in a clear sense, *impossible.*

If Cohen's program were capable of "dropping" one of the limbs (as a geometer may drop Euclid's fifth axiom, or Schoenberg the notion of the home key), it could then draw one-armed, or one-legged, figures. A host of previously unimaginable possibilities, only a subset of which might ever be actualized, would have sprung into existence at the very moment of dropping the constraint that there must be (say) a left arm.

A superficially similar but fundamentally more powerful transformation might be effected if the numeral "2" had been used in the program to denote the number of arms. For a numeral is a *variable,* in the sense that one numeral may be replaced by another. So "2" can be replaced by "1"—or, for that matter, by "7." And depending on the role played by the numeral in the relevant computational system, the result might be a superficial or a fundamental change. We have seen, for instance, that a prairie house may have one fireplace or several, and that the basic architectural form of the whole house depends on how many fireplaces there are.

A general purpose tweaking-transformational heuristic might look out for numerals, and try substituting varying values. Kekule's chemical successors employed such a heuristic when they asked whether any ring molecules could have five atoms in the ring, not six. (They also treated carbon as a variable—as a particular instance of the class of elements—when they asked whether molecular rings might include nitrogen or phosphorus atoms.) A program that (today) drew one-armed acrobats for the first time by employing a "vary-the-variable" heuristic *could* (tomorrow) be in a position to draw seven-legged acrobats as well. A program that merely "dropped the left arm" *could not*.

Suppose that Cohen's program (or Cohen himself) were to allow the left arm to be omitted, without making any other change to the program. The resulting pictures might not be so plausible, nor so pleasing.

The reason is that the program's current world model contains rules dealing with human stability and picture balance, some of which may implicitly or explicitly assume that all people have four limbs. If so, a three-limbed person (one limb having been "dropped") might be drawn in a physically impossible bodily attitude. Human artists drawing a one-armed person would not do this, unless they were deliberately contravening the laws of gravity (as in a Chagall dreamscape). Likewise, a one-armed person placed carefully on the page might look *visually* unbalanced, if the aesthetic criteria governing that placement currently assume a two-armed person. (This is an example of the fact mentioned earlier: evaluative criteria can enter into the generation of a conceptual structure, as well as into its selection/rejection post hoc.)

The psychological interest of Cohen's work is that the constraints—anatomical, physical, and aesthetic—written into his programs are perhaps a subset of those which human artists respect when drawing in comparable styles. A host of questions arise about just what those constraints may be. And a host of issues can be explored by building additional or alternative rules into Cohen's programs, and examining the range of structures that result. Such experiments cannot be done by hand without begging the very questions we are interested in. To understand the potential (and some of the limits) of this genre clearly, we must rely on the computational power of the computer.

It must be admitted, however, that Cohen's programs are like hack artists, who can draw only in a given style. The style may be rich enough (the generative system powerful enough) to make their drawings individually unpredictable. But the style itself is easily recognized. At present, only Cohen can change the constraints built into the program, so enabling it to draw pictures of a type that it could not have drawn before. But some programs, perhaps including some yet to be written by Cohen, might do so for themselves.

To be able to transform its style, a program would need (among other things) a metarepresentation of the lower-level constraints it uses. For the creative potential of a self-transforming system depends on how it represents its current skills (drawing "a left arm and a right arm" or drawing "two arms"), and on what heuristics are available to modify those representations and thereby enlarge its skills. We have already seen that if Cohen's program had an explicit representation of the fact that it normally draws four-limbed people, and if it were given very general "transformation heuristics" (like "drop a constraint," "consider the negative," or "vary the variable"), it might sometimes omit, or add, one or more limbs.

These remarks about creative potential apply to humans as well as to computer programs. Recent evidence from developmental psychology suggests that this sort of explicit representation of a lower-level drawing skill is required if a young child is to be able to draw a one-armed man, or a seven-legged dog (Karmiloff-Smith 1990). Comparable evidence has been found with regard to other skills, such as language and piano playing; here too, imaginative flexibility requires the development of generative systems that explicitly represent lower-level systems (Karmiloff-Smith 1986; Clark and Karmiloff-Smith, in press). As for historical evidence, it is clear that the invention of new systems of representation, such as arabic numerals or musical notation, enormously increases the creative range of people using that representation.

Modeling Musical Creativity

An example of an "artistic" program grounded firmly in ideas about human psychology is the jazz improviser written by Philip Johnson-Laird (1988, 1993). This has appeared in no concert halls, and at first hearing seems much less impressive than Cohen's programs (Johnson-Laird likens its performance to that of "a moderately competent beginner"). However, it raises some highly specific questions—and provides some suggestive answers—about the nature of the complex conceptual space involved, and how about how human minds are able to explore it.

A jazz musician starts with a chord sequence, such as a twelve-bar blues. (The performance will be an improvisation based on a fixed number of repetitions of the chord sequence.) Often, the chord sequence has already been written by someone else. For writing such sequences, unless they are kept boringly simple, typically requires a great deal of time and effort. They are complex hierarchical structures, with subsections "nested" at several different levels, and with complex harmonic constraints linking sometimes far-separated chords. They could not be improvised "on the fly" (where no backtracking is possible), but require careful thought and self-correction.

To take an analogy from language, consider this sentence: *The potato that the rat that the cat that the flea bit chased around the block on the first fine Tuesday in May nibbled is rotting.* You probably cannot understand this multiply-nested sentence without penciling in the phrase boundaries, or at least pointing to them. If someone were to read it aloud, without a very exaggerated intonation, it would be unintelligible. Moreover, you would find it difficult, perhaps impossible, to invent such a sentence without writing it down. For you cannot select the word *is* without remembering *potato*, twenty-two words before. (If you had started with *The potatoes*, you would have needed *are* instead.)

Similarly, jazz composers cannot improvise complicated chord sequences. Indeed, they have developed a special written notation to help them to keep the various harmonic constraints in mind while composing such sequences.

The jazz musician's task, in playing a chord sequence, is more difficult than yours in reading a sentence. For he is improvising, rather than merely reading. The "chords" in the chord sequence are actually classes of chords, and the player must decide, as he goes along, just how to play each chord. He must also decide how to pass to the next chord, how to produce a melody, how to harmonize the melody with the chords, how to produce a bass-line accompaniment, and how to keep the melody in step with the meter.

Johnson-Laird argues that, because of the limited storage capacity of human short-term memory, the rules (or musical "grammar") used for generating these features of the performance must be much less powerful than the hierarchical grammar used to produce chord sequences. Accordingly, his program consists of two parts.

One part generates a simple, harmonically sensible chord sequence (compare "The potato is rotting"), and then complicates it in various ways to produce a nested hierarchical structure (comparable to a grammatically complex sentence). The second part takes that chord sequence as its input, and uses less powerful computational rules to improvise a performance in real time. What counts as an acceptable "melody," for instance, is determined by very simple rules that consider only a few previous notes; and the harmonies are chosen by reference only to the immediately preceding chord.

When more than one choice is allowed by the rules, the program chooses at random. A human musician might do the same. Or he might choose according to some idiosyncratic preference for certain intervals or tones, thus giving his playing an "individual" style. (The same obviously applies for literature and painting.) This is one of the ways in which chance, or randomness, can contribute to creativity. But it is the constraints—governing harmony, melody, and tempo—that make the jazz performance possible in the first place. Without them, we would have a mere random cacophony.

Besides harmony, melody, and tempo, there are other structures that inform music. Piano music, for example, is composed to be played expressively (composers often put expression marks in the score), and human musicians can play it with expression. Indeed, they have to: without expression, a piano composition sounds musically dead, even absurd. In rendering the notes in the score, pianists add such features as *legato, staccato, piano, forte, sforzando, crescendo, diminuendo, rallentando, accelerando, ritenuto,* and *rubato* (not to mention the two pedals).

But how? Can we express this musical sensibility precisely? That is, can we specify the relevant conceptual space? Just what is a *crescendo*? What is a *rallentando*? And just how sudden is a *sforzando*?

These questions have been asked by Christopher Longuet-Higgins (whose earlier work on the conceptual space of tonal harmony was used within Johnson-Laird's jazz program [Longuet-Higgins 1987]). By means of a computational method, he has tried to specify the musical skills involved in playing expressively.

Working with Chopin's *Minute Waltz* and *Fantaisie Impromptu in C Sharp Minor,* Longuet-Higgins has discovered some counterintuitive facts about the conceptual space concerned (Longuet-Higgins in press). For example, a *crescendo* is not uniform, but exponential (a uniform *crescendo* does not sound like a *crescendo* at all, but like someone turning up the volume knob on a radio); similarly, a *rallentando* must be exponentially graded (in relation to the number of bars in the relevant section) if it is to sound "right." Where *sforzandi* are concerned, the mind is highly sensitive: as little as a centisecond makes a difference between acceptable and clumsy performance. By contrast, our appreciation of *piano* and *forte* is less sensitive than one might expect, for (with respect to these two compositions, at least) only five levels of loudness are needed to produce an acceptable performance. More facts such as these, often demonstrable to a very high level of detail, have been discovered by Longuet-Higgins's computational experiments. As he points out, many interesting questions concern the extent to which they are relevant to a wide range of music, as opposed to a particular musical style.

Strictly speaking, this work is not a study of creativity. It is not even a study of the exploration of a conceptual space, never mind its transformation. But it is highly relevant to creativity (as is Longuet-Higgins's earlier computational work on harmony and musical perception [1987]). For we have seen that creativity can be ascribed to an idea only by reference to a particular generative system, or conceptual space. The more clearly we can identify this space, the more confidently we can identify and ask questions about the creativity involved in negotiating it. A pianist whose playing style sounds "original," or even "idiosyncratic," may be exploring and transforming the space of expressive skills that Longuet-Higgins has studied.

Of course, we can recognize this originality "intuitively" and enjoy—or reject—the pianist's novel style accordingly. (Recognizing it and describing it are two different things: the slow tempo of Rosalyn Tureck's performances of Bach is immediately obvious, but many other expressive characteristics of her playing are not.) Likewise, we can enjoy—or reject—drawings done by human artists or by computer programs. But understanding, in rigorous terms, *just how these creative activities are possible* is another matter. If that is our aim, computational concepts and computer modeling can help.

Literary Spaces

Literature involves many different conceptual spaces, mutually integrated in sensible—and sometimes surprising—ways. One of these concerns human motivation, the various psychological structures that are possible—and intelligible—within human action and interaction. Most novels and short stories are less concerned with transforming this space than with exploring it in a novel and illuminating fashion.

Current computer programs that write stories are woefully inadequate compared with human storytellers. But the best of them get what strength they possess from their internal models of very general aspects of motivation. Consider this example, written by a program asked to write a story with the moral "Never trust flatterers":

> *The Fox and the Crow.*
>
> Once upon a time, there was a dishonest fox named Henry who lived in a cave, and a vain and trusting crow named Joe who lived in an elm tree. Joe had gotten a piece of cheese and was holding it in his mouth. One day, Henry walked from his cave, across the meadow to the elm tree. He saw Joe Crow and the cheese and became hungry. He decided that he might get the cheese if Joe Crow spoke, so he told Joe that he liked his singing very much and wanted to hear him sing. Joe was very pleased with Henry and began to sing. The cheese fell out of his mouth, down to the ground. Henry picked up the cheese and told Joe

Crow that he was stupid. Joe was angry, and didn't trust Henry any more. Henry returned to his cave. THE END. (Schank and Riesbeck 1981)

Exciting this little tale is not. But it does, as requested, show us that trusting flattery can lead to disappointment. The story has a clear structure and a satisfactory end. The characters have goals, and can set up subgoals to achieve them. They can cooperate in each other's plans, and trick each other so as to get what they want. They can recognize obstacles, and sometimes overcome them. They can ask, inform, reason, bargain, persuade, and threaten. They can even adjust their personal relationships according to the treatment they get, rewarding rescue with loyalty or deception with mistrust. And there are no loose ends left dangling to frustrate us.

The reason is that this program can construct hierarchical plans, ascribing them to the individual characters according to the sorts of motivation (food preferences, for example) one would expect them to have. It can think up cooperative and competitive episodes, as it can give one character a role (either helpful or obstructive) in another's plan. These roles need not be allocated randomly, but can depend on background interpersonal relations (such as competition, dominance, and familiarity). And it can represent different sorts of communication between the characters (such as asking or bargaining), which constrain what follows in different ways.

All these matters (like the body models in Cohen's line-drawing programs) are represented as abstract computational schemata. In addition, there are procedures and heuristics for integrating these schemata in sensible ways. The program as a whole is a generative system capable of producing a story structure, or plot, and of instantiating it in respect of specific incidents and characters.

A story writer equipped not only to do planning, but also to juggle with psychological schemata such as escape, ambition, embarrassment, or betrayal could come up with better stories still. To design such a program would be no small feat. Every psychological concept involved in the plots of its stories, whether explicitly named in the text or not, would need to be defined—much as "stability" had to be defined for the acrobat-drawing program, and "melody" for the jazz improviser.

Ideally, these psychological concepts should allow for several different varieties, which could enter into story plots in significantly different ways. Consider betrayal, for instance, a concept that figures in many stories—from the court of the Moor of Venice to the Garden of Gethsemane. A very early computationally inspired definition of betrayal was: *Actor F, having apparently agreed to serve as E's agent for action A, is for some reason so negatively disposed toward that role that he undertakes instead to subvert the action, preventing E from attaining his purpose* (Abelson 1973). Suppose that the story writer had some representation of the facts that actors *in general* may vary in power, and that goals *in general* may vary in importance to one (specifiable) actor or another. The conceptual space of betrayal could then be explored by varying the importance (to one actor or the other) of the actions involved.

We can understand *abandonment* and *letting down*, for example, as distinct species of betrayal by "tweaking" the definition given above. To accuse F of abandoning E is to say that he was acting initially as E's agent for action A (this action being crucial to E's welfare); that he has now deliberately stopped doing so; and that this amounts in effect, if not necessarily in intent, to the deliberate subversion of E's purposes—because E (by hypothesis) is helpless without F. In contrast, to say that F let E down implies neither the urgency of A nor the helplessness of E. In short, whereas anyone can let down or be let down, only the strong can abandon and only the weak can be abandoned. This is why abandonment is a peculiarly nasty form of betrayal.

Human authors, and readers, tacitly rely on such facts about the psychological structure of betrayal in writing and interpreting stories about it. They do likewise with respect to other psychological concepts. Some authors have the ability to make us recognize aspects of the relevant conceptual spaces that we had not seen before (much as Dickens reminds us that seven adjectives may accompany one noun). Henry James's novella *The Beast in the Jungle*, for example, is a superb depiction of a familiar motivational category instantiated in a subtly unfamiliar way. Not until the penultimate page does the reader realize just what the story has been about, just what psychological space it has been exploring. At that point, however, the matter becomes glaringly obvious (compare: "*Of course* a noun can have seven adjectives!").

These sorts of conceptual exploration could, in principle, be done by story-writing computer programs too. But the complexities are so great (and the background knowledge of the world so extensive) that it is unrealistic to expect there to be a computerized story writer that can perform at better than a hack level—if that. Our interest, however, is not in getting computers to do our creative acts for us, but in using the computational approach to help us understand what is involved when we do them.

Analogy

Analogy is widely employed in the arts. Literary analogies abound in prose and poetry, visual analogies enliven paintings, and kinetic analogies inform the ballet (think of the jerky actions of the doll Coppelia, or the feline movements of Puss-in-Boots).

Scientific thinking exploits analogy, too. In an earlier section, for example, we took for granted that Kekulé was capable of recognizing the analogy between string molecules and "long rows," and between twisting rows and snakes. Historians and philosophers of science have noted the importance of analogies in scientific discovery and theory (Hesse 1988). And Koestler (1964) held that the most creative moments in science involve the recognition of a novel analogy between previously unrelated fields.

How is analogical thinking possible? An analogy links two previously unrelated concepts. To understand how it arose, we must detail the psychological structure of the two concepts concerned, and specify processes whereby these two spaces can be simultaneously retrieved, compared, and linked. Computational psychology offers some suggestions about what such processes might be like.

Relatively close analogies—family resemblances, Kekulé's rows-as-snakes, and much poetic imagery as well (Boden 1990, ch. 6)—may depend on processes broadly similar to those built into "connectionist" computer systems. These parallel-processing systems, often called "neural networks," are composed of many simple computational units, each coding one semantic feature (Rumelhart and McClelland 1986). The units are linked by excitatory and inhibitory connections (as are neurons in the brain). Units coding for mutually consistent features tend to excite each other's activity, whereas mutually inconsistent units inhibit each other. For instance, a unit coding for "white" may excite both "cream" and (less strongly) "yellow," but it will inhibit "blue," "red," and (above all) "black."

Because of their basic design, connectionist systems can take many different constraints into account simultaneously, where no constraint is necessary but a large number are sufficient for making the judgment concerned. It follows that they are inherently tolerant of noise (missing or spurious information), and superior to traditional AI programs in their ability to associate similar but nonidentical patterns. A connectionist system that has already learned the pattern *Mary had a little lamb*, for instance, will "naturally" be able to retrieve that entire pattern if presented with the fragment *Mary had a. . . .* Likewise, it will "spontaneously" recognize that *Martha had a little luck* is similar. In other words, the system can be reminded of a familiar idea by encountering a fragment of it, or by coming across a similar idea.

Those analogies in art and science that seem most creative, however, do not rely on reminding of this common type. They are more surprising, not to say highly counterintuitive. Consider Macbeth's description of sleep:

Sleep that knits up the ravelled sleeve of care,
The death of each day's life, sore labour's bath,
Balm of hurt minds, great nature's second course,
Chief nourisher in life's feast.

This passage works because Shakespeare's readers, like him, know about such worldly things as knitting, night and day, and the soothing effects of a hot bath. In addition, they are able to understand analogies, even highly unusual or "creative" analogies, such as comparing sleep with a knitter. But how can this be? A knitter is an animate agent, but sleep is not. How can the human mind map "sleep" onto "knitter" so as to realize the link: that both can repair the ravages of the previous day?

Similarly, how can we understand Socrates' remark (in Plato's *Theaetetus*) that the philosopher is "a midwife of ideas"? A philosopher is not (usually!) a midwife. And while a new idea is indeed new, vulnerable, and perhaps flawed—like a baby—it is nevertheless very different from a baby. Like sleep, ideas are not even animate. How, then, can someone create, or creatively interpret, such a strange comparison? Such a thought seems to be *impossible*.

Analogical thinking has been widely studied by psychologists, some of whom have produced computational models of it (Vosniadou and Ortony 1989). A number of connectionist systems have been specifically designed to interpret "surprising" analogies, as opposed to mere family resemblances (Holyoak and Barnden, in press).

One such system was given structured representations of the concepts of philosopher and midwife, and was then presented with Socrates' analogy (Holyoak and Thagard 1989). It mapped "idea" onto "baby" as required. The model includes a large semantic network in which concepts are associated, as the concepts stored in human memory seem to be, somewhat in the way of a thesaurus. They bear links to synonyms, defining properties, and less closely related words such as opposites (so this network could support many different uses of "consider the negative"). The analogy mapper compares concepts in terms of structural similarity, semantic centrality, and pragmatic (contextual) importance. On being told that there is some (unspecified) analogy between "philosopher" and "midwife," this program mapped "baby" onto "idea" even though it recognized that a central feature of a baby (its being alive) does not hold of an idea.

This analogy interpreter has a "sister system" that comes up with analogies, as opposed to interpreting ready-made analogies input to it (Thagard et al. 1988). It does come up with some fairly "surprising" analogies (for instance, it notes the resemblance between the schematized plots of *Romeo and Juliet* and *West Side Story*). But in its current form, it would not spontaneously generate either the idea–baby or the sleep–knitter comparison, because it looks for the "best"—that is, the closest—analogy it can find. Even if it were told to ignore the twenty best comparisons, it would not come up with either of these notions. Part of the reason is that its designers were most interested in analogy in science, where closeness is in general an advantage. In poetry, by contrast, *distance* between the two poles of the analogy is often preferred.

Even poetic distance, however, has to be kept within the bounds of intelligibility. Poets help us to interpret a far-distant analogy by providing additional constraints within the context of the poem. In the four-line fragment of Macbeth's speech, for instance, there is a succession of images for sleep each of which (even "death") suggests some alleviation of previous troubles. The wildness of each individual analogy is thus tempered by the mutually reinforcing semantic associations set up by all the others.

Creative scientists, likewise, justify bold analogies by reference to the theoretical context concerned. Moreover, to accept a new scientific analogy is thenceforth to perceive the experimental situation in a new way. William Harvey's description of the heart as a pump changed not only what experiments were done, but how experimental events (such as systole and diastole) were perceived. The theory-laden nature of observation is a commonplace within the philosophy of science.

A psychology of analogy should be able to show how aptness to the current context can be achieved, and how a new analogy and a new perception can develop together. The analogy programs described above cannot help here, because their contextual sensitivity is shallow and their representations are fixed. After "philosopher" has been mapped onto "midwife," it is represented in exactly the same way as before; but Socrates' aim in introducing the analogy was not merely to point out a likeness, but to alter Theaetetus' perception of what a philosopher is. A computational model of analogy that focuses on these issues of context sensitivity and altered perception is Douglas Hofstadter's "Copycat" (Hofstadter, Mitchell, and French 1987; Hofstadter and Mitchell, in press; Mitchell 1993; Chalmers, French, and Hofstadter 1991).

Hofstadter stresses that one's perception of a situation is normally biased by high-level concepts and aims. Imagine three observers in the same room: the first may see the person in the corner as a woman holding wooden knitting needles, the second as a loving mother carefully mending her child's torn garment, and the third as a proletarian sweatshop worker exploited by the capitalist system. Indeed, these three observers may all be inside a single head: depending on one's interests at the time, one may see the scene in any of these ways. A fourth observer, currently writing a poem about overwhelming guilt, may focus on the steadily lengthening sleeve and be reminded of the refreshing powers of sleep. In each case, the representation of the situation is relevant to the beliefs and interests of the perceiver. Moreover, it is hard to say where perception ends and analogizing begins.

The Copycat project takes these facts about human psychology seriously. The program allows for the generation of many different analogies, where contextually appropriate comparisons are favored over inappropriate ones. It does not rely on ready-made, fixed, representations, but constructs its own representations in a context-sensitive way: its new analogies and new perceptions develop together.

Copycat's "perceptual" representations of the input patterns are built up dialectically, each step being influenced by (and also influencing) the type of analogical mapping that the current context seems to require. A partially built interpretation that seems to be mapping well onto the nascent analogy is maintained and developed further. A partially built representation that seems to be heading for a dead end is abandoned, and an alternative one started that exploits different aspects of the target concept. Varying degrees of conceptual "slippage" are allowed, so that analogies of differing closeness can be generated.

The domain actually explored by Copycat is a highly idealized one, namely, alphabetic letter strings. But the computational principles involved are relevant to analogies in any domain. In other words, the alphabet is here being used as a psychological equivalent of inclined planes in physics.

Copycat considers letter strings such as *ppqqrrss*, which it can liken to strings such as *mmnnoopp, tttuuuvvvwww*, and *abcd*. Its self-constructed "perceptual" representations describe strings in terms of descriptors like *leftmost, rightmost, middle, same, group, alphabetic successor,* and *alphabetic predecessor*. It is a parallel-processing system, in that various types of descriptor compete simultaneously to build the overall description.

The system's sense of analogy in any particular case is expressed by its producing a pair of letter strings that it judges to be like some pair provided to it as input. In general, it is able to produce more than one analogy, each of which is justified by a different set of abstract descriptions of the letter strings.

For instance, Copycat may be told that the string *abc* changes into *abd*, and then asked what the string *mrrjjj* will change into. As its answer, it may produce any of the following strings: *mrrjjd*, *mrrddd*, *mrrkkk*, or *mrrjjjj*. The last one is probably the one that you prefer, since it involves a greater level of insight (or abstraction) than the others. That is, it involves seeing *mrrjjj* as *m-rr-jjj*, and seeing the lengths of the letter groups, and then in addition seeing that the group lengths form a "successor group" (1-2-3), and then finally seeing that "1-2-3" maps onto *abc*. At one level of abstraction, then, the analogy is this: *abc* goes to *abd*, and 123 goes to 124; but at the letter level (the level it was actually posed at), the analogy is this: *abc* goes to *abd*, and *mrrjjj* goes to *mrrjjjj*. But if this is the "best" answer, the other answers are quite interesting. Is *mrrjjd* better than, worse than, or equivalent to *mrrddd*? Why is *mrrkkk* better than both of those? Why is *mrrjjjj* better than all of them? And why is *mrrkkkk* (with four letters *k*) *inferior* to *mrrjjjj*?

The mapping functions used by Copycat at a particular point in time depend on the representation that has already been built up. Looking for *successors* or for *repetitions*, for instance, will be differentially encouraged according to the current context. So the two letters *mm* in the string *ffmmtt* will be mapped as a sameness pair, whereas in the string *abcefgklmmno* they will be perceived as parts of two different successor triples: *klm* and *mno*.

Even in the highly idealized domain of alphabetic letter strings, interesting problems arise. Suppose, for instance, that Copycat is told that *abc* changes into *abd*, and it must now decide what *xyz* changes into. What will it say? (What would you say?)

Its initial description of the input pair, couched in terms of alphabetic successors, has to be destroyed when it comes across *z*—which has no successor. Different descriptors then compete to represent the input strings, and the final output depends partly on which descriptors are chosen. On different occasions, Copycat comes up with the answers *xyd*, *xyzz*, *xyy*, and others. However, its deepest insight is when (on approximately one run out of eight) it chances to notice that at one end of one string it is dealing with the *first* letter of the alphabet, and at the other end of the other string, it is dealing with the *last*. This suddenly opens up a radically new way of mapping the strings onto each other: namely, with *a* mapping onto *z*, and simultaneously *left* onto *right*. As a consequence of this conceptual reversal, *successor* and *predecessor* also swap roles, and so the idea of "replacing the rightmost letter by its successor," which applied to the initial string, metamorphoses under this mapping into "replace the *leftmost* letter by its *predecessor.*" This gives the surprising and elegant answer, *wyz.*

You will have noticed that the initial description in this case is not merely adapted, but destroyed. Hofstadter compares this example with conceptual revolutions in science: the initial interpretation is discarded, and a fundamentally different interpretation is substituted for it.

These ideas about the interdependence of analogy and perception can be informally applied to our previous example. A painter, looking at the knitting woman, might sense some analogy to the portrait of Whistler's mother. In building his perceptual representation, he might therefore concentrate in turn (guided by his memory of the portrait) on the living woman's bodily attitude, hairstyle and hair color, and skirt length. A political activist would find nothing of interest in such matters. His representation of the scene might ignore the physical details entirely, focusing instead on the vulnerability, powerlessness, and political ignorance of nonunionized female workers—going like lambs to the slaughter, as he might (analogically) say.

Neither of these observers would pick out the currently relevant aspects of the entire situation immediately, for neither (we assume) came to the scene with detailed foreknowledge of what he would find, still less of what analogical associations he would be wanting to make. Rather, they would pick out the relevant aspects continuously, by a dialectical process of interpretative-analogical thinking. Much, perhaps even all, of this context-sensitive construction would occur subconsciously. But conscious inference might play a role, especially if someone were puzzling to interpret an analogy as opposed to generating one spontaneously (maybe the politician heard the painter say "Look! Whistler's mother!").

This constructive process can be "telescoped." Suppose that the painter and politician were told, before entering the room, that they would see something very like Whistler's mother. In that case, they would enter the room with certain mapping rules already prepared, and would see the expected analogy very quickly. Such telescoping enabled a positivist philosopher in the 1950s to play a practical joke on a group of "ordinary language" philosophers. Positivists had been arguing for some years that when we look at a straight stick half-immersed in a glass of water, we *see* only "sense data" (which include the appearance of a bend), and we then use our knowledge about refraction to *infer* that the sense data are caused by a straight stick, not a bent one. Their opponents had countered that there are no "sense data," and that we can properly be said to *see*, and even to *know*, that the stick is straight. Predictably, when the positivist lecturer held up a glass of water with a stick in it, the linguistic philosophers in the audience looked at it and insisted that the stick was obviously straight. In fact, it was bent. (Copycat's processing can be telescoped too: if the relevant descriptors are marked beforehand, the system will use those descriptors in preference to others—even though it is still potentially capable of perceiving its data in many ways.)

Culturally based telescoping of this sort explains why a schoolchild can quickly understand, perhaps even discover, an analogy that took the relevant H-creative thinker many months or years to grasp. The particular analogy, we assume, is new to the child. But its general type is familiar. The notion that simple linear equations, for example, capture many properties of the physical world may already be well established in the pupil's mind. It is hardly surprising, then, if this analogical mapping mechanism can be activated at the drop of the teacher's chalk.

As Hofstadter points out, most current computational models of analogy (and of problem solving, including scientific discovery) put the computer in the place of the schoolchild. That is, the relevant representations and mapping rules are provided ready-made to the program. It is the programmer who has done the work of sifting and selecting the "relevant" points from the profuse conceptual apparatus within his mind. Copycat, preliminary though it is, shows that a computational theory of creative thinking need not take relevance for granted in this way.

Transformation in Models of Scientific Discovery

Computational work on scientific thinking is commoner than work on artistic skills. Several "inductive" programs have come up with useful (in some cases, H-novel) scientific ideas. For instance, a suite of programs designed to find simple mathematical and classificatory relations has "rediscovered" many physical and chemical laws (Langley et al. 1987; Zytkow 1990). And an expert system (dealing with a strictly limited area of stereochemistry) has drawn chemists' attention to molecules they had not previously thought of (Lindsay et al. 1980). This system has even been listed as co-author of a refereed paper published in the journal of American Chemistry Society (Buchanan et al. 1976). Like most current AI systems (except Copycat), however, these "discovery programs" depend on the programmers' prior handcrafting of the relevant data. What's more, like the systems discussed in the previous sections, they are exploratory rather than transformational.

Programs capable of *transforming* their own conceptual space are still few and far between. One such is the "Automatic Mathematician"

(AM) (Lenat 1983). This system does not produce proofs, nor solve mathematical problems. Rather, it generates and explores mathematical ideas, coming up with new concepts and hypotheses to think about.

AM starts out with 100 very primitive mathematical concepts drawn from set theory (including sets, lists, equality, and operations). These concepts are so basic that they do not even include the ideas of elementary arithmetic. To begin with, the program does not know what an integer is, still less addition, subtraction, multiplication, and division.

Also, AM is provided with about 300 heuristics. These can examine, combine, and transform AM's concepts—including any compound concepts built up by it. Some are very general, others specific to set theory, and they enable AM to explore the space potentially defined by the primitive concepts. This exploration involves conceptual change, by means of various combinations and transformations.

For example, AM can generate the *inverse* of a function. This heuristic (a mathematical version of "consider the negative") enables the program to define multiplication having already defined division, or to define square roots having already defined squares. Another transformation generalizes a concept by changing an "and" into an "or" (compare relaxing the membership rules of a club, from "anyone who plays bridge and canasta" to "anyone who plays bridge or canasta").

However, AM does not consider *every* negative, nor change *every* "and" into an "or." Time and memory do not allow this. Like all creative thinkers, AM needs hunches to guide it along some paths rather than others. And it must evaluate its hunches, if it is to appreciate its own creativity. Accordingly, some of AM's heuristics suggest which sorts of concept are likely to be the most interesting. If it decides that a concept is interesting, AM concentrates on exploring that concept. For example, it takes note if it finds that the union of two sets has a simply expressible property that is not possessed by either of them. This is a mathematical version of the familiar notion that *emergent* properties are interesting. In general, we are interested if the combination of two things has a property that neither constituent has.

AM's hunches, like human hunches, are sometimes wrong. Nevertheless, it has come up with some extremely powerful notions. It produced many arithmetical concepts, including *integer, prime, square root, addition*, and *multiplication*. It generated, though of its nature could not attempt to prove, the fundamental theorem of number theory: that every number can be uniquely factorized into primes. And it suggested the interesting idea (Goldbach's conjecture) that every even number greater than two is the sum of two different primes.

It defined several concepts of number theory by following unusual paths—in two cases, inspiring human mathematicians to produce much shorter proofs than were previously known. It has even originated one minor theorem that no one had ever thought of before (concerning "maximally divisible" numbers, which AM's programmer knew nothing about). In short, AM appears to be significantly P-creative, and slightly H-creative too.

Some critics have suggested that this appearance is deceptive, that some of the heuristics were specifically included to make certain mathematical discoveries possible. In reply, AM's programmer insists that the heuristics are fairly general ones, not special-purpose tricks. On average, he reports, each heuristic was used in making two dozen different discoveries, and each discovery involved two dozen heuristics. Even so, a given heuristic may have been used only once, in making an especially significant discovery. (A detailed trace of the actual running of the program would be needed to find this out.) The question would then arise whether it had been put in for that specific purpose, or for exploring mathematical space in a more general way. The precise extent of AM's creativity, then, is unclear. But we do have some specific ideas about what sorts of questions are relevant.

Whereas AM has heuristics for altering concepts, a successor program (EURISKO) possesses heuristics for changing heuristics. As a result, EURISKO can explore and transform not only its stock of concepts, but its own processing style.

For example, one heuristic asks whether a rule has ever led to any interesting result. If it has not (given that it has been used several times), it is marked as less valuable—which makes it less likely to be used in future. What if the rule has occasionally been helpful, though usually worthless? Another heuristic, on noticing this, suggests that the rule be specialized. The new heuristic will have a narrower range of application than the old one, so will be tried less often (thus saving effort). But it will be more likely to be useful in those cases where it is tried.

Moreover, the "specializing heuristic" can be applied *to itself*. Because it is sometimes useful and sometimes not, EURISKO can consider specializing it in some way. The program distinguishes several sorts of specialization, and has heuristics for all of them. Each is plausible, for each is often (though not always) helpful. And each is useful in many different domains. One form of specialization requires that the rule being considered has been useful at least three times. Another demands that the rule has been *very* useful, at least once. Yet another insists that the newly specialized rule must be capable of producing all the past successes of the unspecialized rule. And a fourth heuristic specializes the rule by taking it to an extreme. Other heuristics work not by specializing rules, but by generalizing them. Generalization, too, can take many forms. Still other heuristics can create new rules by analogy with old ones. Again, various types of analogy can be considered.

With the help of various packets of specialist heuristics to complement these general ones, EURISKO has been applied in several different areas. It has come up with some H-novel ideas, concerning genetic engineering and computer-chip (VLSI) design. Some of its ideas have even been granted a U.S. patent (the U.S. patent law insists that the new idea must not be "obvious to a person skilled in the art").

The general principles of heuristic embodied within EURISKO have nothing specifically to do with science. They could, in theory, be applied to artistic spaces too. So some future version of the acrobat drawing program, for example, might be able to alter—and even to transform—its graphic style by using methods like those described above. Like analogy, then, heuristic transformation is a general strategy of creative thinking that can be applied in many different fields of thought.

To be sure, scientific ideas have to fit the world in a way in which artistic ideas do not. But AM and EURISKO are not concerned with validation, or proof: their role is simply to come up with potentially interesting new ideas. The selection of the best ideas, and the weeding out of the worst, must be done by their human users.

Genetic Algorithms

The preceding remark should not be taken to mean that *only* humans, in principle, are able to sort the wheat from the chaff. But this is a very common view. It is expressed, for instance, in the following poem, fictionally ascribed by Laurence Lerner to an imaginary computer program called ARTHUR (Automatic Record Tabulator but Heuristically Unreliable Reasoner) (Lerner 1974):

> *Arthur's Anthology of English Poetry*
> To be or not to be, that is the question
> To justify the ways of God to men
> There was a time when meadow grove and stream
> The dropping of the daylight in the west
> Otters below and moorhens on the top
> Had fallen in Lyonesse about their Lord.

There was a time when moorhens on the top
To justify the daylight in the west,
To be or not to be about their Lord
Had fallen in Lyonesse from God to men;
Otters below and meadow grove and stream
The dropping of the day, that is the question.
A time when Lyonesse and grove and stream
To be the daylight in the west on top
When meadow otters fallen about their Lord
To justify the moorhens is the question
Or not to be the dropping God to men
There was below the ways that is a time.
To be in Lyonesse, that is the question
To justify the otters, is the question
The dropping of the meadows, is the question
I do not know the answer to the question
There was a time when moorhens in the west
There was a time when daylight on the top
There was a time when God was not a question
There was a time when poets
                    Then I came

Lerner appears to believe that transformations that could be carried out by a computer program, such as "mechanical" cut-and-paste, could not possibly generate anything sensible—and that no program could tell sense from nonsense anyway. The implication, so far as theoretical psychology is concerned, is that no computational theory could describe the generation of valuable new ideas, and that only an unanalyzable faculty of "intuition" or "insight" could recognize their value. None of these beliefs is justified.

Consider, for example, a computer program that uses IF-THEN rules to regulate the transmission of oil through a pipeline in an economical way (Holland et al. 1986). It receives hourly measurements of the oil inflow, oil outflow, inlet pressure, outlet pressure, rate of pressure change, season, time of day, time of year, and temperature. Using these data, it continually alters the inlet pressure to allow for variations in demand, infers the existence of accidental leaks, and adjusts the inflow accordingly.

So far, so boring. But—what is not boring at all—this program is a self-transforming system. It was not told which rules to use for adjusting inflow, or for detecting accidental leaks. It discovered them for itself. It started from a set of randomly generated rules, which it repeatedly transformed in part random, part systematic ways. To do this, it used heuristics called genetic algorithms. These enable a system to make changes that are both plausible and unexpected, for they produce novel recombinations of the most useful parts of existing rules.

As the name suggests, these heuristics are inspired by biological ideas about how the "creative" process of evolution is effected. Some genetic changes are isolated mutations in single genes. But others involve entire chromosomes. For example, two chromosomes may swap their left-hand sides, or their midsections (the point at which they break is largely due to chance). If a chromosome contained only six genes, then the strings *ABCDEF* and *PQRSTU* might give *ABRSTU* and *PQCDEF*, or *ABRSEF* and *PQCDTU*. Such transformations can happen repeatedly, in successive generations. The strings that eventually result are unexpected combinations of genes drawn from many different sources. Genetic algorithms in computer programs produce novel structures by similar sorts of transformation.

Psychological applications of such simple combinatorial methods may seem doomed to failure. Indeed, these very methods are used by Lerner to ridicule the idea of a computer-poet. Almost all the lines in *Arthur's Anthology of English Poetry* are derived, by cut-and-paste recombinations, from the sixfold miscellany of the first verse. Starting with Shakespeare and Milton, the path runs steeply downward: the imaginary computer tells us that "To justify the moorhens is the question," and produces the gnomic utterance "There was below the ways that is a time."

Lerner's mockery of what are, in effect, genetic algorithms is not entirely fair, for many potentially useful structures were generated by his combinatorial method. Almost every line of his poem would be intelligible in some other verbal environment. "To justify the moorhens is the question" might have occurred in *The Wind in the Willows*, if Ratty's friends had been accused of wrongdoing. Even "Or not to be the dropping God to men" might have featured on Mount Olympus: "Pick up your thunderbolt, Zeus! Do you want to be, or not to be, the 'dropping God' to men?" Only one line is utter gibberish: "There was below the ways that is a time."

The explanation is that Lerner swapped grammatically coherent fragments, rather than single words. A similar strategy was followed by those eighteenth-century composers (including Mozart) who wrote "dice music," in which a dozen different choices might be provided for every bar (as opposed to every note) of a sixteen-bar piece. In general, the plausibility of the new structures produced by this sort of exploratory transformation is increased if the swapped sections are coherent minisequences.

However, there is a catch—or rather, several. The first is that a self-adapting system must somehow identify the most useful "coherent minisequences." But these never function in isolation: both genes and ideas express their influence by acting in concert with many others. The second is that coherent minisequences are not always *sequences*. Co-adapted genes (which code for biologically related functions) tend to occur on the same chromosome, but they may be scattered over various points within it. Similarly, potentially related ideas are not always located close to each other in conceptual space. Finally, a single unit may enter more than one group: a gene can be part of different co-adaptive groups, and an idea may be relevant to several kinds of problem.

Programs based on genetic algorithms help to explain how plausible combinations of far-distant units can nevertheless happen. They can identify the useful parts of individual rules, even though these parts never exist in isolation. They can identify the significant interactions between rule parts (their mutual coherence), even though the number of possible combinations is astronomical. And they can do this despite the fact that a given part may occur within several rules. Their initial IF-THEN rules are randomly generated (from task-relevant units, such as *pressure, increase,* and *inflow*), but they can end up with self-adapted rules rivaling the expertise of human beings.

The role of natural selection is modeled by assigning a "strength" to each rule, which is continually adjusted according to its success (in controlling the pipeline, for instance). The relevant heuristic is able, over time, to identify the most useful rules, even though they act in concert with many others—including some that are useless, or even counterproductive. The strength measure enables the rules to compete, the weak ones gradually dropping out of the system. As the average rule strength rises, the system becomes better adapted to the task environment.

The role of variation is modeled by heuristics (genetic operators) that transform the rules by swapping and inserting parts in ways like those outlined above. For instance, the "crossover" operator swaps a randomly selected segment between each of two rules. Each segment may initially be in a rule's IF section or its THEN section. In other words, the crossover heuristic can change either the conditions that result in a certain action, or the action to be taken in certain conditions, or both.

One promising strategy would be to combine the effective components of several high-strength rules. Accordingly, the genetic operators pick only rules of relatively high strength. But the effective components must be identified (a rule may include several conditions in its IF side and several actions in its THEN side). The program regards a component as effective if it occurs in a large number of successful rules. A "component" need not be a sequence of juxtaposed units. It may be, for instance, two sets of three (specified) neighboring units, separated by an indefinite number of unspecified units. The huge number of possible combinations do not have to be separately defined, nor considered in strict sequence. In effect, the system considers them all in parallel (taking into account its estimate of various probabilities in the environment concerned).

Contrary to Lerner's rhetorical intention, *Arthur's Anthology* shows that simple recombinations of ideas and conceptual themes can sometimes lead to potentially valuable ideas. To that extent, a combination theory may help to explain some examples of creative thinking. But, as remarked in the first section, a combination theory should show how these combinations can come about, and how the results can be selectively sifted. Work on genetic algorithms suggests that unconscious, nondeliberative psychological processes might enable largely random (but useful) combinations and sensible selections to be made in human minds.

Some visual artists are using evolutionary programs to help them produce images that—they assure us—they could not have imagined otherwise. Karl Sims's computer graphics program, for instance, uses genetic algorithms to generate new images from preexisting images (Sims 1991; see also Todd and Latham 1992). In this case, the selection of the "fittest" examples is not automatic. Instead, the programmer selects the images that are aesthetically pleasing, or otherwise interesting, and these are used to "breed" the next generation. (Sims could provide automatic selection rules, but has not yet done so—not only because of the difficulty of defining aesthetic criteria, but also because he aims to provide an interactive graphics environment in which human and computer can cooperate in generating otherwise inconceivable images.)

In a typical run of the program, the first image is generated at random (but Sims can feed in a real image, such as a picture of a face, if he wishes). Then the program makes nineteen independent changes (mutations) in the initial image-generating rule, so as to cover the VDU-screen with twenty images: the first, plus its nineteen ("asexually" reproduced) offspring. At this point, the human uses the computer mouse to choose either *one* image to be mutated, or *two* images to be "mated" (through crossover). The result is another screenful of twenty images, of which all but one (or two) are newly generated by random mutations or crossovers. The process is then repeated, for as many generations as one wants.

How does Sims's program manage to tweak and transform image space? It starts with a list of twenty very simple LISP functions. A "function" is not an actual instruction, but an instruction schema: more like "$x + y$" than "$2 + 3$." Some of these functions can alter parameters in preexisting functions: for example, they can divide or multiply numbers, transform vectors, or define the sines or cosines of angles. Some can combine two preexisting functions, or nest one function inside another; so multiply nested hierarchies (many-leveled spaces) can eventually result. A few are basic image-generating functions ("maps" or images), capable for example of generating an image consisting of vertical stripes. Others can process a preexisting image, for instance by altering the light constrasts so as to make "lines" or "surface edges" more or less visible.

Significantly, one may not be able to say just why *this* image resulted from *that* LISP expression. Sims himself cannot always explain the changes he sees appearing on the screen before him, even though he can access the miniprogram responsible for any image he cares to investigate, and for its parent(s) too. Often he cannot even "genetically engineer" the underlying LISP expression so as to get a particular visual effect. This is partly because his system makes several changes simultaneously, with every new generation.

Where human minds are concerned, we may similarly have multiple interacting changes (and no program explanation at our fingertips). These multiple changes and simultaneous influences arise from the plethora of ideas within the mind. Think of the many different thoughts that arise in your consciousness, more or less fleetingly, when you face a difficult choice or moral dilemma. Consider the likelihood that many more conceptual associations are being activated unconsciously in your memory, influencing your conscious musings accordingly. Even if we had a listing of all these influences, we might be in much the same position as Sims, staring in wonder at one of this nth-generation images and unable to say why *this* LISP expression gave rise to it. In fact, we cannot hope to know about more than a fraction of the ideas aroused in human minds (one's own, or someone else's) when such choices are faced. The notorious unpredictability, and even post hoc inexplicability, of human creativity would therefore be expected, if processes like genetic algorithms are going on in the mind.

This is not to say that the variational/combinatorial processes in human minds are closely similar to those in the pipeline program or Sims' computer graphics system. Like the other programs discussed earlier, these two examples are crude at best and mistaken at worst, when compared with human thinking. But current computational models do offer us some promising, and precise, ideas about how to identify, map, explore, and transform conceptual spaces. And that, I have argued, is what the psychology of creativity is all about.

Can Creativity Be Measured?

Assuming that creativity can be identified, and even explained, can it also be measured? The basic meaning of the term applies to ideas. People and social groups are called creative only if they are thought to have produced creative ideas. If we could measure creative ideas, we could develop some way of "counting" them so as to measure the creativity of individuals or cultures.

Our question, then, is whether—and if so, how—we can say that one creative idea is more, even much more, creative than another. To put the question in a more paradoxical way, but one which seems justified by the account of creativity given above, how can one impossible idea be more impossible than another?

One common usage of "more creative" can be discarded, for present purposes, immediately. We saw in the first section that *creative* may be used as an honorific label reserved for H-creativity, as opposed to P-creativity. In that case, any H-creative idea is "more creative" than any merely P-creative idea. Indeed, the latter would not be regarded as creative at all.

This restrictive sense of the term, applicable only to first-time historical novelty, is unhelpful here. Quite apart from the ubiquitous problem of the reliability of historical evidence, the point at issue here is not "Who thought of X first?" but "Is X a creative idea, and if so, how creative is it?" Our concern (as in previous sections) must be with P-creativity in general, of which H-creativity is a special case. If one wants to measure H-creativity (in comparing cultures, for instance), one must first find a way of measuring P-creativity and then apply it selectively to H-novel cases.

If by "measurement" is meant the application of a numerical scale, based on one or a few numerically describable dimensions, then my account of creativity implies that the creativity of an idea cannot be measured. One cannot capture the interesting differences between the *Mona Lisa* and the *Demoiselles d'Avignon*, for instance, by a set of measurements. Certainly, the spatial area of Nicholas Hilliard's miniatures, or the light reflectance of Rembrandt's portraits, might be relevant to judgments about the originality of those two artists. But the most significant aesthetic questions about their paintings concern other features, grounded in structural properties of various kinds. The same is true of originality in science. In general, one cannot assess creative ideas by a scalar metric.

Some form of complexity measurement, as used by computer science, would be useful. However, depth within the space must be recognized too. The appropriate method of assessment would have to take into account the fact that conceptual spaces are multidimensional structures, where some features are "deeper," more influential, than others. The prairie house fireplace, for example, is architecturally deeper than the bedroom, and much deeper than the (merely ornamental) balcony. Analogously, the linguist's *NP* is syntactically deeper than *determiner*, and much deeper than *red*. And the home key is harmonically deeper than a modulation from major to minor, and much deeper than a plagal cadence.

Moreover, daring harmony can coexist with conservative melody: how is the one to be weighed against the other? What about novels and poems: does the originality lie in the plot, the theme, the language, the meter, the imagery, the psychological insight, the political awareness . . . all or none of these, and/or something else? To compare the degree of creativity of two ideas, we would have to weigh depth against number: novelty in one deep feature (a core dimension of the space) might outweigh several simultaneous novelties in more superficial features.

Creative transformations would have to be compared in respect of their depth, and distinguished from mere superficial tweaking. This could best be done for ideas within a single domain, where the conceptual space is shared. But chalk could sometimes be compared with cheese: to put seven fireplaces in a prairie house is clearly more daring (it results in more significant structural differences) than to put seven adjectives with one noun, or to superimpose seven decorative trills on a melody.

This is not to dismiss the more superficial aspects of our thinking as evaluatively irrelevant. Balconies can be not only well placed (in relation to the overall structure), but beautifully wrought. Dickens's seven adjectives for the sinner Scrooge were well chosen (and well ordered). And baroque music delights us with its profuse ornamentation. Indeed, these "superficialities" have their own internal structural principles. The wrought-iron balcony can be aesthetically evaluated as an object in itself, quite apart from its relation to its parent building. Musical ornamentation has its own structure, quite apart from its relation to the melody: our delight at Alfred Deller's singing, for instance, is elicited partly by his daring—and teasing—mordants, appoggiaturas, and trills.

Comparative assessments of creativity must recognize that many creative achievements involve exploration, and perhaps tweaking, of a conceptual space, rather than radical transformation of it. The more complex the space, the greater its exploratory potential, the more "mere" exploration will be valued. (This is true only up to a point: if the space is so complex as to be unintelligible to us, even in an intuitive way, its generative products will be rejected. The common phenomenon of initial scorn followed by universal acceptance reflects the difficulty people sometimes have of relating a new idea to the underlying space that generated it.)

The exploratory activities of normal science, for instance, are not uncreative, even though they do not involve the fundamental perceptual reinterpretations typical of scientific revolutions. Nobel Prizes are not awarded for revolutionary work in the Kuhnian sense, but for ingenious and imaginative problem solving that may involve fairly deep theoretical transformations (of string molecule to ring molecule, for instance). To call this scientific work mere puzzle solving is to risk losing sight of the distinction between following a well-marked path for three (or three hundred) more steps, and carving out a new path within territory that has been mapped only on a large scale.

It is significant, here, that some musicians regard Mozart as a greater composer than Haydn *even though* they allow that Haydn was more adventurous, more ready to transform contemporary musical styles. Mozart's superiority, on this view, lay in his fuller exploration (and tweaking) of musical space, his ability to amaze us by showing us what unsuspected glories lie within this familiar space. Whether this musical judgment is faithful to Haydn's and Mozart's work is irrelevant. The point is that it is one which can intelligibly be made. It follows that no creativity metric could be adequate that ignored structural exploration, focusing only on structural transformation.

Computational models of concepts within connectionist semantic networks sometimes provide a basis for a metric of conceptual distance. But "metric" is perhaps a misleading term, because this is a structured distance. Copycat's measurements of analogical similarity between letter strings, for instance, take note of various sorts of structural likeness and dissimilarity. It is therefore able, as presumably you are too, to see that the alphabet-reversing *wyz* is a more creative response than is *xyd* to the input problem *abc*--> *abd; xyz*-->???. Two concepts may be compared, for example, in terms of their abstractly defined internal structure and/or their specific semantic content and/or their customary associations. These comparisons may make it possible to compare two theories said to be incommensurable by Kuhnians. (A co-author of the program presented with the philosopher–midwife analogy has argued that a computational definition of "explanatory coherence" can show how the "incommensurable" theories of phlogiston and oxygen can be rationally compared [Thagard 1989].)

Lacking any explicit account of the relevant conceptual spaces, someone may nevertheless make intuitive judgments about creativity. ("I don't know anything about art, but I know what I like!") Some of those judgments may be well grounded, and the more experience the person has of the relevant genre, the more sensitive they are likely to be. But even the well-grounded judgments will be largely indefensible, in the sense that the person is unable to defend them in terms of explicitly identified features of the conceptual space concerned. The intuitions of someone with access to verbal descriptions of the nature and history of the genre will, in general, be more discriminating (so the study of art history can increase one's appreciation of art, not merely one's knowledge about it).

For the purpose of comparing ("measuring") creativity, however, verbal descriptions may not be enough. The more explicit we can be in describing the creativity concerned, the better.

In a few cases, computational analyses exist that make clear the depth and mutual influences of different parts or dimensions of the relevant conceptual space. The creativeness of using seven prairie fireplaces may have been sensed by architectural historians, able only to remark on the "occult" properties of spatial balance involved. But now it can be explicitly described and explained in terms of the architectural grammar of prairie houses. Similarly, a musical grammar of jazz can show which chord sequences are structurally more complex than others (and how), and which improvisations relate to which aspects of the chord sequence. And a model of inductive reasoning within stereochemistry may show, more clearly than the preexisting chemical theory, how different molecular structures are related to each other.

Such analyses draw on conventional (noncomputational) work in aesthetics, musicology, and the history and philosophy of art and science—all of which aim to uncover the styles, genres, and theoretical forms of human achievement. This is hardly surprising, for only an expert in a given domain can write interesting programs modeling that domain. It is no accident that Cohen is an acclaimed painter in his own right, that Johnson-Laird is a good amateur jazz pianist, or that the designers of the stereochemistry and "explanatory coherence" programs include philosophers of science. Traditional work in the humanities is highly relevant to the computational understanding of creativity.

In sum: The computational approach to creativity is grounded in the more familiar disciplines. But it has a higher standard of explicitness and rigor, and a fiercer discipline of theory testing. The price it pays for these theoretical goods is limitation. As yet there are very few computational models of interesting conceptual spaces, and still fewer of creative transformations. Today's computational psychology is therefore of limited use in comparing the creativity of different creative products. Its contribution is to help point the way to the sorts of comparisons that we should be making.

References

Abelson, R. P. 1973. "The Structure of Belief Systems." In R. C. Schank and K. M. Colby, eds., *Computer Models of Thought and Language*. San Francisco: Freeman, pp. 287–340.

Boden, M. A. 1990. *The Creative Mind: Myths and Mechanisms*. London: Weidenfeld and Nicolson.

Brannigan, A. 1981. *The Social Basis of Scientific Discoveries*. Cambridge: Cambridge University Press.

Buchanan, B. G., D. H. Smith, W. C. White, R. Gritter, E. A. Feigenbaum, J. Lederberg, and C. Djerassi. 1976. "Applications of Artificial Intelligence for Chemical Inference. XXII Automatic Rule Formation in Mass Spectrometry by Means of the Meta-Dendral Program." *Journal of the American Chemistry Society* 98: 6168–6178.

Chalmers, D. J., R. M. French, and D. R. Hofstadter. 1991. *High-Level Perception, Representation, and Analogy: A Critique of Artificial Intelligence Methodology*. CRCC Technical Report 49. Center for Research on Concepts and Cognition, Indiana University, Bloomington, Indiana.

Clark, A., and A. Karmiloff-Smith. In press. "The Cognizer's Innards," *Mind and Language*.

Hesse, M. B. 1988. "Theories, Family Resemblances, and Analogy." In D. H. Helman, ed., *Analogical Reasoning*. Amsterdam: Kluwer, pp. 317–340.

Hofstadter, D. R., M. Mitchell, and R. M. French. 1987. *Fluid Concepts and Creative Analogies: A Theory and its Computer Implementation*. CRCC Technical Report 18. Center for Research on Concepts and Cognition, Indiana University, Bloomington, Indiana.

Hofstadter, D. R., and M. Mitchell. In press. "An Overview of the Copycat Project." In K. J. Holyoak and J. A. Barnden, eds., *Advances in Connectionist and Neural Computation Theory, Vol. 2: Analogical Connections*. Norwood, NJ: Ablex.

Holland, J. H., K. J. Holyoak, R. E. Nisbett, and P. R. Thagard. 1986. *Induction: Processes of Inference, Learning, and Discovery*. Cambridge, MA: MIT Press.

Holyoak, K. J., and J. A. Barnden, eds. In press. *Advances in Connectionist and Neural Computation Theory, Vol. 2: Analogical Connections*. Norwood, NJ: Ablex.

Holyoak, K. J., and P. Thagard. 1989. "Analogical Mapping by Constraint Satisfaction." *Cognitive Science* 13: 295–356.

Johnson-Laird, P. N. 1988. *The Computer and the Mind: An Introduction to Cognitive Science*. London: Fontana.

Johnson-Laird, P. N. 1993. "Jazz Improvisation: A Theory at the Computational Level." In P. Howell, R. West, and I. Cross, eds., *Representing Musical Structure*. London: Academic Press, pp. 291–326.

Karmiloff-Smith, A. 1986. "From Meta-processes to Conscious Access: Evidence from Children's Metalinguistic and Repair Data." *Cognition* 23: 95–147.

Karmiloff-Smith, A. 1990. "Constraints on Representational Change: Evidence from Children's Drawing." *Cognition* 34: 57–83.

Koestler, A. 1964. *The Act of Creation*. London: Hutchinson.

Koning, H., and J. Eizenberg. 1981. "The Language of the Prairie: Frank Lloyd Wright's Prairie Houses," *Environment and Planning B* 8: 295–323.

Langley, P., H. A. Simon, G. L. Bradshaw, and J. M. Zytkow. 1987. *Scientific Discovery: Computational Explorations of the Creative Process*. Cambridge, MA: MIT Press.

Lenat, D. B. 1983. "The Role of Heuristics in Learning by Discovery: Three Case Studies." In R. S. Michalski, J. G. Carbonell, and T. M. Mitchell, eds., *Machine Learning: An Artificial Intelligence Approach*. Palo Alto, CA: Tioga.

Lerner, L. A. 1974. *A.R.T.H.U.R.: The Life and Opinions of a Digital Computer*. Hassocks, Sussex: Harvester Press.

Lindsay, R., B. G. Buchanan, E. A. Feigenbaum, and J. Lederberg. 1980. *DENDRAL*. New York: McGraw-Hill.

Longuet-Higgins, H. C. 1987. *Mental Processes: Studies in Cognitive Science*. Cambridge, MA: MIT Press.

Longuet-Higgins, H. C. In press. "The Structural Determinants of Musical Expression." In M. A. Boden and A. Bundy (eds.), *Artificial Intelligence and the Mind: New Breakthroughs or Dead-Ends?* London: The Royal Society and The British Academy.

McCorduck, P. 1991. *Aaron's Code*. San Francisco: W. H. Freeman.

Mitchell, M. 1993. *Analogy as Perception*. Cambridge, MA: MIT Press.

Rumelhart, D. E., and J. L. McClelland, eds. 1986. *Parallel Distributed Processing: Explorations in the Microstructure of Cognition*. 2 vols. Cambridge, MA: MIT Press.

Schank, R. C., and C. K. Riesbeck, eds. 1981. *Inside Computer Understanding: Five Programs Plus Miniatures*. Hillsdale, NJ: Erlbaum Press.

Sims, K. 1991. "Artificial Evolution for Computer Graphics," *Computer Graphics* 25 (no.4), July 1991: 319–328.

Stiny, G. 1977. "Ice-Ray: A Note on the Generation of Chinese Lattice Designs," *Environment and Planning B* 4: 89–98.

Stiny, G. 1991. "The Algebras of Design," *Research in Engineering Design* 2: 171–181.

Stiny, G., and J. Gips 1978. *Algorithmic Aesthetics: Computer Models for Criticism and Design in the Arts*. Berkeley: University of California Press.

Stiny, G., and W. J. Mitchell. 1978. "The Palladian Grammar." *Environment & Planning B* 5: 5–18.

Stiny, G., and W. J. Mitchell. 1980. "The Grammar of Paradise: On the Generation of Mughul Gardens," *Environment & Planning B* 7: 209–226.

Thagard, P. 1989. "Explanatory Coherence." *Behavioral and Brain Sciences* 12: 435–502.

Thagard, P., K. J. Holyoak, G. Nelson, and D. Gochfeld. 1988. "Analog Retrieval by Constraint Satisfaction." Research paper, Cognitive Science Laboratory, Princeton University.

Todd, S., and W. Latham. 1992. *Evolutionary Art & Computers*. London: Academic Press.

Vosniadou, S., and A. Ortony, eds. 1989. *Similarity and Analogical Reasoning*. Cambridge: Cambridge University Press.

Zytkow, J. M. 1990. "Deriving Laws Through Analysis of Processes and Equations." In P. Langley and J. Shrager, eds., *Computational Models of Discovery and Theory Formation*. San Mateo, CA: Morgan Kaufmann, pp. 129–156.

Chapter 5

Creativity: Beyond the Darwinian Paradigm

David N. Perkins

Zippers and Zen koans, Post-its and *Paradise Lost*, Kool-Aid and supercolliders—we live in an invented world. But that world does not stop at the edges of human science, culture, and commerce. Beyond the boundaries of human inventions as such, inventionlike ingenuity appears. The "creativity" of evolution has been celebrated by innumerable watchers of nature from Charles Darwin and before to Lewis Thomas and after. From the familiar fulcrum of the human thumb to the exotic lifestyle of spiders that throw their webs like nets, nature displays its genius.

If both individual human beings and nature invent, so does society. Languages are a case in point. The subjunctive mode of English was not contrived by immigrant Sub Jun, who several centuries ago saw a greater need for the expression of counterfactuals. Languages develop over the centuries through the texture of human interactions.

The creativity of nature has inspired efforts to give a Darwinian account of human creativity. For example, Donald Campbell (1960, 1974) proposed that human creativity depends on the random generation and selective retention of ideas. The more creative the outcome—the more it departs from precedent—the more so this would be the case.

But is nature really creative? It's easy to be uneasy with the notion of nature as an inventor. Michael Ruse (1986), in his *Taking Darwin Seriously*, cautions against too close an analogy between the generativity of nature and the creativity of human beings. Decrying attempts to explain scientific and technological progress on a Darwinian model, Ruse highlights the intentionality of science, its progressive truth-oriented character. In the true Darwinian context, the concept of "progress" makes little sense. Certainly progress cannot be considered as the development of greater complexity and sophistication, culminating in—ahem!—us. In his *Wonderful Life*, Stephen Jay Gould (1989) issues just such a warning amid numerous examples of how an inappropriately progressive image of evolution has distorted both popular understanding and professional research. Progress toward higher and more complex organisms is human wishful thinking. Nature cares only about survival, where sharks, cockroaches, and an innumerable array of one-celled organisms have it all over human beings, the nouveau riche of the biosphere.

Many words could be spent arguing about whether nature's generativity—the Darwinian evolutionary process—is "real" creativity. But such debates risk circularity, because they typically identify "real" creativity with the human model, and who is to say what the right model should be? Trying to decide how authentically creative natural selection is may not tell us the most about creativity.

Instead, let us be generous about what we count as creative. Let us recognize several of what might be called "creative systems." Nature is one of them. The mind of an inventor is another. Social processes of the sort that yield highly developed languages give yet a third example. We can ask of these creative systems: How do they pull creative rabbits out of the hat of the ordinary? And do they do the trick the same way?

Adaptive Novelty and Klondike Spaces

Before dismantling several hats to see how they work, it's useful to develop some tools for the purpose. First of all, any creative system deals in what might be called "adaptive novelty." A creative system produces something on the one hand novel and on the other adaptive in its context. In the biological world, such products of evolution as the Oriental epicanthic fold, a cold-weather adaptation, fit the definition. In the world of human invention, everything from the can opener to Ezra Pound's *Cantos*. In social evolution, grammatical forms such as the subjunctive or customs such as shaking hands. All now *are* but previously were *not*. All constitute adaptations—not the only or even necessarily the best ones to meet the challenges they address, but adaptive novelties nonetheless.

But how novel should "novel" be for creativity? In her recent *The Creative Mind*, Margaret Boden (1991) suggests that an established set of similar products of invention, say conventional mousetraps, reflects an often-tacit "rule set." We recognize true innovation because we explicitly or tacitly detect a move beyond the "rule set," an outcome that could not have emerged from the paradigm defined by those rules. I do not want to limit the present discussion to innovations in this strong sense, but I certainly want to emphasize them. In particular, evolution appears to meet Boden's standard. Evolution "discovers" organisms that play by very different rules. The basic distinction between the plant and animal kingdoms may be the most dramatic example. Plants and animals solve the fundamental problem of energy capture in profoundly different ways, plants extracting energy from sunlight and animals from plants and other animals.

With Boden, I also conceptualize the process of arriving at adaptive novelty as a process of search through a space of possibilities. This move evokes one of the most productive paradigms of modern cognitive psychology, the notion of search in a problem space pioneered by Alan Newell, Herbert Simon, and their colleagues during early work on artificial intelligence (Newell and Simon 1972).

Newell and Simon dealt with formal problems, such as playing chess or proving theorems in logic. In such possibility spaces, both what constitutes a step in the search and what constitutes a solution are well defined. For example, in chess, steps are legal moves of the game, actually made or anticipated in thinking ahead. The ultimate solution is checkmate. In more typical circumstances of invention—either by human beings or nature—neither the steps nor the solution criteria have formal definitions, and the solution criteria themselves often develop considerably in the course of the search. Nonetheless, in a loose sense, both human beings and nature search through possibilities, often achieving adaptive outcomes novel in Boden's rule-breaking sense.

To speak of search through a space of possibilities does nothing to mark out what makes a creative challenge peculiar. How, for example, does the challenge of inventing an electronic mousetrap—or nature's challenge of adapting to a very new environment—differ from the challenge of accommodating four houseguests who suddenly appear for the weekend? It's not that the guest problem proves entirely routine and algorithmic. You may have to exercise some ingenuity, borrowing couch cushions from a neighbor to create a place on the floor, for instance. But broadly speaking the contrast seems to be this: You know how to begin to tackle the guest problem and make fairly steady progress on it. You know that beds, couches, mattresses, and cushions are directly relevant resources. You know the mix and match rules: Let's keep couples together if we can.

What gives a quest a more rule-breaking character than this? What if the problem situation invites or demands reaching beyond the patterns that have served well enough in the past? Some of these circumstances can be captured in a metaphor, the "Klondike space."

Imagine that you are searching for gold in the Klondike. You look from this stream bed to that, in this deposit of gravel and the next. You are guided by a fundamental principle: Gold is where you find it.

That is, although you can look in more likely and less likely places, you have no reliable strategy that will lead you to the gold.

You have to invest considerable search in a relatively clueless realm. You also know that searching in a particular region (metaphorically, sticking to the same old rule set) may not serve you well. You may need to look over the hill into the next valley.

Figure 5.1 helps us to single out what might be called the four basic "Klondike problems" of creative systems, as follows. Let us look at them in the literal Klondike context, the biological context, and the context of human invention.

The Rarity Problem.   Payoff is sparsely distributed in a vast space of possibilities. In the Klondike metaphor, gold is scarce. In the possibility space of imaginable biological organisms, very few are actually viable. In the space of possible electronic circuit layouts, few do anything at all, much less anything useful.

As the examples of biological organisms and electronic circuits make plain, the possibility spaces of biological or human invention are vast for *combinatorial* reasons: Proteins or transistors can be assembled in innumerable configurations. In discussions of heuristic search, this is often called the problem of "combinatorial explosions," which generate far too many combinations to be explored by exhaustive search processes in reasonable periods of time. Figure 5.1 captures something of the rarity problem, although it does not really represent how very rare rare is. The darkest and next darkest regions, representing high payoff and some payoff, occupy little of the total.

The Isolation Problem.   Regions of payoff often lie isolated or semi-isolated. In the Klondike metaphor, pockets of gold occur here and there, unconnected with one another. In the possibility space of imaginable biological organisms, some imaginable biological organisms, viable in principle, might be quite unlike anything that exists. In the world of inventions, a fruitful invention might lack close precedent. Thus in figure 5.1, some regions like region F lie completely isolated from others by blank areas of no promise. Other regions, like E, connect only by thin bridges of promise.

The Oasis Problem.   This is the flip side of the isolation problem, which says that some regions are hard to get to. The oasis problem says that regions of payoff or even promise are hard to leave. In the Klondike metaphor, even if a rich area becomes nearly mined out, it's tempting to stay and rework it. After all, when will one really find another? In the world of biology, why should nature try out new experimental forms when a number of established forms already function well? In

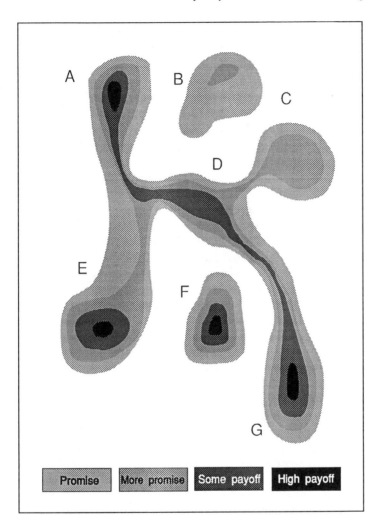

Figure 5.1
A sample "Klondike space."

the world of inventions, why seek a better mousetrap of a very different kind, rather than refine the ones we have? Thus in figure 5.1, regions of high payoff are surrounded by regions of declining payoff and promise.

The Plateau Problem. In many regions, directions toward greater promise are not clear. In the Klondike metaphor, a prospector may find no gold, or traces of gold uniformly across a wide area. In what direction does the mother lode lie? In the world of biology, a whole range of biological forms may be more or less equally adaptive with no natural "direction" for evolution to pursue (although of course evolution does not really pursue directions, as we shall see). In the world of inventions, many alternative ideas may seem equally promising, or do an equally adequate if not ideal job. Thus, in figure 5.1, there are some large regions of blankness, and of uniform promise, or uniform ordinary but not high payoff.

What do these topographical features of Klondike spaces have to do with creativity? Remember, creative systems discover adaptive novelty through search. Each of these characteristics of a Klondike space works against the discovery of adaptive novelty. The sheer rarity of adaptive novelty makes searches long and rewards sparse. The isolation problem means that many worthwhile discoveries lie "off the beaten track." The oasis problem creates a temptation for search processes to linger fruitlessly in areas of promise but no payoff, or some but not high payoff. The plateau problem means that search processes often cannot tell in what direction to search for increasing promise or payoff.

To put the matter another way, problems of low creative challenge involve possibility spaces not dominated by these features. Let us revisit the problem of accommodating the four guests, for instance. In the possibility space of possible sleeping arrangements, many patterns will not serve, but solutions are not all that sparse. Rather than isolated, solutions are closely related to one another: John could sleep on the living room sofa, or downstairs on the playroom sofa, or upstairs on the attic cot. Because solutions neighbor one another, it's unlikely that the search will get trapped by the marginal oasis of a barely adequate solution. And, because solutions lie close to one another, there are no extended plateaus: It's easy to cast about and find promising directions.

The rarity, isolation, oasis, and plateau problems are very abstract properties of a possibility space. They inevitably miss many nuances of specific creative enterprises such as the Wright brothers' work on powered flight or Beethoven's struggles with the Ninth Symphony.

However, in their abstractness, these properties capture some important features of the general puzzle of the emergence of adaptive novelty, and allow us to compare and contrast how different creative systems address the Klondike problems.

The Evolutionary Creative System

The crows strutting arrogantly about your lawn may have a good reason. Perhaps through some genetically coded racial memory, they dream of their days as dinosaurs. While to think of crows' dreams is a whimsy, there is this much truth: Contemporary paleontology holds that dinosaurs did not completely die; they took to the air instead.

Birds, it seems, are the most direct living descendants of dinosaurs. The evolutionary tale goes something like this. Contrary to popular perception, certain reptiles in the days of the dinosaurs were warm rather than cold blooded. This characteristic helped them evade the torpid behavior of normal cold-blooded reptiles in cold weather and darkness, keeping the biochemical engines turning over at a steady pace and the organism active, as with mammals today (Gould 1980).

Body heat regulation is the principal adaptive challenge of warm bloodedness, solved in mammals by hair to insulate and sweat to cool off, among other means. Feathers did not evolve initially for flight. They were certain dinosaurs' answer to the cooling problem, as much insulation then for those creatures as for birds today.

What happened then could have been something like this. Many dinosaurs walked on two legs, leaving two free for grasping. Feathers along the two "arms" may have afforded an adaptive advantage in giving balance. So the feathers lengthened.

By chance, the longer feathers afforded some lift and glide, at first perhaps just allowing slightly longer jumps, then, as the feathers lengthened still more, glides, and eventually true flight. So the wing feathers traversed three roles: as insulation, then for balance, then for flight—at each turn the adaptive advantage that drove evolution forward until dinosaurs filled the air.

This episode of evolution certainly seems to fit Boden's criterion of breaking a rule set. Aerial mobility demands a whole new range of adaptation and offers a whole new range of opportunities, yielding organisms of radically different morphology and behavior. What can it and episodes like it teach us about evolution as a creative system?

Just as with any creative system, we can envision the process of evolution as search in a Klondike space. Of course, the space of evolution is not a literal physical layout, like the Klondike where prospectors grub about. It is a space of different biological forms that might or might not prove viable.

We can imagine a piece of this space centered around the early feathered dinosaurs. Here are a few of its dimensions relevant to insulation, stability in running, and flight:

- Total quantity of feathers.
- Length and stiffness of feathers.
- Distribution of stiff, long feathers: on the arms versus elsewhere.
- Total mass (larger dinosaurs are too heavy to fly for physics reasons).

Evolution "searches" the possibilities by trial adaptations: a small dinosaur well insulated, then one that runs using arm feathers for balance, then one that glides, then one that flies. Original and intermediate forms may die out (as the dinosaurs did) but in their day they proved viable.

We take as the mechanism of evolution Darwin's three classic principles of natural selection: (1) spontaneous variation (now, but not by Darwin, understood as variation in genes); (2) selection (a matter of survival long enough to breed); (3) preservation of traits (parents tend to pass on traits to offspring). Each generation yields a range of variation, for instance, feathered dinosaurs with more or less glide potential. The more viable forms survive and breed.

Although contemporary views of evolution such as the punctuated equilibrium theory elaborate the implications of this basic Darwinian mechanism, by and large they do not challenge the mechanism itself (Ruse 1986). However, Wesson (1991) recently has offered an elaborate critique of natural selection, questioning on a number of technical grounds whether it can account for the range of organisms actually found in nature. Although Wesson's stance is provocative, we will focus on natural selection here. In writings on creativity at least, it is natural selection that has been put forth as a mechanism not only for creativity in the biological world but, by analogy, for aspects of human invention.

How Evolution Solves the Rarity Problem.   Like any creative system, the creative system of natural selection must deal with the four Klondike problems outlined earlier. Its solution to the problem of rarity is double: time and parallelism. For the first, evolution operates over geological time. Even the punctuated equilibrium theory, which holds that evolution occurs in spurts, does not fundamentally change the point. The "spurts" still occupy tens of thousands of years and innumerable breeding cycles. As to parallelism, evolution tries many things at the same time. Each generation of an organism yields a range of variants, each variant constitutes a parallel trial.

How Evolution Solves the Isolation Problem.   The creative system of evolution does not deal well with the isolation problem. Paths of evolution are paths of viable forms, each one in its day an at least marginally successful organism.

Looking to figure 5.1, imagine an evolutionary process with its ancestor organism starting in the middle of region A. Other payoff regions in figure 5.1 represent other organisms that might evolve from A. Descendent organisms might eventually appear in region D and later G. But evolution cannot achieve the potential organisms in region F or even region E, because they do not connect to region A by paths of viable intermediate organisms. Paths of "promise" as between A and E are not enough.

Another way to put this is to say that evolution does not "leap" as human inventors may. Evolution inherently has a more incremental character. This does not mean, however, that evolution cannot devise exotically divergent forms or that evolution progresses slowly on a geological time scale. In *Wonderful Life,* Stephen Jay Gould acquaints us with the remarkable fossil finds in the Burgess Shale of British Columbia, Canada, small sea creatures of more than 500 million years ago that show far *more* diversity in the top levels of the taxonomy of animals than exists today. Organisms that emerged nearly at the beginning of multicellular life, they testify to the far-reaching power of nature to experiment.

How Evolution Solves the Oasis Problem.   The search performed by evolution radiates outward in all viable directions, even in directions of lesser viability. Imagine, for instance, small feathered dinosaurs at A in figure 5.1, well adapted for a vigorous life as warm-blooded predators.

Among many variants and variants of variants, mutation eventually produces a small dinosaur with stiff wing feathers that help with balance, but do not suffice for flight. This dinosaur might be *less* viable than dinosaurs without stiff feathers. Place it at D in figure 5.1, a dark gray (some payoff) but not a black (high payoff) region. This dinosaur has its own niche, taking advantage of its better balance to feed on a flying insect population that evades other small dinosaurs. But the wing feathers impair the use of its "arms" for defense, so it falls to predators more often. Its population expands and diversifies very slowly.

No matter. Evolution "doesn't care" that this intermediate form proves less well adapted than its region A ancestors without stiff feathers, who are still thriving. So long as it can barely survive, that suffices. Variants gradually strengthen the feathers further. Finally, glides are possible. This variant can not only feed on aerial insects but can escape its enemies—a strong adaptation with room for great diversification. We can think of it as a form in the center of region G.

How Evolution Solves the Plateau Problem.   This problem falls to the mainstays of evolution: time and parallel search. Viable variants radiate out from the ancestor form generation by generation, covering plateaus.

The Meme Creative System

As a dessert toward the end of his *Selfish Gene,* Richard Dawkins (1976) develops an analog of evolution not for biological forms but for the ideas of human beings. Daniel Dennett (1991) picks up the same theme and develops it further in *Consciousness Explained.* The meme analogy follows the mechanism of evolution closely, but applies it to the human mind and society. Thus Dawkins gives us a language for talking in Darwinian terms about the social evolution of ideas.

Imagine, for example, Benjamin Franklin making up homilies. One says, "A penny saved is a penny earned." Another says, "A stitch in time saves seven." Another says, "Pay your debt to tomorrow." All three are "memes"—mental rather than genetic forms tossed into the environment of human society. They will survive, or mutate and survive, or "die" and become forgotten.

"Pay your debt to tomorrow" lacks poetry and compelling meaning. People forget it. "A penny saved is a penny earned" clicks. People remember it and pass it on. Like the shark and the cockroach, unaltered for millions of years, it hardly changes. "A stitch in time saves seven" does okay for a while. But at some point, someone makes up the variant, "A stitch in time saves nine." The greater euphony lets the mutant form propagate more widely, driving out the weaker competing "seven."

Presumably such a mechanism underlies the social evolution of languages. From time to time, individuals spontaneously try out variations, typically with little thought. Some of the variations—contractions, for example—catch people's fancy and get adopted and passed along. They in turn become the basis for other variations.

A key implication of Dawkins's "meme" notion is that the evolution of ideas does not depend on truth or excellence, but instead reflects survival power. The memes that thrive in the environment of mind and society are not necessarily the memes that make the most profound statements or express the richest artistic ideas. Just as insects are a bigger success story in the animal kingdom than the more sophisticated and intelligent mammals, so disco music takes the day while fusion jazz only does okay.

My favorite example of a vigorous but obtuse meme is the "right brain–left brain" notion. Popularized a few years ago, this notion has spread into the minds of almost everyone even idly concerned with psychology, creativity, or education. The general precept holds that the right side of the brain exercises the holistic creative functions, while the left side takes responsibility for the more analytic and linguistic functions. This is, of course, a gross oversimplification and parody of the actual findings and does not even make logical sense (Gardner 1975; Perkins 1981). Nonetheless, the idea has enormous magnetism. People love to believe it and draw questionable implications from it.

In keeping with Dawkins's analogy, the meme system solves the four Klondike problems in much the same manner as genetic evolution. But with some interesting differences.

How Memes Solve the Rarity Problem.   As with genetic evolution, the search done by memes occurs in parallel, each viable meme passing "descendants," which may be variants, to several people. Many of these people in turn pass second-generation descendants and variants to other people. Unlike genetic evolution, things happen quickly. Teen slang comes and goes, and fashions of dress change over years and decades. The pace is fast because social evolution works in a Lamarckian rather than Darwinian way. The host mind for a particular meme often tinkers with it, making it more viable. For instance, in our Benjamin Franklin story, "A stitch in time saves seven" does not have to wait upon a slip of the tongue—the analog of a random mutation— to produce "nine." Some poetic soul remakes the homily.

How Memes Solve the Isolation Problem.   As with genetic evolution, memes evolve only through viable forms, ideas that survive in one person's mind long enough to get passed to other minds in the original form or a variant. Thus the meme creative system per se solves the isolation problem no better than does the evolution creative system. Within an individual mind, however, leaps may occur that bring isolated regions into play.

How Memes Solve the Oasis Problem.   As in genetic evolution, less viable forms can spread too. For instance, suppose a person knows "A stitch in time saves nine" and, through a slip of the tongue, repeats it as "A stitch in time saves seven" to a visitor from another English-speaking country where the homily has no prevalence. Upon returning home, the visitor passes it around. With the more viable "nine" form not known there, the "seven" form spreads.

How Memes Solve the Plateau Problem.   As in genetic evolution, meme variants radiate in parallel from the ancestor.

As must be clear by now, the role that individual intentionality plays in meme variation puts a limit on the explanatory power of the meme view. Like other creative systems, the meme system helps to explain how adaptive novelty comes about. To the extent that the adaptive novelty in question involves the capturing of chance variations, the meme system explains well.

The meme system thus illuminates much about the evolution of linguistic forms, where intentional invention figures minimally. The meme system explains much less, but something worthwhile, about more Lamarckian situations like homilies and the left brain–right brain notion. For instance, it helps us to understand why the left brain–right brain notion proves most prevalent in its most simpleminded forms. The meme system explains little about intensively engineered technical inventions that see mindful improvement by others and adoption for calculated reasons: for example the Dolby scheme for encoding the volume of low-pitched sound, variants of which are now used on virtually all high-fidelity recordings.

This point recommends a look at the world of true human invention.

The Inventor Creative System

One of my most intriguing professional experiences in recent years was a small conference organized by my colleague Robert Weber and me to include a few cognitive psychologists, some historians of technology, and several world-class inventors. In the latter category, four of the several who participated were James Hillier, one of the developers of the electron microscope; John Wild, the principal developer of ultrasound; William Campbell, head of the team that developed the antibiotic *Ivermectin*, important in preventing the African parasitic disease river blindness and in treating heartworm and other related animal parasitic disorders; and Edward Rosinsky, one of the inventors of the Zeolite catalyst for cracking petroleum, which increased the yield of gasoline from petroleum by 30 percent.

These inventors joined the historians and cognitive psychologists for two days of discussion, presenting papers about their own thinking in arriving at their principal discoveries. One thing we learned was that inventors—or at least these inventors—were anything but your stereotypical reclusive basement tinkerers. They proved generally to be lively, witty, sociable, and broadly humanistic. Another thing we learned was something about the process of invention.

The details of the story appear in *Inventive Minds* (Weber and Perkins, 1922), a collection of articles from all participants including the inventors. Here I will draw in a few highlights around the theme of search.

One striking feature of almost all the inventions reviewed—not only the contemporary ones but the work of the Wright brothers, Edison, and others, seen through the historians' eyes—was the duration of the enterprise. There were no cases of instant breakthrough and prototypes on the table in a matter of weeks. In fact, nearly every tale of invention unfolded over several years, with many false starts and dead ends.

Another important feature concerned the grain of progress. Although the image of the creative leap dominates much everyday thinking about creativity (in fact, it is one of those persistent "memes," more notable for its magnetism than its descriptive accuracy), we saw no cases of inventions resulting from a single leap plus working out the details. There were leaps in plenty—some smaller, some larger—but never so large as to constitute the whole story.

Robert Weber and I found it illuminating to articulate a spectrum of styles of search around the role of chance, as follows (Perkins and Weber, 1992):

1. *Sheer chance.* An invention not particularly sought gets discovered by an active searcher exploring widely and incidentally.
2. *Cultivated chance.* The searcher deliberately opens himself or herself to a variety of semirandom input, harvesting the occasional useful connections.
3. *Systematized chance.* The searcher systematically surveys a sizable number of options that fall within a defined set, seeking ones with the target characteristics.
4. *Fair bet.* The searcher conceives and develops one or a few prototypes, relying on science and craft, with reasonable expectations that one or another will serve.
5. *Good bet.* The searcher conceives and develops a prototype from principle and experience that probably will work.
6. *Safe bet.* The searcher deduces with formal methods something that almost certainly will do the job.

All these styles of search could be found one place or another in the corpus. But the trend lay toward the middle, categories (3), (4), and (5). Rarely did sheer chance figure. Although some of the inventors employed cultivated chance, which sometimes made a contribution, it was hardly the mainstay. At the other end of the spectrum, safe bet reasoning through formal methods only operated to solve certain technical problems from time to time.

As one would expect, there was extensive crafting and testing of prototypes, in the spirit of (4) and (5). For instance, extensive work on prototypes occurred around the development of the electron microscope and of ultrasound.

But we also found a surprising amount of systematized chance. For example, the development team for *Ivermectin* scanned thousands of soil samples with mechanical means, looking for bacterial cultures with potentially useful antibiotic powers. Edward Rosinski and a colleague systematically tested hundreds of combinations of conditions in seeking to optimize the use of Zeolite catalysts. The classic case that many have heard of concerns Thomas Edison: as W. Barnard Carlson and Michael Gorman describe, Edison from time to time employed what he called a "drag hunt," for instance having his laboratory staff test hundreds of substances as potential filaments for the electric light (Carlson and Gorman, 1992).

So the inventor's search process involves a mix of chance and craft, with even the chance a craft of sorts. The balance between the two depends on the circumstances. Systematized chance has a more evolutionary flavor, but proceeds far more systematically than evolution does. The fair and good bet search styles involve constructing something toward a purpose, a Lamarckian rather than Darwinian enterprise. A Darwinian trial-and-error element remains, of course: conceptual or actual prototypes constructed toward a purpose do not necessarily serve; they may fail. But, in contrast to evolutionary variation, they are far more calculated than rolls of the genetic dice.

How Inventors Solve the Rarity Problem.   Unlike evolution, inventors cannot take tens of thousands of years. However, remember the category of "systematized chance." More often than one might think, inventors examine large numbers of variations by automation and by systematic parallel investigation of possibilities using teams of people or banks of equipment. These processes of systematized chance are much more parsimonious than the profligacy of nature.

Inventors also deal with the rarity problem by following promise. They do not spend time in regions of low promise. They look for patterns of increasing promise. To put this in terms more familiar to cognitive science, inventors "hill climb" by clues in the possibility space, using heuristics to ignore large parts of the possibility space and focus on more rather than less plausible inventions.

Robert Weber, for instance, has analyzed a number of the heuristics that appear to figure in inventive search (Weber 1992; Weber and Dixon 1989; Weber and Perkins 1992). For example, he notes the widespread pattern of combining something with its "inverse" to form a single invention. The claw hammer joins the nail-driving mechanism with the nail-removal mechanism. The pencil with eraser combines marking and unmarking functions.

For yet more help with the rarity problem, inventors search through abstract ideas for inventions sketchily and broadly envisioned. Carlson and Gorman (1992), writing about the development of the telephone, emphasize how both Bell and Edison thought in terms of schematic mental models of what a telephonic mechanism might be like, working back and forth between their mental models and prototypes to test their ideas.

In contrast, evolution only searches through particular organisms. There is no generalized primate, for example, only the various particular primate species. Inventors can think in terms of general forms. The part of an inventor's possibility space concerned with general forms is, of course, much smaller than the part concerned with particular forms. By moving back and forth between the general and particular conceptions, inventors can avoid the worst effects of a combinatorial explosion of possibilities.

How Inventors Solve the Isolation Problem.   Unlike evolution, inventors can search through nonviable forms. A concept or sketch of an invention need not be functional as conceived. It need only have initial promise. An actual prototype need not work to be fruitful; the inventor can learn from its failure. Taking advantage of figure 5.1 again, the inventor's path of thought can travel not just through the dark gray and black regions of payoff, but also through the gray regions of promise, not only from a starting point at C to G or A, but also to E.

But what about truly isolated regions, such as F? Inventors will not get to such regions even by systematic chance, because they lie isolated in a wilderness of no promise. An inventor cannot afford to poke around in such areas.

To ask this question is to ask how genuine mental leaps occur. Indeed, the idiom of search in possibility spaces and the notion of the isolation problem attach a more precise operational meaning to the notion of a leap. What is leapt over are no-promise regions in the possibility space, as the inventor passes from one region of promise to another. However, putting a name to the phenomenon does not explain it. The question is, how can such leaps happen successfully, at least now and then?

Part of the answer is that (1) sheer chance and (2) cultivated chance help. One might call this the prepared mind effect, after Pasteur's well-known remark that "Chance favors the prepared mind." For instance, when Alexander Fleming noticed that mold on a petri dish held in bay the advance of a bacterial culture, he recognized its potential significance. Had Fleming been searching for medical treatments to kill bacteria, it's unlikely he would have turned to molds. The idea of molds helping would lie in a region of zero promise from his viewpoint. Thus chance coupled with the prepared mind gives the inventor an occasional reach that more conservative systems do not have.

Another part of the answer looks to the abstract models and images inventors often think in, as mentioned regarding Edison and Bell. In figure 5.1 again, when we are focusing on actual functioning inventions, potential inventions as in region F may lie isolated in the midst of a region of little promise. An inventor working directly from existing inventions in region E would be unlikely to get to F. But at a high enough level of abstract principle, regions E and F may actually merge. For example, the automobile engine and the jet engine seem about as different as engines could be; but both depend on harnessing the power of hot expanding gases.

Still another answer recognizes the importance of paradigm changes in science. Such changes in effect redraw the possibility space in which the inventor works. In the redrawn space, regions previously disconnected may overlap or at least connect through a bridge of promise. This answer of course generates the further question of how paradigm changes occur. The brief answer is that entire paradigms may be seen as alternatives in a yet more abstract possibility space. Discovery of new paradigms has to solve rarity, isolation, oasis, and plateau problems just as in ordinary invention—and does so by the same sorts of mechanisms.

How Inventors Solve the Oasis Problem.   Inventors solve the problem by knowing about it. Aware of the risks of getting trapped by convention, they cast about. They consider odd angles. They expose themselves to novelty. Rather than trying to improve the present mousetrap, they often try to rethink the mousetrap. In other words, unlike evolution, inventors can deliberately change points of entry. In terms of figure 5.1, an inventor could work in region B for a while and, finding nothing, simply cast about for a new start in a new region. Or an inventor could work in region G for a while, and, finding already well-established inventions, seek a new start.

One manifestation of this is sometimes called "problem finding." As articulated by Getzels and Csikszentmihalyi (1976), problem finding involves early search for what goals to pursue and midcourse openness to doubts about the chosen course and reframing of the problem pursued. This may lead to very different outcomes than originally anticipated. Although Getzels and Csikszentmihalyi were investigating the behavior of artists, they suggested that problem finding figures universally in creativity across all fields. Certainly abundant biographical evidence speaks to the problem-finding orientation of creative scientists (e.g. Barron 1969; Mansfield and Busse 1981; Roe 1952a, b; 1963).

Problem finding can be seen as a way of escaping from oases of promise or partial payoff. The reconstruction of what is construed as the problem amounts to the finding of new entry points in the search process, entry points perhaps quite different from the original initiative.

How Inventors Solve the Plateau Problem. Sometimes systematized chance is the answer: the inventor plows through a large number of possibilities, seeking higher promise or payoff—Edison's drag hunt again.

But also, inventors can control the grain of their search. If ideas in a region seem much the same, equally promising and equally limited, inventors can jump to another region of the search space, trying to reenter the problem from another direction. To turn to figure 5.1, an inventor pondering ideas in the plateau between A and E could simply start over in C or D.

But how could the inventor find a new starting place of promise in C or D? This question is essentially the same as that raised around the isolation problem and mental leaps. The same mechanisms apply: the prepared mind effect via sheer chance and cultivated chance; thinking in models and images, in effect an augmented possibility space that includes a level of abstraction showing patterns of promise not apparent when thinking in terms of particular concrete inventions; and paradigm change in science, which redraws the possibility space.

Can We Measure Creativity?

This chapter outlines a creative systems perspective on creativity, one that recognizes creative systems other than the individual human being and compares and contrasts them in search of insight about the nature of creativity. One way to test this creative systems perspective further is to see whether it can illuminate standing puzzles about creativity. One such puzzle concerns measurement: Can creativity be measured? The notion that one might put any sort of yardstick to so supposedly ineffable a trait has always aroused controversy.

For a crude first-cut answer, we do not have to turn to the creative systems perspective at all. The answer is already in, at least for human beings. Yes, creativity can be measured, because it has been measured. The best predictors of real-world creative achievement in the sciences and related domains are (1) biographical inventories and (2) personality profiles (Mansfield and Busse 1981; Wallach 1976, 1985). Both are considerably better predictors of creative achievement than cognitive measures of divergent thinking and the like, so long as the people concerned are reasonably able to start with. Cognitive abilities seem more of a necessary than a sufficient condition for creative achievement.

All this is fine as far as it goes. But one might ask whether scores added up from biographical inventories and personality profiles are truly measures. It may be worth distinguishing a weak and a strong sense of measure. In the weak sense, a measure is simply a predictive correlate. In this weak sense, we already know that creativity can be measured, because biographical inventories and personality profiles do so. In the strong sense, a measure measures an underlying one-dimensional characteristic. For example, kilograms measure weight, a one-dimensional continuously variable quantity. To underwrite the logic of the measure, we have a theory of weight: It is the force exerted by inertial mass in a gravitational field.

Plainly there is room for skepticism about biographical inventories and personality profiles as strong-sense measures of creativity. They do not reveal whether creativity varies along a single dimension. Nor do they come with a theory like the theory of inertial mass that tells us what they really represent. Instead, both these measures make a simple, almost atheoretical, point: Creative people are those who invest their cognitive resources in a creative direction—as shown either by track record (the biographical inventories) or personality profiles (which in effect reveal dispositions to behave in a certain way).

Just here is where the creative systems model might help, because it offers a very general theory of the nature of creativity. To review, creative endeavor can be viewed as a process of search through possibility spaces. The four characteristics discussed earlier make a possibility space creatively challenging: the rarity, isolation, oasis, and plateau problems. A system (human beings, natural selection, or whatever) is creative to the extent that it copes with these four challenges. Creativity *is* the ability and tendency to cope with them.

If we were to base measures of creativity on these four challenges, what would such measures be like? Taking a cue from biographical inventories, we could look at the history of system performance. Taking a cue from studies of personality and cognitive skills, we could look at system mechanism. In both cases, though, we would want to look in a more differentiated way, attentive to the four demands. These are the sorts of questions we might ask.

Rarity.   Regarding past performance, does the system have a good "hit rate?" Has it commonly achieved satisfactory outcomes? Does an inventor, for example, have record of successful inventions? Regarding mechanism, does the system display parallelism, go through many many cycles, capitalize on "the prepared mind" effect or analogs of it for nonhuman systems, use systematized chance in any sense, follow gradients of promise ("hill climbing" in the idiom of artificial intelligence), and search in abstract or model spaces? Any of these might help with the rarity problem.

Isolation.   Regarding past performance, has the system usually explored only a narrow range of possibilities, or has it ranged widely? For example, does the inventor show diversity? Regarding mechanism, does the system capitalize on sheer, cultivated, or systematized chance in any sense? Does it utilize abstract models and images to range more widely? Do circumstances (for example, scientific paradigm changes for inventors, or environmental changes for biological organisms) reconfigure the problem space in which the system searches, thereby creating new opportunities?

Oases.   Regarding performance, has the system gotten hung up on success or continued wide-ranging exploration? For example, has the inventor continued to explore other directions after a major success, or rested on his or her laurels, focusing on minor improvements? Regarding mechanism, are there mechanisms that recognize oases and calculatedly invest in some exploration away from them? Is the basic mechanism simply indifferent to oases and therefore not trapped by them, as in the case of natural selection?

Plateaus.   Regarding past performance, has the system wandered at length in large, marginally satisfactory regions, or moved quickly beyond them? For example, has the inventor gotten stuck overworking ideas that yield little progress or instead sought new entries to problems or new directions altogether? Regarding mechanisms, are there mechanisms that increase the grain of search when little progress occurs? Are there mechanisms such as abstraction and modeling that allow for "leaps?" Does parallel processing and numerous cycles of processing help to solve the plateau problem, as in the case of evolution?

All this points up a clear moral. Biographical inventories and personality profiles may sum up to yield single scores, but these certainly are no more than weak-sense measures of creativity. Because, according to the present model, creativity is plainly not a single simple trait such as intelligence is supposed to be (but almost certainly is not; e.g., Gardner 1983; Horn 1989; Sternberg 1985). The four challenges of rarity, isolation, oases, and plateaus invite somewhat different resolutions, and each allows multiple resolutions. It's perfectly possible for different creative systems to handle those challenges effectively in different ways and for a given system to handle some of the four challenges better than others. Creativity, in short, is multidimensional, not monolithic.

To offer an analogy, measuring creativity by a single index is a little like measuring basketball prowess by baskets per game or height. To be sure, both certainly have some predictive value. They are weak-sense measures. But both are very partial indicators and neither rests on a deep theory of the game and its play. Neither is a measure of basketball prowess in the strong sense. Indeed, sports managers and statisticians show their wisdom by routinely relying on multiple, not single, indices of prowess in a sport. They recognize the inherently multidimensional character of sports performance. Odd that for as complex an attribute as creativity it takes us so long to reach the same conclusion.

In sum, there can be no strong-sense measure of creativity. Weak-sense measures may be useful as indices of overall performance. But their partial nature must be recognized. And, in the end, a measure is no substitute for an understanding of mechanism.

The Evolution of Invention

This chapter stays well away from important nuances of the human creative experience, for example, how Einstein's obsession with symmetry in nature helped lead him to relativity (Holton 1973); how Coleridge may have produced *Kubla Khan* in an opium-induced dream, but did not disclose how much he fiddled with his first draft afterward (Schneider 1953); or how Darwin found the truth of evolution in his voyage on the *Beagle*, but labored for months thereafter to conceive a mechanism to explain it (Gruber 1974).

However, the ambition here is to draw a bead on a particular problem about creativity: the role of Darwinian natural selection and variations of it such as the meme creative system in explaining the emergence of adaptive novelty. The discussion takes as its backdrop the startling inventiveness of nature, circumstantial evidence that nature's way might explain the human way as well. How much, then, of human invention reflects in some analogical form the Darwinian mechanism?

The discussion of three creative systems highlights some fundamental differences. The meme perspective does explain some important adaptive novelties of human society in a basically Darwinian way, with some qualifications. However, the inventor creative system introduces a host of features that have no Darwinian precedent.

By and large, they fall into two categories. First, while both evolution and inventors work in Klondike spaces vexed by the Klondike problems, inventors work in a space vastly richer and yet more manageable. Inventors have access to nonfunctional possibilities, whereas evolution only searches through the viable. Nonfunctional possibilities can be stepping stones to functional ones. Moreover, inventors spend much of their time with abstract mental models rather than prototypes. Evolution only "reasons" in the concrete, through producing organisms. This abstract level of human reasoning constitutes a second story to the Klondike space, another layer where the space is smaller and where forms isolated from one another in their concrete realizations may fall into the same more encompassing category.

This higher level of search is familiar to artificial intelligence research on more formal problems. It amounts to what Newell and Simon (1972) called a "planning problem space," a logical structure abstracted from the base space, more schematic and consolidated and hence more compressed and easier to search. The mechanisms of search find solutions in the planning space and then try to map them down into more detailed resolutions in the original base space. This effort to translate a planning space solution into a base space solution may fail, of course, because to gain parsimony and highlight principle the planning space leaves out considerable information. Nonetheless, the idea is that the tactic succeeds often enough, and search entirely in the base space is vexed enough, to make planning spaces worthwhile.

The second major contrast between the inventor and the evolution creative systems concerns the management of search. Evolution, of course, manages nothing. It simply happens. The mainspring of variation, selection, and preservation ticks along generation after generation.

In contrast, our analysis of inventors discloses a great deal of thoughtful management of search as such. Inventors are metacognitive, aware of their own process. Inventors move back and forth between real inventions and prototypes and the virtual space of ideas, seeking reality tests in the one and a smaller space of high-leverage principles in the other. Inventors devise schemes for systematized chance when they see no option. They employ heuristics to "follow promise," ignoring large chunks of the Klondike space that may contain occasional nuggets but that do not prove cost-effective to search. They modulate the grain of their search and shift starting points to avoid the traps of oases and plateaus. Inventors would not put this in such language, but it seems to be what they do.

As all this makes clear, human invention in its most human form—the inventor creative system but not the meme creative system—displays radical contrasts with the Darwinian paradigm.

Michael Ruse (1986) and Rupert Riedl (1984) among others argue that not only the morphology but the epistemology of human beings can be seen as a product of Darwinian evolution. Ruse, for example, urges that notions of causality, basic ideas about number, principles of conservation in the Piagetian sense, analogy making, and the notion that claims are verified by a convergence of evidence from various sources all are likely consequences of evolutionary processes, all very fundamental adaptive characteristics of mind with a genetic basis. To these elements of abstraction in thought, one might well add the power of self-management, including the management of searches.

But what environment is the mind adapted *to*? As angel fish move through a topography of coral and foxes a topography of brush and briar, the mind moves through a topography of ideas, seeking ones that serve a mosaic of purposes. We think in terms not just of actualities but possibilities of varying payoff and promise.

In short, the mind moves through a Klondike space. And as angel fish and foxes have adapted through evolution more ideally to their physical environments, so very likely has the mind to its mental one. In the spirit of Ruse and Riedl, we can suggest that human powers of abstraction and search management are in part consequences of the genetic evolution of intelligence, selection specifically for characteristics facilitative in the search of Klondike spaces. By this measure, evolution has produced a mechanism far more sophisticated than itself in playing its own Klondike game.

Acknowledgment

This paper was prepared for the *Achievement Project Symposium*, Kent, England, December 13–15, 1991. Some of the ideas in this paper were developed with support from the

MacArthur Foundation and the Spencer Foundation. I include the standard disclaimer that the ideas expressed here are not necessary the position or policy of the conference or supporting agencies.

References

Barron, F. 1969. *Creative Person and Creative Process.* New York: Holt, Rinehart, & Winston.

Boden, M. 1991. *The Creative Mind: Myths and Mechanisms.* New York: Basic Books.

Campbell, D. 1960. "Blind Variation and Selective Retention in Creative Thought as in Other Knowledge Processes." *Psychological Review* 67 (6): 380–400.

Campbell, D. 1974. "Evolutionary Epistemology." In P. A. Schilpp, ed., *The Philosophy of Karl Popper,* vol. 14, I and II. LaSalle: Open Court Publishing Co.

Carlson, W. B., and Gorman, M. 1992. "A Cognitive Framework to Understand Technological Creativity: Bell, Edison, and the Telephone." In R. J. Weber and D. N. Perkins, Eds., *Inventive Minds: Creativity in Technology.* New York: Oxford University Press. Pp. 48–79.

Dawkins, R. 1976. *The Selfish Gene.* New York: Oxford University Press.

Dennett, D. C. 1991. *Consciousness Explained.* Boston: Little, Brown and Company.

Gardner, H. 1975. *The Shattered Mind.* New York: Knopf.

Gardner, H. 1983. *Frames of Mind.* New York: Basic Books.

Getzels, J., and Csikszentmihalyi, M. 1976. *The Creative Vision: A Longitudinal Study of Problem Finding in Art.* New York: John Wiley & Sons.

Gould, S. J. 1980. *The Panda's Thumb: More Reflections in Natural History.* New York: Norton.

Gould, S. J. 1989. *Wonderful Life: The Burgess Shale and the Nature of History.* New York: W. W. Norton.

Gruber, H. 1974. *Darwin on Man: A Psychological Study of Scientific Creativity.* New York: E. P. Dutton.

Holton, G. 1973. "On Trying to Understand Scientific Genius." Chapter 10 in G. Holton, *Thematic Origins of Scientific Thought: Kepler to Einstein.* Cambridge, MA: Harvard University Press.

Horn, J. 1989. "Models of Intelligence." In R. Linn, ed., *Intelligence: Measurement, Theory, and Public Policy* (pp. 29–73). Chicago: University of Illinois Press.

Mansfield, R. S., and Busse, T. V. 1981. *The Psychology of Creativity and Discovery.* Chicago: Nelson-Hall.

Newell, A., and Simon, H. 1972. *Human Problem Solving.* Englewood Cliffs, NJ: Prentice-Hall.

Perkins, D. N. (1981). *The Mind's Best Work.* Cambridge, MA: Harvard University Press.

Perkins, D. N., and Weber, R. J. 1992. "Effable Invention." In R. J. Weber and D. N. Perkins, eds., *Inventive Minds: Creativity in Technology.* New York: Oxford University Press. Pp. 317–336.

Riedl, R. 1984. *Biology of Knowledge: The Evolutionary Basis of Reason.* New York: Wiley.

Roe, A. 1952a. "A Psychologist Examines 64 Eminent Scientists." *Scientific American* 187(5): 21–25.

Roe, A. 1952b. *The Making of a Scientist.* New York: Dodd, Mead & Co.

Roe, A. 1963. "Psychological Approaches to Creativity in Science." In M. A. Coler and H. K. Hughes, eds., *Essays on Creativity in the Sciences.* New York: New York University.

Ruse, M. (1986). *Taking Darwin Seriously: A Naturalistic Approach to Philosophy.* New York: Basil Blackwell.

Schneider, E. 1953. *Coleridge, Opium and Kubla Khan*. Chicago: University of Chicago Press.

Sternberg, R. J. 1985. *Beyond I.Q.: A Triarchic Theory of Human Intelligence*. New York: Cambridge University Press.

Wallach, M. A. 1976. "Tests Tell us Little about Talent." *American Scientist* 64: 57–63.

Wallach, M. A. 1985. "Creativity Testing and Giftedness." In F. D. Horowitz and M. O'Brien, eds., *The Gifted and Talented: Developmental Perspectives*, pp. 99–123. Washington, D.C.: American Psychological Association.

Weber, R. 1992. *Forks, Phonographs and Hot-Air Balloons: A Fieldguide to Inventive Thinking*. New York: Oxford University Press.

Weber, R. J., and Dixon, S. 1989. "Invention and Gain Analysis." *Cognitive Psychology* 21: 283–302.

Weber, R. J., and Perkins, D. N. 1992. *Inventive Minds: Creativity in Technology*. New York: Oxford University Press.Wesson, R. *Beyond Natural Selection*. Cambridge, MA: MIT Press.

Chapter 6
The Creators' Patterns
Howard Gardner

In the human sciences, a useful distinction has often been drawn between idiographic and nomothetic research (Allport 1961). In idiographic work, the focus falls sharply on the individual case study, with its peculiar emphases and wrinkles. In nomothetic work, the focus falls instead on a search for general laws; such work, by its very nature, overlooks individual idiosyncracies, searching instead for those patterns that appear to apply to all, or to the vast majority of cases.

One can readily find this distinction echoed in research in the human sciences that has been centered on creative individuals, works, and processes. Because, as it is usually construed, "the creative" is an unusual occurrence, there have been several efforts to study a creative entity in great depth. In recent times this work has been epitomized by Gruber's important studies of Charles Darwin and Jean Piaget (Gruber 1981; Gruber and Davis 1988). Befitting the fact that such case studies have been done in a social-scientific rather than humanistic spirit, there have been efforts to tease out more general principles at work (Langley et al. 1986; Perkins 1981; Wallace and Gruber 1990). In contrast to this idiographically tinged work, there have been frank efforts to go beyond the individual, to examine the processes at work in large numbers of creative individuals, texts, or processes. This line of study has been pursued most rigorously and vigorously by Dean Keith Simonton (1984, 1988a, 1988b) and by others working in this historiometic tradition, such as Martindale (1990, this volume).

In this chapter I seek to begin the construction of a bridge that spans the usually separate realms of idiographic and nomothetic lines of work on creativity. I report on a set of case studies that examine the creative lives of seven individuals who lived around 1900 and who have deliberately been drawn from disparate domains of accomplishment. These case studies are detailed in a recent book, entitled *The Creators of the Modern Era* (Gardner 1993). My focus falls on those patterns that seem to characterize all, or at least a sizable majority of these individuals. As such, the chapter constitutes a modest effort to tease out generalizations that may obtain more generally to highly creative individuals in our time.

Approaches to Creativity

Until recently, social-scientific work in the area of creativity has been dominated by psychology, and particularly by two subdisciplines within psychology. On the one hand, there is an extensive amount of work in the psychometric tradition. Since World War II, much effort has been expended in an attempt to measure creative processes in normal and in unusually talented individuals (Guilford 1950, 1967). The basic model has been to administer creativity tests that are loosely modeled after intelligence tests. While some useful information has been gleaned from this research (Torrance 1988), it has failed to establish itself as sufficiently valid and has been abandoned by some of its strongest supporters (Wallach 1976, 1985).

Complementing the psychometric work have been efforts to determine the psychological traits of creative individuals. Some of this work has been empirical, as creative individuals have described themselves or been described by close peers (Barron 1969; MacKinnon 1962). Other work has come more directly out of the psychoanalytic tradition; such work has stressed the neurotic or sublimatory foundations of creative efforts (Freud 1958; Kubie 1958). From this line of work has emerged one or more descriptions of the creative personality; as in the case of psychometric efforts, some useful generalizations have emerged, but only limited understanding of creative efforts in their fine structure.

My own review identifies two promising approaches in recent years. From the point of view of motivation, important research has been carried out on the centrality of intrinsic, as compared to extrinsic motivations, in the conduct of creative work (Amabile 1983; Hennessey and Amabile 1988). In related work, Csikszentmihalyi (1988a, 1988b, 1990) has highlighted the reinforcing character of "flow states"; those pleasurable periods of complete immersion in the activity of creation that come to characterize the creative individual. Fresh energy has also been conferred upon creativity research by the efforts of individuals drawn from cognitive psychology, developmental psychology, and cognitive science (Feldman [with Goldsmith] 1986; Langley et al. 1986; Perkins 1981; Simon 1988). This latter group of researchers has highlighted the rule-governed nature of much creative work; provided a detailed information-processing approach to the delineation and solution of problems; identified intriguing parallels between "ordinary " and "exceptional" creativity and between problem solving as carried out by human beings and by artificial computational systems. These lines of work have been recently reviewed in a number of publications (Boden 1990; Briggs 1989; Gardner 1988; Ochse 1991; Runco and Albert 1990; Sternberg 1988; Weisberg 1986) as well as the present volume.

The Present Approach

In my own work, I have sought to build upon the strengths of recent work in creativity. Reflecting my own training, the stress has fallen particularly on cognitive and developmental psychological approaches, but I have sought to take into account as well social and motivational aspects of creation and perspectives taken from the other human sciences.

According to my definition, a creative individual solves problems, fashions products, or poses new questions within a domain in a way that is initially considered to be unusual but is eventually accepted within at least one cultural group. In its mention of problem solving, and its contrast between initial novelty and ultimate acceptance, this definition conforms closely to that put forth by other researchers. Its somewhat different accent is conveyed by a few phrases:

1. I focus equally on problem solving, problem finding, and the creation of products, such as scientific theories, works of art, or the building of institutions.
2. I emphasize that all creative work occurs in one or more domains. Individuals are not creative (or noncreative) in general; they are creative in particular domains of accomplishment, and require the achievement of expertise in these domains before they can execute significant creative work.
3. No person, act, or product is creative or noncreative in itself. Judgments of creativity are inherently communal, relying heavily on individuals expert within a domain.

This definition also has implications with respect to methodology. In my view, the study of creativity is inherently interdisciplinary; in addition to being rooted in psychology, the student of creativity must be informed about epistemology (the nature of knowledge in different domains) and about sociology (the ways in which judgments are reached by experts in different domains).

Moreover, this perspective on creativity draws attention away from questions of who and what is creative and instead to the question of where is creativity. As formulated by Csikszentmihalyi (1988b), creativity emerges in virtue of a dialectical process among individuals of talent, *domains* of knowledge and practices, and *fields* of knowledgeable judges. If one wants to understand phenomena of creativity, one cannot simply focus on the individual—his brain, her personality, their motivations. Instead, one must broaden one's focus to include a study of the area in which that creative individual works and the procedures by which judgments of originality and quality are rendered.

To this general position, I bring two further perspectives. The first perspective posits the existence in human beings of a number of separate faculties or intellectual strengths, which I have labeled the seven human "intelligences" (Gardner 1983, 1992). It is my claim that all normal human beings can develop at least seven different intelligences, and that individuals differ from one another in the strengths and configurations of these intelligences.

The second perspective involves the claim that creative individuals are characterized particularly by a tension, or lack of fit, between the elements involved in productive work—a tension that I have labeled *fruitful asynchrony* (Gardner and Wolf 1988). This concept is best illustrated by a contrast with the case of the prodigious individual. In the case of a prodigy, a talented individual fits very well with a domain that exists in his society and his work is immediately recognized as highly competent by members of the relevant field (Feldman [with Goldsmith] 1986). In contrast, the creative individual is marked by one or more asynchronies: an unusual configuration of talents, and an initial lack of fit among abilities, the domains in which the individual seeks to work, and the tastes and the prejudices of the current field. Of course, in the end, it is the conquering of these asynchronies that leads to the establishment of work that comes to be cherished.

Against this background of assumptions, I launched my study of the seven "creators of the modern era." I chose to work with seven individuals, each an acknowledged creator, each exemplifying at least one of my seven intelligences: Sigmund Freud was the exemplar of intrapersonal intelligence; Albert Einstein represented logical-mathematical intelligence; Pablo Picasso, spatial intelligence; Igor Stravinsky, musical intelligence; T. S. Eliot, linguistic intelligence; Martha Graham, bodily-kinesthetic intelligence; and Mahatma Gandhi, interpersonal intelligence. And I deliberately elected to work with individuals who are roughly contemporaries of one another, so that any differences observed could not be attributed simply to their existence at different historical moments.

In what follows, I begin with a sketch of E. C., an Exemplary Creator. E. C. is exemplary in the sense of Weber's "ideal type": that is, E. C. captures a number of the powerful generalizations that obtained across all or the majority of my seven creators. I then mention some of the more striking findings that emerged when I focused on the specific elements of the creative process. I conclude by indicating the two most surprising results of the investigation and by noting some limits of, and some future directions for, this line of work that seeks to close the idiographic-nomothetic gap.

E. C.: An Exemplary Creator

E. C. comes from a zone somewhat removed from the actual centers of power and influence in her society, but not so far away that she and her family are entirely ignorant of what is going on elsewhere. The family is not wealthy, but neither is it in dire financial circumstances; and life for the young creator is reasonably comfortable in a material sense. The atmosphere at home is better described as correct than warm; the young creator often feels a bit estranged from her biological family. Even when there are close ties to one or another parent, these are laced with ambivalence. Intimate ties are more likely to obtain between E. C. and a nanny, nursemaid, or more distant member of the family.

The family of E. C. may not be highly educated, but it values and has high expectations with respect to learning and achievement. Usually, the child's area of strength (her dominant intelligence) emerges at a relatively young age, and the family encourages these interests, though there may be ambivalence about a career that falls outside the established professions. There is a moral if not religious atmosphere around the home, and the child develops a strict conscience, which can be turned against herself but also, and especially in later life, against others who do not adhere to desired behavioral patterns.

There comes a time when the growing child—now an adolescent—seems to have outgrown her home environment. Often, the adolescent has already invested a decade of work in the mastery of a domain and is near its forefront; she has little to learn from her family and from local experts, a quickened impulse to test herself against the leading young persons in the domain. And so, the adolescent or young adult ventures toward that city which is seen as a center of vital activities. (Around 1900, London, Paris, Berlin, and Zurich were favorites.) With surprising speed, the future creator discovers a set of peers who share the same interests; together these "young Turks" explore the terrain of the domain, often organizing institutions and issuing manifestos, stimulating one another to new heights. Sometimes E. C. proceeds directly to work in a chosen domain; not infrequently, there are flirtations with a number of different career lines until a crystallizing moment occurs.

Experiences within domains differ from one another, and there is no point in glossing over them. Still, with greater or lesser speed, E. C. discovers a problem area or line of production of special interest, one that promises to take the domain into uncharted waters. This is a highly charged moment. At this point E. C. generally becomes isolated from peers and must work on her own. She senses that she is on the verge of a breakthrough that is as yet little understood, even by her. At this point, some kind of support from others is crucial.

In the happy circumstances that I studied, E. C. succeeds in effecting at least one major breakthrough, one that is recognized with relative rapidity by the relevant field. E. C. finds herself to be different from others and goes to extraordinary lengths to retain this difference. E. C. works nearly all the time, making tremendous demands on herself and on others, constantly raising the ante. She is self-confident, able to deal with false starts, proud and stubborn, reluctant to admit mistakes to others though usually willing to shift course, when such a tack seems indicated.

In general, given such enormous energy and commitment, the opportunity arises for at least one more breakthrough. That breakthrough occurs about a decade after the first. As I shall show, the possibility for future breakthroughs is closely tied to the nature of the domain. In any event, E. C. seeks to retain her creativity; she will seek marginal status, or heighten the ante of asynchrony, to maintain freshness and secure the "flow" that accompanies formidable challenges and exciting discoveries. In cases where there is an outpouring of works, a few of them will stand out as *defining*, both for E. C. herself and for members of the encompassing field.

Inevitably, with the onset of advanced age, limits emerge in the powers of the creative individual. Younger persons are sometimes cultivated or exploited as a means of rejuvenation. Often, even if original new works prove elusive of production, an important role as critic, commentator, or sage remains. Some creators die young, but in the case of E. C., she lives on until late in life, gains many followers, and continues to make significant contributions until the time of her death. Moreover, because her life's work has transformed the domain and the field, her effect continues to be felt for many years afterward.

Of course no single creator, let alone the seven that I've studied, conforms exactly to this pattern. The patterns proposed here are illustrative rather than definitive; one would need larger samples, and more precise measures, to establish the validity of any proposed pattern—to effect the course from idiographic to nomothetic. Nonetheless, the "ideal type" portrait at least conveys the kinds of generalizations that one hopes to obtain from studies of these kind. I turn now to some of the more specific patterns that emerged from the intensive studies I have carried out.

Cognition

Each of my creators was selected because of a suspected strength in a particular intelligence, and so, not surprisingly, each of them has a distinctive cognitive profile. What I had not suspected was that the creative individual is characterized as much by an *unusual combination* of intelligences as by a single outstanding intelligence. Thus, for instance, Freud had the combination, unusual for a scientist, of linguistic and personal intelligences; Stravinsky combined musical with other artistic intelligences; Einstein featured a strong spatial intelligence to complement his logical-mathematical strengths. With the possible exception of Stravinsky, each of the creators also had definite areas of intellectual weakness, though it remains speculation whether that form of asynchrony contributed to their specific creative course.

It has been appreciated for some time that it takes approximately a decade for an individual to master a domain, to come to the level of technical expertise that is expected of an adult professional (Hayes 1981). Generally the most pronounced breakthrough occurs within a decade after this initial mastery: I speak here of such works as Freud's account of the unconscious processes in dreams, Einstein's theory of relativity, Gandhi's *Satyagraha*, and the breakthroughs captured in Picasso's *Les desmoiselles d'Avignon*, Stravinsky's *Le sacre du printemps*, Eliot's *The Waste Land*, and Martha Graham's *Frontier*.

Not infrequently, a second breakthrough occurs, about a decade later. While still radical, this additional breakthrough involves a reconciliation between creator and the broader traditions of the domain. I cite here Freud's work in social psychology, Einstein's general theory of relativity, Gandhi's well-orchestrated large-scale protests, Picasso's *Guernica*, Stravinsky's *Les Noces*, Eliot's *Four Quartets*, and Graham's *Appalachian Spring*. Some creators continue to have breakthroughs over several more decades, but Einstein and Eliot did not. I speculate that the possibility for breakthroughs beyond the first is a function, on the one hand, of the nature of the domain (arts being more susceptible than the sciences), and on the other, of the personality of the creator (some content to rest on the laurels of their first breakthrough, others determined to surpass themselves).

Other Psychological Dimensions

It has always been known that creative individuals are highly energetic and extremely demanding of themselves and others. Their work stands above all else. I had not fully appreciated, however, the extent to which these individuals are frankly difficult. All of them were quite prepared to use individuals and then to discard them when their utility was at an end. A legacy of destruction and tragedy surrounds those who enter into the orbit of the creative individual; the excitement of being in the company of such individuals is great but the decompression afterward can be quite trying. There is also much self-promotion and, often, a concomitant deprecation of others.

Two other personal dimensions are worthy of comment. The first is the distinct marginality of creative individuals. In most cases, the marginality was there from the start—by place of birth, by religion, by gender. But even when it was not there initially—as in the case of T. S. Eliot—it becomes possible to lead one's life so as to become and remain determinedly marginal. And this is what each of our creators was determined to do. Indeed, when acceptance appears at hand, there is a temptation—usually accepted—to raise the ante so that one's marginal status is again firmly established.

The second dimension concerns the extent to which creative individuals retain features of their childhood. Sometimes this retention stresses some of the less appealing aspects of childhood—selfishness, self-centeredness, intolerance, silliness, stubbornness. But even when these traits are not salient, the creative individual retains a ready access to what might be called childlike traits—the ability to ignore convention, to follow a lead where it goes, to ask questions that adults usually have stopped asking, to go directly to the essence of an issue. It is not surprising that, whether or not they had children themselves, each of the creators was quite fascinated by childhood and actively sought to retain some of the cognitive, affective, emotional, and social strands of their own childhood.

Domain

Many investigators of creativity, including myself, have been attracted by the possibility of creating a scheme that pertains to all creative activity (Gardner and Nemirovsky 1991; Wallas 1926). Indeed, when I first began this study, I sought such an integrative framework. I have become convinced, however, that there exist at least five different kinds of creative activity. It is important to understand the dimensions of each activity before one searches for generalizations that may obtain across these varieties:

1. *The solution of a well-defined problem.* This kind of work is often pursued in the course of training, as when Stravinsky was asked by his teacher to orchestrate well-known melodies. However, it

has the potential to be highly creative, when the problem is important and has not yet been solved. A modern example is the discovery of the double helix by James Watson and Francis Crick. In their early scientific work, both Freud and Einstein exhibited this form of creativity several times.

2. *The devising of an encompassing theory.* We see the development of a widely incorporative theory in the examples of Freud studying the unconscious, and of Einstein pondering the riddles of relativity. In creating such a theory, the scholar not only reconfigures existing data and concepts, but points the way to future lines of research. Certain important artistic movements, such as cubism or twelve-tone music, bear something of an analogy to what is usually achieved in this kind of scientific work.

3. *The creation of a "frozen work."* Most artists, working alone or in collaboration, create some kind of a work in a symbolic system. That work can then be examined, performed, exhibited, evaluated by others who are knowledgeable in the domain. In any event, there is a distance between the occasion of creation and the times when the work is encountered and evaluated. In this respect, the work differs from the fourth variety of creation.

4. *The performance of a ritualized work.* Some works can only be apprehended in performance, and the creativity inheres chiefly in the particular characteristics of the specific performance. The prototypical example is the performance of a dance by Martha Graham. While the dance can in principle be notated and performed by someone else, in fact Graham's creativity adhered significantly in her capacity to perform in a distinctive and valued way. In art forms where notations do not exist, or where the notations fail to capture important aspects of the performance, the performance *is* the work.

5. *A "high-stakes" performance.* In the fifth variety, an individual actually carries out a series of actions in public in order to bring about some kind of social or political change. Our prototypical instance here are the protests, fasts, and nonviolent confrontations engaged in by Gandhi and his followers. In contrast to ritualized artistic performances, where the steps can be worked out in advance, this performance is determinedly "high stake." It is not possible to work out the details of the performance in advance because much of it depends upon the reactions of the audience or the combatants.

There is clearly a relationship between the kinds of creative activities outlined here and the domains in which creative work can be achieved.

Scientific domains highlight the first two kinds of activity; the second pair of activities are particularly associated with artistic work; and the final kind is most likely to occur in the political domain. Anyone who wishes to enter into the space of creative individuals needs to take into account these domains, these kinds of activities, and the overlap and non-overlap among them.

One further significant aspect of domains is the extent to which they are paradigmatic. This notion, building on the well-known concept of Kuhn (1970), calls attention to the extent to which individuals working in a domain agree about the delineations of problems and solutions within that domain. In the case of well-developed sciences, there is generally agreement about what constitutes appropriate problems, methods, and solutions; and in art forms where practices have been well established, such as classical painting or the nineteenth-century novel, a similar consensus can obtain. However, at certain times in the sciences, and currently in the arts, one encounters a situation where there obtains little agreement about paradigms. Such moments are particularly ripe for breakthroughs, and yet the dispersed nature of the domain makes it less likely that the breakthroughs can be immediately appreciated.

Field

In some respects, the concept of field is the social counterpart to the concept of the domain. The domain is a set of practices associated with an area of knowledge; the field consists of the individuals and institutions that render judgments about work in the domain. An important feature of the field is the extent to which it is hierarchical: that is, the extent to which a few powerful individuals can render influential judgments about the quality of work.

Such hierarchical domination occurred, for example, in the area of physics early in the century, when the editors of the leading physics journals played a major role in determining which ideas were published and which received attention. Einstein owed much to the support of Max Planck and a few other powerful figures. But it occurred equally prominently in modern dance in the 1930s, when a few powerful critics brought attention to the performance of Martha Graham. To the extent that the field is hierarchical, it is possible quickly to be recognized and to gain influence; the costs of this hierarchization is that one runs the risk more quickly of becoming "dated," as younger figures master the art of addressing the field appropriately.

Another dimension of the field involves the relation of aspiring creators to others who are pursuing the same line of work. I have been impressed by the rapidity and ease with which aspiring creators locate their peers at an early age and, at least for awhile, work together cooperatively with them. However, competition and isolation eventually become powerful factors, and the recognized creator generally searchers for followers and for promoters rather than for challenging competitors. And in the case of our titans, they often come to identify with great figures from other eras, or from distant domains, rather than with the few peers in their own chosen area of specialty.

Fruitful Asynchrony

My study of creators provided ample evidence in support of the notion of fruitful asynchronies. One could almost plot out the seven target lives in terms of the numbers and types of "lacks of fit" that characterized them. These include powerful tensions with the nodes (Picasso's strong spatial intelligence in contrast to his weak scholastic intelligences; the tension in the domain of physics between an approach that was built upon the concept of the ether and one that questions its utility; the tension within the musical field between supporters of Stravinsky's chromatic music and devoteés of Schoenberg's twelve-tone music). And it includes powerful tensions among the nodes: the lack of fit between Freud's intelligences and those usually honored in the sciences; the tensions between Picasso's cubist works and the earlier dominance of representational works; the tensions between the poetry prized in the nineteenth century and the contrasting pulls of elite and mass literary taste in the twentieth century.

The problem with the concept of fruitful asynchrony is not, then, a question of locating support for it; rather its very ubiquity in the lives of human beings itself becomes a problem. Perhaps asynchrony is everywhere potentially fruitful and it is only a question of making use of it. My study does not resolve this question, but it raises two interesting possibilities.

First, it seems that creators, more so than other mortals, search for asynchronies, thrive on them, receive flow from them. This is exemplified by the findings on that type of asynchrony termed *marginality:* when marginality is not given to creators, or when it appears to be disappearing, the creators—unlike many others—actually attempt to reestablish the asynchrony.

The second point has to do with the amount of asynchrony. It is possible to have too much asynchrony. Indeed, all of our creators seem to have suffered some kind of breakdown when they were still relatively young; this dysfunction suggests a degree of asynchrony that was beyond endurance. The creator may stand out for the *amount* and *type* of asynchrony that she can endure and exploit without being overwhelmed in the process.

Two Unexpected Findings

Though all have their pet hypotheses, researchers usually are most grateful if their studies turn up a result that is a surprise for them and will, hopefully, constitute a surprise for others as well. In the case of my study of *Creators*, two findings stand out.

1. Cognitive and Affective Support Systems.   First, at the time of the greatest breakthrough, our creators were in one sense very much alone. Often they had physically withdrawn from other individuals; and, at least in their exploration of the farthest reaches of their domain, they were venturing into areas where no one had gone before.

Somewhat paradoxically, however, it was precisely at these times that our creators needed, and were fortunate enough to be able to secure, strong support from other individuals. The support needed to be both cognitive (from someone who could understand the nature of their breakthrough) and affective (from someone who could assure them that they were all right as human beings and that they had not departed from their senses). In the majority of the cases, the support came from the same individual—for example, Louis Horst provided both forms of support for Martha Graham, just as Wilhelm Fliess provided both forms for Sigmund Freud. However, a division of labor is also possible: Einstein received cognitive support from a group called the Olympiad and from his friend Michelangelo Besso, and affective as well as some cognitive support from his wife Mileva.

2. A Faustian Bargain.   Another unexpected finding concerns the extent to which creators are willing, so to speak, to sell their souls in order that their creative juices can continue to flow. In the cases of each of the creators, I found evidence that they had made bargains with themselves—and with their makers—which struck me as quite extreme. Sometimes the arrangements were ascetic, almost masochistic in nature; at other times, they were frankly exploitative, even sadistic in character. But in either instance, these arrangements seem to have been made so that the creator had the best opportunity to continue to work in her domain.

On the masochistic side, one finds Freud and Gandhi taking vows of celibacy at a young age; Eliot, Graham, and Gandhi pursuing extremely ascetic kinds of existences. More exploitative forms of bargains were struck by Picasso, who ruthlessly exploited those about him, and especially "his" women; and Stravinsky, who engaged in tireless litigation against nearly everyone in his personal and professional circle, as if determined that no advantage ever be taken of him. In some cases, one can find evidence of both forms of bargain—Freud was as severe with reference to other individuals as he was with himself. And even the individual least involved in the world of other human beings, Albert Einstein, essentially gave up family life and intimate relations so that he could pursue his work—though, paradoxically, he retained a keen if distanced interest in the broader world of other human beings.

Final Reflections

In the course of this whirlwind tour of a set of case studies about the founders of the modern era, I have conveyed a set of impressions and trends. Each of these, it should be stressed, arises from the idiographic study of a well-documented life; yet it is only by examining such lives together that one begins to discern those patterns that may strain toward, and perhaps even reach, the status of a nomothetic finding: the "creators' patterns" of my title.

The limitations of such a study are evident. I have selected but seven individuals for study, all living within the same time compass, and all influenced primarily by Western Europe; the very factors that make for some comparability at the same time constrain the reach of the generalizations. We simply do not know to what extent similar patterns would have obtained if I had selected other exemplars from the era—say, Henri Matisse, Virginia Woolf, or Mao Zedong; individuals drawn from other domains, such as Thomas Edison, Ludwig Wittgenstin, or Barbara McClintock; let alone individuals drawn from a different historical era, such as Mozart, St. Augustine, or Dante. Above all, generalizations obtained on the basis of five, six, or seven cases can easily be undone by the next dozen cases, or for that matter, by a somewhat different set of criteria or scoring decisions than the ones I have chosen to employ.

A more delicate issue concerns the kinds of creativity I have examined. Clearly there is a bias toward individuals who have been revolutionary rather than evolutionary—individuals who took the dramatic steps of *Le sacre du printemps* or *Les Noces*, rather than the more evolutionary changes associated with a Bach from another era, or a less radically-oriented composer, like Bela Bartok or George Gershwin from our own era. There is a possible confound with the factors of success and of self-promotion: Pierre Janet made many of the same discoveries as Freud, Braque contributed as much to cubism as did Picasso; Doris Humphrey was possibly a more outstanding choreographer than Martha Graham; and yet relatively few studies have been carried out of the less illustrious of each pairing. In a sense each of the individuals I studied became an icon of the domain during the modern era; that decision was made as much by the field, for its own purposes, as by the "objective" factors of the creators' achievement.

Though case studies have their limitations, I believe that the present ensemble of cases in particular helps to illustrate two possibly important phenomena of a more general nature. First, I believe that creative individuals of each era make some kind of a raid upon their childhood, preserving certain aspects of their own earlier life in a way that advances their work and makes sense to their peers. In the case of the creators of the modern era, each of them seems to me to have made contact with the years of early childhood—the preschool years. Whether it is Einstein peering at the erratic behavior of the needle of a compass, Stravinsky experimenting with the rhythms that had struck him when he was barely capable of speaking, or Freud looking at the dreams and wishes of early childhood, the creators of the modern seem drawn to the same basic, elemental, simple forms that attract the mind of the child before it has been too influenced by the conventions of his society.

Second, in considering creative work it is important to be sensitive to two contrasting trends: a tendency to question every assumption and to attempt to strike out on one's own as much as possible, and a countervailing tendency to exhaust a domain, to probe more systematically, deeply, and comprehensively than anyone has probed before. One can distinguish cultures and eras that are determinedly iconoclastic, such as the high Renaissance; and one can counterbalance these instances with the work produced during the medieval era or with the traditions that are so valued in China. From my vantage point, the changes that took place in Europe around the turn of the century represent an extreme in the challenging of given assumptions about life, work, progress, value; even compared to the succeeding postmodern era, that heroic and epoch-making time continues to stand out. In that sense, at least, it may signal some of the outer limits of which human beings are capable during the very few years that each of us has been allotted.

Note

This paper summarizes some of the major themes of a recently completed book, entitled *The Creators of the Modern Era* (New York: Basic Books, 1993). Portions of the paper were discussed at the Workshop of the Achievement Project, Ashford, Kent, England, January 13–15, 1992. I am grateful to Margaret Boden, Penelope Gouk, and the others in attendance at the conference for their helpful feedback.

References

Allport, G. 1961. *Pattern and Growth in Personality.* New York: Holt, Rinehart and Winston.

Amabile, T. 1983. *The Social Psychology of Creativity.* New York: Springer Verlag.

Barron, F. 1969. *Creative Person and Creative Process.* New York: Holt, Rinehart and Winston.

Boden, M. 1990. *The Creative Mind.* New York: Basic Books.

Briggs, J. 1989. *Fire in the Crucible.* New York: St. Martins Press.

Csikszentmihalyi, M. 1988a. "Motivation and Creativity: Towards a Synthesis of Structural and Energistic Approaches to Cognition." *New Ideas in Psychology* 6, 2: 159–176.

Csikszentmihalyi, M. 1988b. "Society, Culture, and Person: A Systems View of Creativity." In R. J. Sternberg, ed., *The Nature of Creativity.* New York: Cambridge University Press, pp. 325–338.

Csikszentmihalyi, M. 1990. *Flow.* New York: Harper Collins.

Feldman, D. 1980. *Beyond Universals in Cognitive Development.* Norwood. NJ: Ablex.

Feldman, D. (with L. Goldsmith). 1986. *Nature's Gambit.* New York: Basic Books.

Freud, S. 1958. *On Creativity and the Unconscious.* (Edited by B. Nelson). New York: Harper and Row.

Gardner, H. 1983. *Frames of Mind.* New York: Basic Books.

Gardner, H. 1988. "Creativity: An Interdisciplinary Perspective." *Creativity Research Journal* 1: 8–26.

Gardner, H. 1992. *Multiple Intelligences: The Theory in Practice.* New York: Basic Books.

Gardner, H. 1993. *The Creators of the Modern Era.* New York: Basic Books.

Gardner, H., and Nemirovsky, R. 1991. "From Private Intuitions to Public Symbol Systems: An Examination of Creative Process in Georg Cantor and Sigmund Freud." *Creativity Research Journal* 4 (1): 1–21.

Gardner, H., and Wolf, C. 1988. "The Fruits of Asynchrony: A Psychological Examination of Creativity." *Adolescent Psychiatry* 15: 106–123.

Gruber, H. 1981. *Darwin on Man.* Chicago: University of Chicago Press.

Gruber, H., and Davis, S. N. 1988. "Inching Our Way up Mount Olympus: The Evolving Systems Approach to Creative Thinking." In R. J. Sternberg, ed., *The Nature of Creativity.* New York: Cambridge University Press, pp. 243–270.

Guilford, J. P. 1950. "Creativity." *American Psychologist* 5: 444–454.

Guilford, J. P. 1967. *The Nature of Human Intelligence.* New York: McGraw-Hill.

Hayes, J. 1981. *The Complete Problem-Solver.* Philadelphia: Franklin Institute Press.

Hennessey, B., and Amabile, T. 1988. "The Conditions of Creativitity." In R. J. Sternberg, ed., *The Nature of Creativity.* New York: Cambridge University Press, 11–38.

Kubie, L. 1958. *The Neurotic Distortion of the Creative Process.* Lawrence, KA: University of Kansas Press.

Kuhn, T. S. 1970. *The Structure of Scientific Revolutions* (second edition). Chicago: University of Chicago Press.

Langley, P., Simon, H., Bradshaw, G. L., and Zytkow, J. 1986. *Scientific Discovery: Computational Explorations of the Creative Process.* Cambridge, MA: MIT Press.

MacKinnon, D. 1962. "The Nature and Nurture of Creative Talent. *American Psychologist* 17: 484–495.

Martindale, C. 1990. *Clockwork Muse.* New York: Basic Books.

Ochse, K. 1991. *Before the Gates of Excellence.* New York: Cambridge University Press.

Perkins, D. N. 1981. *The Mind's Best Work.* Cambridge, MA: Harvard University Press.

Runco, M., and Albert, R., eds., 1990. *Theories of Creativity*. Newbury Park, CA: Sage Publishers.

Simon, H. 1988. "Creativity and Motivation: A Response to Csikszentmihalyi." *New Ideas in Psychology* 6, 2: 177–182.

Simonton, D. K. 1984. *Genius, Creativity, and Leadership*. Cambridge, MA: Harvard University Press.

Simonton, D. K. 1988a. *Scientific Genius*. New York: Cambridge University Press.

Simonton, D. K. 1988b. "Creativity, Leadership, and Chance." In R. J. Sternberg, ed., *The Nature of Creativity*. New York: Cambridge University Press, pp. 386–426.

Sternberg, R. J., ed., 1988. *The Nature of Creativity*. New York: Cambridge University Press.

Torrance, E. P. 1988. "The Nature of Creativity as Manifest in Its Testing." In R. J. Sternberg, ed., *The Nature of Creativity*. New York: Cambridge University Press, pp. 43–75.

Wallace, D., and Gruber, H. 1990. *Creative People at Work*. New York: Oxford University Press.

Wallach, M. 1976. "Tests Tell Us Little about Talent." *American Scientist* 64: 57–63.

Wallach, M. 1985. "Creativity Testing and Giftedness." In F. Horowitz and M. O'Brien, eds., *The Gifted and Talented: Developmental Perspectives*. Washington, DC: American Psychological Association.

Wallas, G. 1926. *The Art of Thought*. New York: Harcourt, Brace.

Weisberg, R. 1986. *Creativity, Genius, and Other Myths*. New York: Freeman.

Chapter 7

How Can We Measure a Society's Creativity?

Colin Martindale

Before asking how to measure the creativity of an entire society, we should consider the more tractable question of how to measure creativity in given areas of endeavor. Creative productions occur in structured social contexts rather than in isolation. A creative idea is generally defined as one that is novel and, in some sense, useful or appropriate for the situation in which it occurs. Given this definition, creativity is rare, if not impossible, in most lines of endeavor. Most of the work done in a society is supposed to be routine. For example, a police officer may think of a novel interpretation of existing laws, but it would not be appropriate to impose this new interpretation on people even if it were potentially useful. A worker on an assembly line may think of a new way of doing things, but that is not what he or she was hired to do. Of course, the police officer can become a politician or the assembly-line worker an entrepreneur. The point is that the way creativity is defined restricts it to only some social institutions. Thus the term "creative" is commonly used in reference to scientists and artists, but rarely in reference to many other occupations. In this chapter I shall focus on creativity in poetry simply because I have studied the topic. With appropriate modifications, the theory I outline could be applied to creativity in other domains (Martindale 1990).

A number of evolutionary theories of sociocultural change have recently been proposed (e.g., Cavalli Sforza and Feldman 1981; Pulliam and Dunford, 1980). For example, Campbell (1974) argues for a direct extrapolation of the principles of Darwinian evolution to change in cultural systems and products. Such change, he holds, is a product of "blind" variation and selective retention. The three factors necessary for either biological or sociocultural evolution are (1) presence of variation, (2) consistent selection criteria favoring one sort of variant over others, and (3) mechanisms for preserving the selected variants. At any point in time, a number of variants of a cultural artifact are produced and the most useful or pleasing is chosen. Then, at the next point in time, there is variation of the new form and the process continues. Such theories provide a general framework for thinking about innovation in literature and the arts, but they do not tell us why aesthetic variation exists in the first place. What is the motivation for the trial-and-error or blind variation that produces the alternatives upon which the selective forces operate? In science or technology, there is often a clear problem to be solved, but the problem to be solved in art is unclear, especially if we follow Kubler (1962) in defining works of art as useless objects (or the useless aspects of useful objects). These general theories also tell us nothing specific about the direction of change in aesthetic forms. However, they do give us a general framework for explaining change in the arts.

A Psychological Theory of Aesthetic Evolution

Aesthetic Variability
The role definition of artist or poet almost always and everywhere calls for the creation of new, different, or original artifacts. A person who produces exact copies of already-existing art works is usually not considered an artist at all. We make a fundamental distinction between a typesetter and a poet or between someone who photographs a painting and the painter who produced it.

Many theorists have pointed out that if art is characterized by factors such as novelty or disruption of expectation, a necessity for change is built into it. If a work of art must be novel, each successive work of art must be different from prior works or it will not qualify as a work of art at all. The Russian and Czech formalists argued that poetic devices involve "estrangement" or "deformation." What gives poetry its effect is the use of words in ways that are unusual or unexpected. The deformed word usages in poetry hypothetically intensify perception or arouse attention. With repetition, linguistic deformations and estrangements gradually become "automatized" (Tynjanov 1924). They lose their effect. Several formalist theorists (e.g., Shklovsky 1919; Tynjanov 1929; Mukarovsky 1940) derived from this fact the hypothesis that literature must necessarily evolve. If aesthetic effects arise from deformations, and if deformations are gradually automatized, then there is a constant pressure on successive artists to produce new deformations. Similar evolutionary theories have been independently proposed by Laver (1950), Meyer (1956), Peckham (1965), and Cohen (1966). These theories have been based upon intuitive or common-sense psychological assumptions. A more comprehensive formulation can be derived from psychological theory.

Selection Criteria

According to Berlyne (1971), preference for any stimulus is based upon the arousal potential or impact value of that stimulus. The arousal potential of a stimulus is determined by collative properties (e.g., novelty, complexity, surprise, unpredictability), ecological properties (signal value or meaning), and psychophysical characteristics (e.g., stimulus intensity). There is a good deal of evidence to support Berlyne's (1971) hypothesis that people prefer stimuli with a medium degree of arousal potential and that they dislike stimuli with either very high or low arousal potential (Berlyne 1967; Schneirla 1959). Berlyne's hypothesis has also been supported by studies of literary and artistic stimuli (Day 1967; Evans 1969; Kamann 1963; Vitz 1966).

Reaction to most of the components of arousal potential habituates. That is, repeated presentation of a given work decreases that work's arousal potential or impact value, so that a work of art—or any stimulus—gradually loses its arousal potential (Berlyne 1971). A work of art with medium arousal potential will not have medium arousal potential forever, but will gradually lose its capacity to elicit interest, liking, and attention. A number of studies have shown that repeated presentation of the same aesthetic stimulus eventually leads to a decline in liking for that stimulus (Berlyne 1970; Skaife 1967).

It follows that, if a series of artists kept producing the same or very similar works of art, liking for their productions would decrease over time. This is true regardless of whether artists feel any conscious desire to produce novel or original artifacts. To compensate for habituation, it is necessary for successive works of art to have more and more arousal potential. In principle, this could be accomplished by manipulating any of the components of arousal potential. Successive composers could create louder and louder musical compositions, or successive painters could paint larger and larger paintings. However, there are practical limits as to how loud a piece of music can be or how large a painting can be. In a medium such as poetry, it is impossible to compensate for habituation of arousal potential by increasing stimulus intensity. Arousal potential can also be increased by increasing the meaningfulness of an artistic work. There are several difficulties with this technique. First, people vary widely in what is meaningful to them. A poet cannot be sure that what is more meaningful for him will also be more meaningful for his audience. Second, there is the problem of ceiling effects. In a religious epoch, where all painters are already painting the crucifixion, the nativity scene, and so on, the maximal amount of meaningfulness has already been reached. On the other hand, collative properties such as novelty or unpredictability are much freer to vary in all of the arts. Thus the necessity to increase the arousal potential of aesthetic products over time eventually comes down to a pressure to increase novelty, incongruity, unpredictability, and other collative variables. This is the reason for the theoretical emphasis on collative properties rather than on other components of arousal potential. Another way of putting things is that the second law of thermodynamics applies to the art world just as to the physical world: Entropy, disorder, or unpredictability must always increase and can never decrease.

Hedonic Selection
The selection criterion in aesthetic evolution is analogous to Darwin's (1871) sexual selection or hedonic selection rather than to his more well-known selection criterion of "fitness" to the environment (Darwin 1859). Both selection criteria operate on artistic products, but their effects are quite different. Selection on the basis of preference has presumably been present ever since works of art were first produced. Habituation is a universal property of nervous tissue. Thus hedonic selection has exerted a constant pressure in the same direction throughout the entire course of human history. On the other hand, social "fitness" has varied wildly across time. Pornography has low fitness in a puritanical society, moralistic literature has low fitness in a licentious society, and so on. What is fit in one epoch may not be in the next. Thus, fitness has not exerted a consistent, unidirectional pressure on works of art.

If there is a constant pressure for change in the art world, there are also countervailing pressures against it. On the sociological level, Martindale (1975) has argued that the rate of change in a poetic tradition is a function of the value placed upon novelty by the poetry-producing system and that the latter is a function of the system's autonomy from its audience. Poetic values competitive with novelty (such as those of beauty, appropriate subject matter, proper syntax, etc.) depend ultimately upon need for communication with an audience. On the psychological level, habituation is something that occurs gradually. An audience should find aversive not only works of art with too little arousal potential but also those with too much arousal potential. The two opposing pressures should lead to orderly and gradual change in the arts.

This view is similar to the "exhaustion" theories of aesthetic change proposed by Göller (1888) and Lange (1903). These theories traced change in the arts to what Göller called "Formermüdung" or form fatigue. Göller argued that aesthetic pleasure arises from the mental effort of what would today be called assimilation of percepts to memory schemata. As this assimilation becomes too easy because of familiarity, pleasure is lessened and preference for new forms increases. This view makes sense in terms of modern theories about arousal. For example, Sokolov (1963) argues that arousal and attention are functions of lack of fit between memory schemata or expectations and perceptual inputs. It makes sense, then, that a too close fit between expectation and perception should yield little arousal and, hence, little attention and pleasure.

It should be made clear that I am not asserting that artists are motivated solely by a quest for novelty. Artists are interested in accomplishing many other things besides making their works novel. However, what these other things are varies quite unsystematically, whereas the pressure for novelty is constant and consistent. Thus, only this pressure can produce systematic trends in artistic form and content. This is true even if need for novelty is a comparatively *unimportant* motive for any specific artist.

The Direction of Aesthetic Evolution
The formalist theorists (Tynjanov and Jakobson 1928; Mukarovsky 1940) agreed that their evolutionary theory could not explain the direction of aesthetic changes, that it is necessary to look to extra-artistic social or cultural forces for an explanation. Similarly, the theories of Peckham, Meyer, and Cohen do not contain predictions about the specific direction that changes in aesthetic content will take. One of the merits of the psychological theory proposed here is that it makes specific predictions concerning the sequence of contents and styles that would be expected in any artistic or literary tradition.

These predictions arise from a consideration of the psychological means whereby works of continually increasing arousal potential could be produced. How do successive poets produce poetry that becomes more and more novel, original, or incongruous over time? To answer this question, it is necessary to ask how novel ideas or works of art are produced in the first place. According to Kris (1952), novel or original ideas arise from a biphasic process. An initial inspirational stage involving "regression" is followed by a subsequent stage of elaboration with a relatively less regressed mode of thought. By regression is meant a movement from secondary process thinking toward primary process thought. The secondary process–primary process continuum is the fundamental axis along which states of consciousness and types of thought vary (Fromm 1978). Secondary process cognition is abstract, logical, and reality-oriented. Primary process cognition is concrete, irrational, and autistic. It is the thought of dreams and reveries. To avoid psychoanalytic connotations, I use the terms "primordial" and "conceptual" cognition rather than the terms "primary process" and "secondary process." It would be just as accurate to have used terms such as Werner's (1948) "dedifferentiated" versus "differentiated," McKellar's (1957) "A-thinking" versus "R-thinking," or Berlyne's (1965) "autistic" versus "directed" thinking. Indeed, one could just as well refer to what Eysenck (1991) calls breadth of associative horizon.

Primordial cognition is free-associative. It thus increases the probability of novel combinations of mental elements, which form the raw material for a work of art. This raw material must then be put into final form (e.g., be made to conform to stylistic rules) in a rational or conceptual state of mind. Novel ideas could emerge in two ways from the inspiration-elaboration process: Holding the amount of elaboration constant, deeper regression toward primordial cognition should lead to more free-associative thought and thus increase the probability of original combinations of ideas. In other words, to produce a novel idea, one must regress to a primordial level. To produce an even more novel idea, one must regress to an even more primordial mode of thinking. To use Eysenck's (1991) terms, the broader one's associative horizon, the more likely it is that a novel idea will occur. Holding the amount of regression constant, decreasing the degree of elaboration can lead to statements that are original by virtue of being "nonsensical" or nonsyntactic in varying degrees.

Because increasing the novelty of utterances by decreasing level of elaboration is more drastic than increasing novelty by increasing depth of regression during inspiration, poets seem to favor the method of increasing depth of regression rather than of decreasing level of elaboration. If possible, successive poets should engage in deeper and deeper regression while maintaining the same level of elaboration. Each poet must regress further in search of usable combinations of words not already used by his or her predecessors. We should expect the increasing remoteness of similes and metaphors to be accompanied by content indicating the increasingly deeper regression toward primordial cognition required to produce them.

Eventually a turning point—caused by audience pressures or the difficulty of deeper regression—will be reached. At that time, further increases in novelty would be much easier to attain by decreasing level of elaboration—that is, by loosening the stylistic rules governing the production of poetry. This corresponds to a period of major stylistic change. Hypothetically, stylistic change allows poets to return to word combinations composed of relatively close associates. This is accomplished either by changes in the poetic lexicon such that entirely new stimulus words are dealt with or by loosening the stringency of poetic rules so that previously forbidden word combinations are allowed.

There should be a partial return from deep to shallow regression during periods of stylistic change: Because the rules have been changed, deep regression is not needed to produce novel ideas. Once such stylistic change has occurred, the process of increasing regression would be expected to begin again.

A clear example of stylistic change can be seen in the history of modern French poetry. Until 1900, French poets accepted the commonsense stylistic rule that the word "like" had to join like words. Thus, if a poet wanted to compose a simile, "A is like B," then "A" and "B" had in fact to be alike in at least some arcane way. By the end of the nineteenth century, a lot of French poets had written a lot of poetry. It had become very difficult to comply with the stylistic rule without repeating what someone else had already said. Around 1900, this rule was quite explicitly abrogated (Martindale 1975). It became acceptable poetic practice to combine unlike words with the word "like." Thus, Eluard's surreal image, "the earth is blue like an orange," was perfectly good poetry. Surreal images tend to be composed of easily accessible word associates such as "blue" and "orange." No great regression is needed think of "orange" given the word "blue." I have elsewhere presented quantitative evidence that successive nineteenth-century poets did in fact regress more and more up to about 1900, when the process was reversed and depth of regression decreased, presumably because of the loosened stylistic rules (Martindale 1975, 1990).

General Predictions

If the theory is valid, several predictions can be made about any series of literary products produced within a given tradition: Indices measuring collative properties such as novelty, complexity, and variability should increase monotonically across time. Indices of primordial cognition should increase over time, but there should also be cycles of increasing and decreasing density of words indicative of primordial cognition thought superimposed on this uptrend. Periods when primordial cognition content decreases should show evidence of stylistic change. These predictions hold only if the autonomy of the artistic subculture remained relatively constant. There are certainly cases where novelty and primordial content have declined over time. Hypothetically, these would be cases where autonomy also declined or the art-producing system was violently disrupted or destroyed by extra-artistic forces.

It should be made explicit that the evolutionary theory concerns trends in word usage rather than trends in meaning. It is not a theory about the meaning of poetry or about how to interpret poetry. It was not meant to be. Humanistic scholars have sometimes misunderstood this and criticized the theory because it does not concern what they take to be the essence of art and literature. This makes as much sense as criticizing, say, quantum mechanics because it is also mute concerning such matters.

Strong and Weak Versions of the Theory
The evolutionary theory can be construed in two ways. The weak version is that the sorts of changes postulated do occur, but along with many others, in the history of any art form. That is, there may be many unrelated trends in subject matter going on simultaneously with the trends predicted by the theory. The strong version is that the theory accounts for most historical changes in content. In this version, any major trends in content or style can be subsumed by the general primordial cognition trends. Espousal of the strong version of the theory is not unreasonable. The main dimension along which works of art are held to vary by many theorists is isomorphic with the primordial conceptual cognition dimension. Examples would be Nietzsche's (1872) Apollonian versus Dionysian, Riegl's (1901) objectivistic versus subjectivistic, Wölfflin's (1915) linear versus painterly, Sorokin's (1937–41) ideational versus sensate, Sachs's (1946) ethos versus pathos, and Worringer's (1957) abstraction versus empathy. In this view, romantic, mannerist, or baroque styles may be seen as local realizations of a general primordial cognition style. They differ in their surface details but not in their "deep structure." On the other hand, classic, neoclassic, or realistic styles would be examples of a general conceptual cognition style.

Retention Mechanisms
The evolutionary theory applies only to a series of artists working within the same tradition. Just as biological evolution is species-specific, aesthetic evolution is tradition-specific. An evolutionary change in kangaroos has no direct implications for elephants. However, artistic traditions are not as clearly defined as species. Sociological investigations (Clignet 1985; Crane 1987; Martindale 1990) suggest that artists working within the same medium tend to form "invisible colleges." That is, they usually know one another, interact with one another, and are aware of each others' work before the general public is exposed to it. At times, there is interaction among artists working in different media, but artistic "invisible colleges" seem usually to be composed mainly of people working in the same medium. If close interpersonal contact and influence are crucial, one might expect aesthetic evolution to be medium-specific. However, it remains an em-

pirical question as to what, exactly, evolves. It is an empirical question whether it is a specific tradition within a specific medium, the entire medium, or perhaps all artistic media. If the last possibility were correct, then we should expect that primary process cycles in all artistic products would be synchronized. If the first or second possibility is correct, then we should expect the cycles to be randomly related. The question is of interest because historians of art and literature have been asking for several centuries whether the arts change in synchrony or not. Perhaps because of the lack of quantitative investigations, two centuries of humanistic inquiry have produced no generally agreed upon answer to the question. In a study of British poetry, painting, and music, Martindale (1990) found that these three art forms evolve fairly independently of each other. In earlier quantitative historical studies, Sorokin (1937–41) and Kroeber (1944) found little evidence for synchronous changes in the arts.

The Timing of Stylistic Change
A complete theory of aesthetic evolution should be able to explain why and when stylistic changes occur. Three possible explanations seem reasonable (Martindale 1990). According to the least-effort hypothesis: poets adopt a new style when it is easier or requires less effort to increase arousal potential in the new style than in the old style (Martindale 1975). In this view, the old style could have been successful continued, but only at the cost of ever-increasing difficulty. An implication of this explanation is that indices of both arousal potential and primordial content should continue to increase across the entire time during which the old style is used. That is, the style yielded the requisite increases in arousal potential due to successive poets engaging in deeper and deeper regression.

Another explanation might be called the exhaustion hypothesis. In this view, the late practitioners of the old style fail to increase the arousal potential of their poetry as compared with that of their predecessors. Arousal potential may decline or its rate of increase may fall too low. This causes new poets to choose or create new styles. It also causes the audience to prefer a new style that produces poetry with the requisite arousal potential. One problem with the least-effort hypothesis is that a new poet could not know that the old style required too much effort without trying to write in it. However, the initiators of new styles are not usually defectors from a previously dominant style. Rather, they tend to begin their careers as practitioners of the new style. This is easy to explain if the old style had produced actual failures, as suggested by the exhaustion hypothesis.

The most obvious reason for exhaustion is that, given the rules of the old style, there are no more usable combinations of ideas left. Simply put, all of the ideas implicit in the old style have been thought of—the area has been "mined out" (compare Holton 1973; Perkins 1994). Not every conceivable poem in the old style will have been written, but those remaining to be written would be too similar to existing ones. On the theoretical level, this is similar to saying that deeper regression is impossible, because it is regression that produces the ideas for poems. Thus to say that no ideas are left implies that regression has reached its maximum depth. Had it not, even deeper regression would produce more new ideas. If this were the problem, then measures of primordial content should level off in the late stages of a style if the exhaustion hypothesis is true.

A third explanation, which I shall call the evolutionary-trap hypothesis, is based on the probability that depth of regression and originality are in fact curvilinearly related. Perhaps there is a point beyond which deeper regression does not lead to more originality or variability, and even deeper regression may lead to *decreased* originality. Very deep regression involves not only disorganization but also simplification of mental contents (Martindale 1981). Thus, there would be fewer mental elements to combine and hence less variability and originality. In this view, the late practitioners of a style are caught in an evolutionary trap: more regression should lead to more originality, but in fact it does not. If this explanation is correct, then primordial content should increase across the entire time span of a style, whereas indices of arousal potential should increase at first and then level off or decline. These three explanations were tested quantitatively in an investigation of English metaphysical poetry (Martindale 1984b, 1990). In that study, the evolutionary-trap hypothesis best accounted for the data.

Empirical Investigations
A number of studies have been conducted to test the evolutionary theory outlined above. Those concerning literature include investigations of nineteenth- and twentieth-century French poetry (Martindale 1975), fourteenth- through twentieth-century British poetry (Martindale 1984a, 1990), seventeenth-century English metaphysical and nonmetaphysical poetry (Martindale 1984b), nineteenth- and twentieth-century American short stories (Martindale and Keeley 1988), and an experimental simulation of literary change (Martindale 1973b). These studies are summarized in Martindale (1990), as are studies of the history of painting, architecture, music, and science. Below I give some details concerning the study of British poetry.

The Evolution of British Poetry

Sampling
Our first task is to decide what constitutes British poetry. Do we want to explain the history of all poetry ever written in Great Britain, or do we want to explain the history of the accepted canon of British poetry. Literary theorists are currently spending a good bit of time arguing about whether a stable canon really exists. Feminist critics, for example, argue that women writers have been unfairly excluded. From the point of view of evolutionary theory, it makes little difference how we define the population of British poets. Any reasonable definition will get us a historical series of poets who were subject to the same evolutionary laws. A number of years ago, I (Martindale 1975) argued that it would be perfectly reasonable to test the theory with random samples from the entire population of British poets. The only reason I have not done this is logistical: It would be extremely difficult to define that population precisely and to obtain the relevant texts. Also, one would end up with a series of poets that was rather at variance with the series dealt with by other literary historians. Depending upon how many poets were included, the series might not be all that different: Unless one is very lenient as to what one is willing to call poetry, there have not been very many British poets.

The epoch from 1290 to 1949 was divided into 33 successive twenty-year periods. For each of these periods, the poets born during the period were ranked on the basis of number of pages devoted to them in the relevant Oxford anthology of English verse (Chambers 1932; Grierson and Bullough 1934; Hayward 1964; Larkin 1973; Smith 1926; Yeats 1936; Sisam and Sisam 1970). For the last twenty periods—1550 to 1949—this caused no difficulties. The seven poets assigned the most pages were included in the sample. For the period 1530–1549, we come up with only six poets. This is certainly sufficient. Unless the reader is an expert on English literature, the list of poets studied (see Martindale 1990) will include almost all the British poets he or she has heard of as well as a number of unfamiliar names. The sixth and seventh most eminent poets in many of these periods are quite deservedly not very eminent. For only a couple of the periods are poets of much worth excluded. For periods 1–12, only two poets per period were included. The simple reason is that this is as many as we can find for most of these periods. For these early periods, birthdates are questionable—even for several of the poets included—or very little of their poetry remains. For these periods, the Oxford anthologies do not provide enough names, so Bennett (1947), Hammond (1927), Renwick and Orton (1939), and Watson (1974) were also consulted. The fact that we only have two poets per period should lead us to regard the results for the early periods as more tentative than those for the later ones. To make matters even more tentative, during the early periods English and Scottish poetic traditions were fairly distinct. However, to get enough poets, we must mingle together English and Scottish poets. Finally, the early poetry was written in Middle English and Middle Scots, so it literally had to be translated into modern English.

It might have been preferable to select poets on the basis of their contemporary fame rather than on the basis of their present-day fame. However, there is no very good objective method of determining contemporary fame. Such an approach would be far too subjective. Furthermore, contemporary fame is not always a good guide to importance. The list is not perfect in other ways. The average reader has never heard of John Cleveland or Edward Benlowes. Because of their importance for the development of English poetry, however, they should be on the list. Thomas Traherne is included but probably should not be. He is a good poet, but his works were not discovered until the twentieth century. Thus he had no impact upon his contemporaries or upon poets who wrote soon after him. This sort of imperfection is the price we pay for objectivity. The Oxford anthologies include poets born in Great Britain who subsequently migrated, as well as poets born elsewhere who wrote for long periods of time in Great Britain. Such poets (e.g., T. S. Eliot) were included. A few exclusions were necessary. Given the method of assigning poets to periods, poets whose birthdates are unknown were excluded. A few poets (e.g., Henry VIII) did not write enough poetry to be included. On the assumption that the computer would make no sense of Lewis Carroll's nonsense verse, he was omitted.

In view of current controversies in the United States concerning how or whether the canon of great works of art or literature should be redefined, it is worth asking whether eminence is a reliable measure of a person's creativity. In investigating the prices of paintings, Reitlinger (1961) found that the prices paid for works by a given painter tend to oscillate, often wildly, for several generations after the painter's death. They then rise or settle down to their "proper" place and stay there. In other words the "test-retest" reliability of a painter's worth is quite high across long periods of time. Farnsworth (1969) studied the amount of space given to works by various composers in the repertoire of the Boston Symphony Orchestra in 1915–24 and 1955–64. The correlation was .89. He found similarly high reliabilities when he examined the amount of space devoted to composers in musical reference works published up to fifty years apart. Simonton (1984) measured the "alternate forms" reliability of eminence by looking at the amount of space devoted to philosophers and composers in different reference works. Again, very high reliability coefficients were found.

Eminence is reliable, but is it valid? There are few quantitative studies of this question, perhaps because it can be answered affirmatively by qualitative means. No one would seriously argue that Marlowe was a greater dramatist than Shakespeare or that Gebel was a greater composer than Bach. There is clearly something in the style of Bach's compositions that sets them above those of Gebel. If it is there, it can be measured: Simonton (1983) studied the melodic originality—note-to-note transitional improbability—of 15,618 themes in the classical repertoire. He found a very clear relationship between a measure of "thematic fame" and melodic originality.

Eminence also has a sort of self-evident "face validity" in the sense that the ideas of eminent creators influence subsequent creators. A history of physics that left out Max Planck would make no sense, as quantum physics would seem to have appeared from nowhere. Those who seek to revise literary or artistic canons seem not to realize that the same is true of literature and the arts. A history of German literature omitting Goethe would make no sense. Pulling obscure authors out of oblivion only creates confusion, as such creators usually had little or no impact upon subsequent writers. Even more than the eminence of creators, the relative importance of innovations is self-evident. Because locomotives, for example, are dependent upon the steam engine, the latter would seem clearly to be a more important innovation.

Once poets had been selected, the most complete and recent available edition of their poetic works was obtained. Fifty random samples were taken by drawing fifty page numbers from a table of random numbers. The first eight lines were counted off and the sample for each page was terminated at the first phrase delimiter ('.',':',';','?', or '!') at or after the end of the eighth line. The mean number of words per poet was about 3,000. The mean number of phrases per poet was about 200. Neither number of words nor number of phrases varied significantly across periods. Some editing was done in order to make the texts compatible with the programs used: All contractions and abbreviations were spelled out and all hyphens and dashes were deleted. Old spellings were consistently modernized to facilitate dictionary look-ups. Modernization was confined to minor spelling changes. Further details and results of earlier studies of this series when it contained a smaller number of poets may be found in

Martindale (1969, 1975, 1978, 1984a). We end up with a sample totaling 521,566 words.

General Method

Because of the large amount of text analyzed, computerized content analysis was employed. To attempt to test the theory using a traditional humanistic or qualitative approach would have been impossible. The task of reading the works of 170 poets and deciding whether arousal potential increased in a monotonic fashion across time completely exceeds the capacities of human memory. Given that a quantitative method was necessary, why were human raters not used? The basic reasons are that content analysis done by humans is not very reliable—raters tend to disagree with one another—and they are very slow. However, people want to be paid a lot of money for their slow and unreliable work. Computerized content analysis suffers from none of these problems.

Programs

The texts were analyzed with a set of computer programs developed by the author. COUNT (Martindale 1973a) is a general purpose content analysis program. It is modeled on the General Inquirer (Stone et al. 1966) and has similar capabilities. SEMIS is a program for modified content analysis. It applies dictionaries containing words rated on up to four dimensions. Rather than only being assigned to a dimension, the degree to which a word "belongs to" the dimension can be specified. COUNT and SEMIS contain routines for removing punctuation and common suffixes before dictionary look-up of text words. To avoid miscategorization due to suffix removal, each word is looked up in an auxiliary dictionary prior to suffix removal. For example, removing the final 's' from 'as' would lead to confusion between 'a' and 'as'. In order to avoid this, words such as 'as' are placed in the auxiliary dictionary. LEXSTAT (Martindale 1974) is a program for computation of standard lexical statistics such as average word length, average sentence or phrase length, type-token ratio, and so on.

Arousal Potential

The first question of interest concerns the prediction that the arousal potential of poetry has increased over time. I constructed a Composite Variability Index to measure the collative properties of texts (Martindale 1978). The goal was to create an index of the degree of complexity, surprise, incongruity, ambiguity, and variability of texts. In creating the index, several steps were involved. First, nonredundant measures with face validity were selected. Then, because many of them are spuriously related to number of words or phrases in a text, the effects of these variables were removed with multiple regression techniques. That is, residual scores with the effects of number of words and number of phrases statistically removed were computed. Finally, a Composite Variability Index was created by adding together the variables in standard score form (to give each equal weighting). The index is composed of the following measures:

1. Polarity (a measure of semantic intensity or strikingness). Heise (1965) had a large number of subjects rate the 1,000 most frequent English words on Osgood, Suci, and Tannenbaum's (1957) connotative dimensions of potency (strong vs. weak), activity (active vs. passive), and evaluation (good vs. bad). Because these dimensions are orthogonal, we can place a word in the three dimensional "semantic space" that they form. Polarity is a measure of the absolute distance from the origin in this space. SEMIS was used to compute average polarity for each poet.

2. Number of Word Associates (a measure of use of words with multiple meanings, and thus, more potential ambiguity). Paivio, Yuille, and Madigan (1968) had subjects produce word associates to 925 common English nouns and computed the number of different responses to each of these words. SEMIS was again used to apply the norms to the texts.

3. Hapax Legomena Percentage (percentage of words occurring only once in a document: an index of complexity or difficulty). In order to compute this and the following measures, I wrote a program called LEXSTAT (Martindale 1974). To compute the hapax legomena percentage the program, rather obviously, tabulates how often each word in a text occurs. It then computes how many of these words was used only once.

4. Mean Word Length (a measure of complexity or difficulty).

5. Coefficient of Variation of Word Frequency (a measure of variability or unpredictability). LEXSTAT computes the average frequency with which words are used as well as the variation around this average. The coefficient of variation is the variance divided by the mean. If a poet used each of his or her words exactly twice, average word frequency would be 2, but the coefficient of variation would be 0. To get a high score on this measure, some words have to be used a lot and some have to be used infrequently. This seems to be a poetic rather than a normal pattern of using words.

6. Coefficient of Variation of Word Length (another measure of variability). This is a measure of tendency to intermix long and short words.

7. Coefficient of Variation of Phrase Length (another measure of variability). This is a measure of unpredictability of phrase length. By a phrase is meant a sentence or a string of words terminated by a colon or semicolon.

The Composite Variability Index is for the most part a measure of unpredictability or entropy. A text that is unpredictable should be surprising. The more unpredictable a poem is, the less certain we are what the poet is going to say next. The Composite Variability Index gets at unpredictability on a very basic linguistic level. Many readers may not pay a lot of attention to whether, say, a poet is intermixing long and short words. Jakobson (1960) notes that poetic language attempts to call attention to itself. This is not always successful, though. We *can* read poetry as if it were prose and miss the interplay of words. I do not claim that linguistic variability is the main aspect of poetry. It certainly is the easiest aspect to measure, though. If the Composite Variability Index is not getting at anything important, it will not show any coherent trend across time. I should merely have gone to a great deal of trouble to generate a set of random numbers.

The Composite Variability Index varies across periods in a highly significant way. Differences among the periods are much greater than differences within the periods. Seventy-one percent of variation in the index is due to differences among periods. As predicted, these differences are due to a monotonic uptrend over time. Mean values of the Composite Variability Index for each period are shown in figure 7.1. The best-fitting trend line is also shown in the figure. The equation for the trend is

$$AP = 10 + \frac{1}{-10.23 + 10.41e^{-.00036P}},$$

where e is the base of the natural logarithm, and P is period. The equation accounts for 76.5% of variation in the mean values. As is obvious from the figure, the rate of change in Arousal Potential has accelerated across time. Note that Arousal Potential has been changing and accelerating according to the above equation since before Chaucer. It is speeding up in its rate of change, but this has always been the case.

As may be seen, the early periods show a lot of variability around the trend line. Some of this variability arises because some components of the Composite Variability Index are not very appropriate for these texts. For example, punctuation in Middle English was capricious and inconsistent by modern standards. In fact, several of the poets did not use it at all. It had to be guessed at in what may have been a too

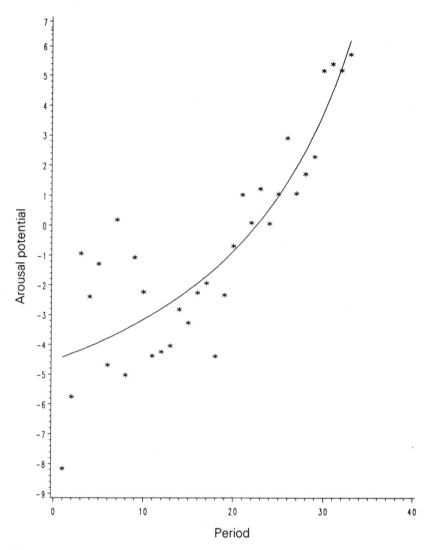

Figure 7.1
Mean arousal potential (Composite Variability Index) in texts of 170 British poets born in thirty-three consecutive twenty-year periods from 1290 to 1949.

conservative fashion. Of course, with only two poets per period, the averages are less stable than those for later periods. Some of the variability is probably real. When a poetic tradition is first coalescing, poets will be less sure of the rules of the game and of who else is playing. They are likely as a consequence to overshoot and under-shoot the mark. That is, to produce somewhat too much or too little variability.

If we disregard the first ten periods because of the uncertainties just mentioned, we find that the best-fitting equation—accounting for 91% of interperiod variation—for the Composite Variability Index is simply a straight line,

$$AP = -10.18 + .47P.$$

In this case, the rate of change is given by the slope of the line—a constant .47 units per period. The acceleration is, of course, zero: The rate of change in the entropy, variability, or arousal potential of British poetry has not appreciably increased or decreased across the last 450 years or so.

Some of the components of the Composite Variability Index show nonlinear trends, but they all show highly significant ($p < .001$) monotonic increases. Poets in different periods prefer to obtain arousal potential in different ways. In some periods, poets use long and infrequent words, whereas in other periods poets obtain their impact by use of words of high polarity. An obvious objection to a theory that takes a quest for novelty and variability as the impetus behind literary history is the existence of movements such as neoclassicism that ostensibly call for simplicity, order, symmetry, and balance. The English neoclassical poets occupy periods 18–21. The Composite Variability Index continued to rise across these periods. An examination of the component indices shows that some of them, such as polarity and the coefficient of variation of phrase length, did decrease. However, these decreases were more than offset by increases in other measures such as the hapax legomena percentage and mean word length. In other words, the neoclassic poets more than compensated for decreases in some of the components by increasing others. These results suggest that the popular view of the neoclassical style as a reversion to order following seventeenth-century excesses is incorrect. On the contrary, it would seem that the neoclassic style shift was in the service of *increased* arousal potential. These poets' rhetoric concerning order with regard to some aspects of poetic practice has obscured their pursuit of disorder in other aspects. By analogy with thermodynamics, greater order and simplicity on one level of poetic practice was bought at the cost of even greater disorder on another level.

Primordial Content
To test the predictions concerning trends in primordial content, we need a measure of the latter. The Regressive Imagery Dictionary (for use with COUNT) contains 2,900 words assigned to thirty-six categories. Each word is assigned to only one category. Table 7.1 presents information on the categories and words in the Regressive Imagery Dictionary. The basic categories are summed to yield two summary categories that measure primordial and conceptual content. The primordial content categories are grouped into subdivisions of Drives, Sensations, Perceptual Disinhibition, Regressive Cognition, and Icarian Imagery. Each of these has been suggested by various theorists as being important in primordial cognition. The categories measuring conceptual content have, likewise, been used by theorists in describing this type of thought. Martindale (1975, 1990) presents evidence concerning the rationale and reliability of the coding scheme. In order to obtain a general measure of primordial content, the five component Primordial Content categories were added together and the conceptual content category was subtracted from this sum.

Evidence for the construct validity of Primordial Content as an index of dedifferentiated thought comes from a number of studies where the measure has behaved as theoretically predicted. Significantly more primordial content has been found in the poetry of poets exhibiting signs of psychopathology than in that of poets not exhibiting such signs (Martindale 1975); in the speech of paranoid schizophrenics as opposed to control subjects (West and Martindale, 1988); in psychoanalytic sessions marked by therapeutic "work" as opposed to those marked by resistance and defensiveness (Reynes, Martindale, and Dahl 1984); in sentences containing verbal tics as opposed to asymptomatic sentences (Martindale 1977); in texts composed by a subject under the influence of psilocybin as opposed to texts composed before and after the drug experience (Martindale and Fischer 1977); in fantasy stories written by subjects under the influence of marijuana as opposed to stories written by subjects given a placebo (West, Martindale, Hines, and Roth 1983); in fantasy stories told by younger as opposed to older children (West, Martindale, and Sutton-Smith 1985); in written fantasy stories of subjects with more right-hemisphere EEG activity (Martindale, Covello, and West 1986); in fantasy stories of hypnotized as opposed to unhypnotized subjects (Comeau and Farthing 1982); and in folktales of more primitive as opposed to more socioculturally complex preliterate societies (Martindale 1976).

Factor analyses of the categories based on the above type of texts, as well as the poetic texts, have consistently yielded a first factor accounting for about 30% of the variance, which loads highly on the

Table 7.1
Regressive imagery dictionary: Summary categories, categories, and sample words

Summary Category
Category (sample words)

Drives
Oral (breast, drink, lip)
Anal (sweat, rot, dirty)
Sex (lover, kiss, naked)
Sensation
General sensation (fair, charm, beauty)
Touch (touch, thick, stroke)
Taste (sweet, taste, bitter)
Odor (breath, perfume, scent)
Sound (hear, voice, sound)
Vision (see, light, look)
Cold (cold, winter, snow)
Hard (rock, stone, hard)
Soft (soft, gentle, tender)
Perceptual Disinhibition
Passivity (die, lie, bed)
Voyage (wander, desert, beyond)
Random movement (wave, roll, spread)
Diffusion (shade, shadow, cloud)
Chaos (wild, crowd, ruin)
Regressive Cognition
Unknown (secret, strange, unknown)
Timelessness (eternal, forever, immortal)
Consciousness alteration (dream, sleep, wake)
Brink-passage (road, wall, door)
Narcissism (eye, heart, hand)
Concreteness (at, where, over)
Icarian Imagery
Ascend (rise, fly, throw)
Height (up, sky, high)
Descend (fall, drop, sink)
Depth (down, deep, beneath)
Fire (sun, fire, flame)
Water (sea, water, stream)
Conceptual Content
Abstraction (know, may, thought)
Social behavior (say, tell, call)
Instrumental behavior (make, find, work)
Restraint (must, stop, bind)
Order (simple, measure, array)
Temporal references (when, now, then)
Moral imperatives (should, right, virtue)

primordial content categories and in a high negative direction on the categories designed to measure conceptual content.

Figure 7.2 presents mean values for Primordial Content for each period. As may be seen, Primordial Content rose over time but a cyclical or oscillatory trend is superimposed on the uptrend. Sixty-two percent of the variance in Primordial Content is accounted for by interperiod differences. The remaining 48% is due to variation among the poets within periods (that is, to individual differences). If we examine the means shown in figure 7.2, we find that 70% of the variation is due to a monotonic uptrend. This trend is purely linear. It does not accelerate or decelerate across time. The other 30% of variation is due to the quasi-periodic oscillations around the trend line. Presumably, the linear uptrend has occurred because more and more primordial cognition has been needed to think of useful word combinations. Theoretically, the oscillations indicate stylistic changes. Primordial Content does tend to begin declining during periods commonly seen as involving initiation of new styles: Chaucerian, Skeltonic, Tudor, Jacobean, Neoclassic, Pre-Romantic, Romantic, Post-Romantic, and Modern. It begins to rise once the new style is established.

Theoretical considerations and the fact that the cycles vary in their periods suggest that they arose from stochastic rather than strictly deterministic causes. Stylistic change allows primordial cognition to decline. After the stylistic change is completed, primordial content begins to increase again. It has to, because poets must engage in more primordial cognition to find the increasingly rare useful word combinations allowed by the style. How far primordial content falls or how long a cycle in primordial content is will depend upon how extreme the style change is and how fruitful it is in producing useful poetry. We would find cycles of exactly the same duration and amplitude only if all style changes were equally useful. This is unlikely because the poets who begin a stylistic change cannot know ahead of time how fruitful the change is going to be. To know this would mean that they already knew all of the useful similes and poetic devices implicit in the style. If they had this knowledge, they would themselves have used all of these poetic devices.

An autoregressive statistical analysis of the cycles is most appropriate. In such an analysis, one attempts to predict the mean score for one period from the mean scores for prior periods. Of course, this is consistent with the evolutionary theory, which involves the assertion that the main cause of poetic content in any period is the poetic content of prior periods. Cycles of the sort observed can arise from a second-order autoregressive process: that is, the mean value for a given period

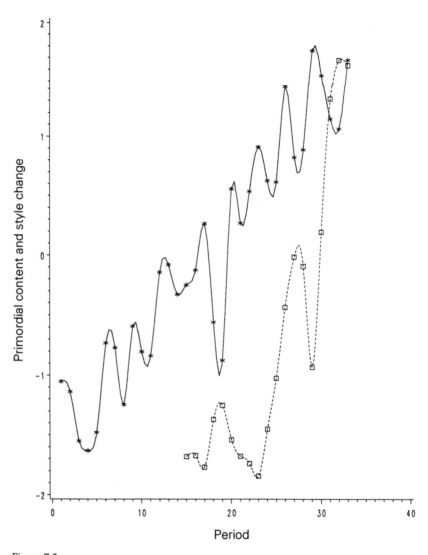

Figure 7.2
Mean amount of Primordial Content (*————*) and Stylistic Change (- - - -) in texts of 170 British poets born in thirty-three consecutive twenty-year periods from 1290 to 1949.

is determined by the values for the prior two periods plus random error (Gottman 1981). Autocorrelation analysis of detrended average Primordial Content scores for the thirty-three periods supports this notion: Autocorrelations at lags from 1 to 10 periods exhibit a damped sinusoidal pattern. On the other hand, partial autocorrelations (the autocorrelation at a given lag partialling out the effect of autocorrelations due to earlier or intervening lags) fall to about zero after a lag of two. This is the pattern expected with a second-order autoregressive process (Gottman 1981). It is of less than incidental interest that a completely different pattern of autocorrelations would be found if reflectionist theories of artistic change (primordial content in a given period is due to extraliterary "shocks" in the current and/or prior periods) were true. If a time series is caused by external "shocks," the autocorrelations decrease with increasing lags until the shock has been absorbed, and then they vanish abruptly (Gottman 1981).

Since the first autoregressive parameter is statistically insignificant, the best autoregressive model for Primordial Content in a given period (PC_t) is $PC_t = -.368PC_{t-2}$. That is, amount of primordial content in the poetry of a given period is a function of primordial content two periods prior (PC_{t-2}) to the period. When Primordial Content scores are correlated with scores predicted from this model, a significant fit is achieved. The fact that the first autoregressive parameter is insignificant suggests that we are dealing with what is called a "seasonal" rather than a second-order autoregressive process. Both processes can produce quasi-periodic oscillations (Gottman 1981).

The autoregressive equation does explain some of the oscillation in primordial content. However, it only explains 16% of it. Clearly, other factors besides prior values of primordial content are causing most of the oscillation. Theoretically, this is what we expect: The cycles are hypothetically being caused primarily by stylistic changes. As I implied, they should vary in their amplitude and duration as a function of how extreme these stylistic changes were.

Stylistic Change

I remarked above that declines in primordial content coincide with introduction of new styles. They do seem to, but we should seek some quantitative evidence to support this statement. After all, literary critics are hardly unanimous as to exactly when stylistic changes occurred in British poetry. Leaving aside pronouncements from poets that they have changed styles, a critic must judge that a new style has been introduced on the basis of changes in the content of poetry. We should be able to measure such changes in an objective manner.

The task of a poet is to combine words in a way that is pleasing or interesting to his or her audience. The audience habituates to old combinations and demands new ones. I have argued that engaging in more primordial cognition makes the poet more efficient at finding such new combinations. However, the audience must also be habituating to the words themselves. Thus there must be continual pressure to change the poetic lexicon by adding new words and dropping old ones. This pressure is compounded by the fact that there is a finite number of useful combinations—no matter how primordial the cognition one engages in—in a given set of words. Thus we would expect that the poetic lexicon should show continual change. An indicator of stylistic change may be the addition and deletion of words at an above average rate. Of course, stylistic change also involves changes in the rules governing poetic practice, that is, in the rules governing how words may be "legally" combined. This aspect of stylistic change, though, is more difficult to measure.

Josephine Miles (1964) argued that stylistic change can be measured by tabulating changes in the poetic lexicon. She held that the first practitioners of a new style tend to add new words to their poetic vocabulary without dropping an abnormally large number of the old words used by prior poets. Once the new style gains a foothold, the old words tend to be dropped. Miles presented some convincing quantitative evidence for her contention. However, she did not do any statistical tests that would allow us to assess the significance of the patterns. We can approach our texts in the same spirit and see what we find.

We want to compute how many unique words the poets in each period used. If this is done for each period, we can compute how many of these words were retained from the prior period, how many were new words, and how many of the words used in the prior period have been dropped. For any period, the number of unique words (types) will depend upon the total number of words (tokens) in the sample. In general, the number of types declines as the number of tokens increases (Herdan 1966). If a text were composed of 10 words, each of them could be unique. This would hardly be possible if the text were 100 words in length, because function words (which account for about 40% of the words in a text) would have to be repeated. This presents a problem. We have two poets per period for periods 1–12, six poets in period 13, and seven poets per period thereafter. Thus, the earlier samples are much shorter—and are thus composed of fewer word types—than the later ones. Because there is no completely satisfactory way to splice together the early and late data, I shall consider only the periods for which there are seven poets per period. Because we want to compute the number of word types in one period relative to the prior one, we cannot use the first period with seven poets. The sample for it is larger than that for the prior period, which had only six poets. This would produce misleading results. For the usable periods, the total number of words (tokens) does not differ significantly. The average number of tokens per period is 20,970, whereas the average number of types (different words) per period is 4,814. In total, we are dealing with a sample of 398,432 tokens and 91,471 types. Because the number of tokens in each period is almost identical, it does not distort the number of types per period.

The first question is how many word types did the poets of each period use. By this I mean how many different or unique words did they use. We disregard whether a word was used once by one poet or many times by all of the poets in the period. I used LEXSTAT to generate the list of words used by each poet and some programs written in SAS for the remaining tabulations and computations. I computed the number of word types added, kept, and dropped in each period. Across time, the percentage of words added to the poetic lexicon has increased at an accelerating rate, whereas the percentage of words dropped or kept has decreased at an accelerating rate. It is apparent that the poetic lexicon has turned over at a faster and faster rate over time. As time passes, a larger and larger percentage of poets' vocabulary consists of new words and a smaller and smaller percentage consists of words retained from the prior period.

Poets will not be able to continue with this rate of addition and deletion much longer. Obviously, poets cannot add more than 100% of their vocabulary or drop more than 100% of the vocabulary of the previous generation. If present trends continued, poets born about 100 years from now would exceed this addition rate. It must be, then, that the rate of addition and deletion will have to decrease as they approach the 100% ceiling; that is, we are looking at the first part of logistic or sigmoid growth curves. A logistic function at first increases at an exponential rate. At some inflection point, rate of increase begins to slow down. Such curves describe the growth of organisms and of populations. If poets have increased addition and deletion rate in order to increase the arousal potential of their poetry, then slowing down the rate of increase would cause arousal potential to decline. A system that thrives on change will die if change is no longer possible. A decrease in arousal potential means poetic failure. To compensate for this, poets would have to engage in more and more primordial cognition until this too reached its limit. Another strategy would be to increase the total number of word types in the poetic lexicon. There is a limit to this as well. The number of types cannot exceed the number of tokens.In a text in which the number of types was equal to the number of tokens, every word would be used only once. Such a text would be incomprehensible because it would not be "glued together" by function words. Of course, poets seem not to aim primarily at comprehensibility.

Addition and deletion rates have increased across time, but all of the data points are not on the trend line. Perhaps the deviations have to do with stylistic changes. If Miles is correct, then either addition or deletion can indicate a stylistic change. I added together the percent of types added and the percent of types deleted in each period and used this as an index of Stylistic Change. This index is plotted above, along with Primordial Cognition, in figure 7.2. In the figure, both measures are shown in standardized form so as to be comparable. The index of Stylistic Change looks as if it is measuring what we want. It tends to increase when primordial content decreases and vice versa. If we partial out the long-term temporal trends in each variable, we find that the correlation between Stylistic Change and Primordial Content is $-.58$, $p < .05$.

Stylistic Change and Primordial Content are not perfect inverses of each other. Part of the reason is that neither is a perfect measure. Let us see what information we can piece together from these measures. Both have increased across time. Theoretically, they have increased because of poets' efforts to counter habituation. Oscillations are superimposed on these increases, and the oscillations tend to be out of phase: Poets seem to favor one or the other method of increasing arousal potential. However, poets can use both methods. This is hardly a startling finding. There is no certainly iron-clad rule that a poet who adds or drops a lot of words is forbidden to engage in primordial cognition when it comes to combining these words in his poetry. There is merely an empirical tendency for this not to be the case.

Once vocabulary has changed to a sufficient degree, poets tend to slow down the rate at which they add and discard words and focus on extracting the useful combinations present in the vocabulary at hand. As this becomes more difficult, they engage in more primordial thinking in order to discover these combinations. If poets had perfect knowledge and acted under no constraints, there should be no oscillations in either Primordial Content or Stylistic Change. That is, poets could "compute" how many words to add and drop so as to increase arousal potential without having to engage in a lot of primordial cognition. One suspects that poets do not do this because the "computation" would force them to add and delete words at a rate that is too fast for whatever audience they have. We can do more than suspect: we can make a few computations. That is, we can see whether the data show any indication that Stylistic Change is held in bounds. I have implied that poets increase arousal potential (AP) by a combination of primordial cognition (PC) and stylistic change (SC). The data support this implication. We find that the equation,

$$AP = .58PC + .25SC,$$

explains 88% of the variation in arousal potential (as measured by the Composite Variability Index) for the periods in question. (In this and the next equation, the variables are in standard score form, so the beta weights are equivalent to correlations.) This is the same percentage of variation explained by an equation relating arousal potential to the mere passage of time.

If primordial cognition and stylistic change caused changes in arousal potential, what caused changes in these variables? Theoretically, the changes are due to habituation (passage of time) and to prior values of these variables. We can use stepwise regression to predict primordial content (PC_t) in a given period (t) from prior values of primordial content (PC_{t-i}) and present (SC_t) and prior (SC_{t-i}) values of stylistic change.

The best prediction equation—best in the sense that no better can be found and all predictors are statistically significant—is

$$PC_t = 12.81 + .51t - .55SC_{t-1} - .52PC_{t-1} - .56PC_{t-2}.$$

The equation explains 91% of the variation in primordial content. In words, the equation says that primordial content increases linearly with time and decreases as a function of stylistic change in the prior period and of amount of primordial content in the prior two periods. All of the scores except period (t) are standard scores with a mean of 0 and a standard deviation of 1. PC_{t-1}, for example, can be either positive or negative. If it is positive, it will drive PC_t down. If it is negative, it will drive PC_t upward. For example, if $PC_{t-1} = -1$, we multiply it by $-.52$ and get $+.52$. This is the contribution of PC_{t-1} to determining what the value of PC_t will be.

The best equation for stylistic change (SC_t) accounts for 94% of the variation:

$$SC_t = -1.027 + .0094e^{.175t} + .57SC_{t-1} - .50SC_{t-2}.$$

The first part of the equation tells us that SC increases exponentially with time. The second part shows that if the value of SC in the prior period was high, the value in the current period will also be high. However, this is held in check by the last term, which tells us that stylistic change at $t-2$ inhibits stylistic change in the current period.

Once stylistic change begins, it tends to persist into the next period, but not into the one after that.

It is not immediately apparent what the relationships in these equations are going to cause. We do know that the equations explain almost all of the variation in arousal potential, stylistic change, and primordial content, so they must cause some oscillation in the last two variables. Indeed, equations of this sort do produce oscillations. The equation for Primordial Content contains several negative feedback terms: If Primordial Content was "too high" in prior periods, current poets decrease it. If it was too low, current poets increase it. This is what a thermostat does to temperature. Because of delay—when the thermostat turns on the furnace, there is a delay before the furnace can get the temperature to the desired level—the target temperature is continually overshot and undershot. The same overshooting and undershooting occurs with primordial content. Primordial Content is also controlled by stylistic change in the prior period: If there was a lot of stylistic change in the prior period, primordial cognition is decreased. It is not necessary, because the new style allows for sufficient increases in arousal potential without a lot of primordial cognition. If there was little stylistic change in the prior period, primordial cognition is increased. It has to be if arousal potential is to be increased sufficiently. On the other hand, the equations do not show primordial content holding stylistic change in check. Primordial content in the same period and the prior period is in fact negatively correlated with stylistic change. However, the correlations are comparatively uninformative, that is, the ones shown in the equations do a better job of explaining trends in stylistic change.

Tests of the Strong versus Weak Versions of the Theory
In the process of examining how many words were added and dropped during each period, it was necessary to compute which words were used by each of the poets in the sample. Because this had to be done anyway, little extra effort was necessary to compute exactly how often each poet used each of these words. These data allow us to correlate each poet with all other poets. If two poets used exactly the same set of words at exactly the same frequencies, we would obtain a correlation of 1.00. To the extent that their word usage differed, the correlation would be lower. The correlations thus tell us how similar poets were in their word usage. This similarity matrix of poets was analyzed with a multidimensional scaling program, ALSCAL (Young, Lewyckyi, and Takane 1980).

Multidimensional scaling provides a spatial representation of the similarities among the group of poets, with more similar poets being placed closer together. The question to be answered is how many dimensions are needed to represent the similarities. Obviously, a perfect spatial representation of the similarities among 170 poets would be provided by a 169-dimensional space. ALSCAL provides an answer to the question of how many of these dimensions are really important by minimizing an index, Kruskal's Stress. Kruskal (Kruskal and Wish 1978) suggests that a solution where this coefficient is .10 or less is adequate. Preliminary scaling of the similarity matrix yielded a stress value of less than .10 for five dimensions. Based on Kruskal's rule, the five-dimensional solution was used. The implication is that the poets in the present sample differ along five basic dimensions. Indeed, 95% of interpoet similarities in word usage are accounted for by these five dimensions.

The question of interest is the extent to which a poet's position in this five-dimensional multidimensional space can be predicted from his or her scores on the two main theoretical variables, Primordial Content and the Composite Variability Index. To answer this question, canonical correlations between these two theoretical variables and the four multidimensional variables were computed. Two highly significant canonical correlations emerged. On the basis of these correlations, Stewart and Love's (1968) measure of redundancy was computed. The measure tells us how much of the variation in one set of variables (the five multidimensional axes in this case) can be accounted for by another set of variables (the two theoretical variables in this case). The redundancy score, 34%, means that about one-third of the overall variation among the poets in the sample can be accounted for by the two theoretical variables.

Specificity of the Trends to Poetic Language
It is clearly necessary to distinguish trends in poetic language from trends in language in general. Thus, for control purposes, it was necessary to analyze some nonliterary texts. The *Annual Register* has been published yearly in England since the mid-eighteenth century. It is a narrative description of world events for the year. There is no reason to think that writers for the *Annual Register* have been under a pressure to increase the arousal potential of their prose. Their job has been simply to report upon what has occurred in the past year. For the period from 1770 to 1970, ten samples from the Annual Register for every tenth year (i.e., 1770, 1780, etc.) were drawn at random. The mean number of words per volume sampled was about 1690. The total sample consists of 56,055 words. To obtain a longer sample of English prose, I took five samples of about 340 words each for every twentieth year from 1510 to 1970 for the *British Statutes* (Acts of Parliament). To

avoid the stylized opening paragraphs of the statutes, samples were taken only from the middle and ending sections. This produces a sample of 40,789 words of legalese. The Composite Variability Index was computed for these nonliterary texts. It showed no statistically significant interperiod differences and no linear trend over time. Likewise, there were no interperiod differences for Primordial Content nor any linear or higher-order trends. Thus trends found in poetry do not appear to be mere reflections of general trends in the English language (Martindale 1990).

Conclusions

Because arousal potential has increased across time, we could say that British poetry has been a creative enterprise for the last several centuries. (Of course, we already knew this.) The arousal potential of British painting and music has also increased for the last few centuries (Martindale 1990). We could say that British society has been "creative" in the sense of *allowing* these art forms to evolve without hindrance. The arousal potential of painting rose throughout most of the Eighteenth Dynasty of ancient Egypt and then declined drastically (Martindale 1990). The cause of the decline was active interference by religious and political institutions. In this case, the natural evolution of Egyptian society was not being creative, or—more precisely—was not allowing creativity. It would be possible to use rate of change in the arousal potential of various art forms to measure how creative different societies are. If this were done in the case of musical compositions, we would conclude that Britain and Germany have fostered more creativity than have France and Italy since the eighteenth century (Martindale 1990). Of course, we would want to measure rate of change of arousal potential in other art forms before concluding that these pairs of countries were in general different in the degree to which these allowed or facilitated artistic creativity.

Sociocultural Correlates of Creativity in Great Britain
The main point of the study described above was to test an evolutionary theory of literary history. In line with theoretical predictions, I found that most aspects of literary content are not related to much if anything in the extrapoetic social and cultural milieu. In order to demonstrate this, literary content was correlated with various extraliterary time series. Quite by chance, I did discover a consistent set of relationships relevant to scientific and technological innovation.

I gathered a large number of extraliterary time series and constructed several more summary indices. The relevant ones were the following:

1. Philosophical emphasis. Sorokin (1937–41, vol. II) measured sensate versus ideational emphasis in several aspects of European philosophy. By sensate, Sorokin meant realistic and empirical (Locke would be an example), whereas by ideational he meant an emphasis on the mental and a priori (Hegel would be an example). Sorokin gives figures for the number of philosophers adhering to sensate versus ideational emphasis in systems of truth, ethical systems, and first principles: temporalism versus externalism, realism versus conceptualism, singularism versus universalism, materialism versus idealism, and indeterminism versus determinism. His measures of sensate emphasis were standardized and added to yield an index of Net Sensate Emphasis. Because we cannot measure the cultural Zeitgeist directly, Sorokin's figures give us at least an indirect measure of it.
2. War. Sorokin (1937–41, vol. III) also provides figures for the number of casualties for battles engaged in by Great Britain.
3. Technological innovations. Sorokin (1937–41, vol. II, p. 136, col. 4) provides tabulations of European technological innovations.
4. Wages relative to prices. Based on their figures for British wages and prices across the last seven centuries, Phelps Brown and Hopkins (1956) computed a measure of wages relative to prices; higher numbers indicate greater purchasing power. The index can be taken as a measure of general prosperity.
5. Industrial productivity. Mitchell (1975) computed an index of British industrial productivity from the eighteenth century to the present. We would expect this measure to give us an idea of the vitality of the British economy.
6. Illegitimacy rate. The ratio of illegitimate to legitimate births may be a measure of moral permissiveness. It was low during the puritan era (the 1650s) and high around 1600, 1800, and the 1960s—all liberal eras. However, it was low throughout the Restoration (1660–1688), which was—at least for the upper class—probably the most licentious era in English history. Figures were taken from (Laslett and Oosterveen 1973, Mitchell and Deane 1962, and Mitchell and Jones 1971.)

Each extraliterary series was aggregated to correspond to twenty-year periods centered thirty years after the birth periods of poets. Most of the series show increases across time, and many of them have increased at an accelerating rate. I therefore removed linear and quadratic secular trends. If two series are really correlated, the relationship will still be there after such detrending. The samples of poetry were analyzed with the Harvard III Psychosocial Dictionary (Stone et al. 1966), a general set of categories of words designed for computerized content analysis. Linear and quadratic trends were also removed from scores for the content categories in this dictionary. I correlated the content-analysis categories with the external series. I lagged the categories and computed another set of correlations to see whether changes in literature can predict changes in the external variables. I also lagged the external variables and did more correlations to see if changes in external forces could predict changes in literature. For all of the series, the correlations at different lags are consistent: if the series correlates significantly with a content category at one lag, correlations at other lags tend almost always to be in the same direction. The correlations shown in table 7.2, between the external series and Harvard III summary categories, tell a quite consistent story. With the exception of the wage-price ratio, the measure of general prosperity, the correlations are almost all in the same direction. There are consistent negative correlations between literary references to collectivities—organized social groups—and innovation, sensate emphasis, illegitimacy, industrial productivity, and war. On the other hand, these variables tend to be positively related to references to Persons—because, in almost all cases, of high usage of the subcategory Self (containing words such as "I," "me," "mine"). This suggests an emphasis on individualism. The other correlations are consistent with this interpretation. The variables are negatively related to references to cultural patterns (words having to do with social norms) and social-emotional actions (the subcategories are "communicate," "approach," "guide," "control," "attack," "avoid," "follow"). In other words, there is an avoidance of references to norms and conformity to them. This, and the positive relation to references to nature suggest that this is what Lévi-Strauss (1964) might call "raw" poetry. It is about the nonconforming or amoral self in a state of nature. Save for the wage-price ratio, all of the extraliterary variables have to do in one way or another with individualism, nonconformity, and freedom. Innovation is by definition a break with old conventions. An innovative idea is like an illegitimate child in that it arises from the mating of ideas that, except in the mind of the creator, do not lawfully belong together. Having an illegitimate child is to defy social and religious mores. Sensate philosophies defy at least religious norms. Sorokin (1937–41) notes that such philosophies are usually antireligious. Both Marxists and free-market economists argue that industrialists—but perhaps not workers—do best in a free market. What is good for industrialists is by definition good for industrial productivity. It is interesting that left-wing social theorists are fond of calling the profits of the entrepreneur "illegiti-

Table 7.2
Correlations between British extraliterary series and Harvard III summary categories[a]

Category	Innovations	Sensate emphasis	Illegitimacy	Industrial productivity	War	Wage-price ratio
Social realm	.36	.49		.69		
Persons	.49**	.60**	-.38			
Roles	-.37				-.31	
Collectivities	-.76**	-.52*	-.54*	-.77*	-.40*	.58
Cultural realm	-.45*	-.47*	-.72**	-.77*		.73
Cultural object						.50
Cultural setting		-.48*				.47
Cultural pattern	-.47*	-.51*	-.72**		-.39*	.52
Natural realm	.37	.48*	.40	.61		-.38
Psychological processes	.46*	.53*				
Emotions			.38			
Thought	.62**	.68*			.34	
Evaluation		-.43				
Behavior			-.63**			.41
Social-emotional	-.55**		-.61**		-.42*	.62
Instrumental	.46*	.38				

[a]Largest correlation from lags of −1, 0, and 1. Correlations without superscripts are significant at $p < .10$.
*$p < .05$
**$p < .01$

mate," because the labor of many results in the enrichment of the individual. Social Darwinists do not deny this. Rather, they present an asocial or antisocial equation of society with a state of nature in which the distinction between legitimate and illegitimate has no meaning. War is an act of the state, but the state needs people to start it and people to fight it. McClelland (1975) has argued that wars are more likely when the people in a nation are more individualistic and concerned with their own power and less concerned with affiliation and other people.

Eras of prosperity—when the wage-price ratio is high—produce poetry that emphasizes social collectivities and avoids references to the self. References to cultural patterns and social-emotional acts are emphasized and those to nature deemphasized. We could call this "cooked" rather than "raw" poetry. That poets are reflecting a general sense of social solidarity and conformity in the larger society seems reasonable, but the data at hand do not assure us that this is the case. In such eras innovation, the illegitimacy rate, and industrial productivity decline. The latter must do so if workers are paid high wages to produce goods sold at low prices. Such eras may give "the greatest good for the greatest number," but they can do so only for a limited amount of time, since they are inherently self-destructive: Lack of innovation, low profits, and high labor costs lead to economic stagnation. As a consequence, general prosperity declines.

The poetry of an era of innovation and illegitimacy is opposite to that of an era of prosperity. If we factor analyze the correlations among the social indices, we find two main dimensions (see table 7.3). The first opposes the wage-price ratio to productivity, innovation, illegitimacy, and sensate emphasis in philosophy. The latter set of variables all tend to be intercorrelated. The second dimension opposed war to the wage-price ratio and industrial productivity. The first factor seems, indeed, to be getting at individualism or social disorganization versus

Table 7.3
Factor loadings of British extraliterary variables

	Factor I	Factor II
Innovations	.82	−.16
Sensate emphasis	.66	.37
Illegitimacy	.61	.11
Industrial productivity	.95	−.51
War	.04	.98
Wage-price ratio	−.81	−.32

social solidarity. Following Eysenck's (1991) theory about individual creativity, we could label it "societal psychoticism." I should emphasize that these results are tentative. They should be replicated for other nations before being given too much weight. They are, however, consistent with theoretical expectations and with the empirical results reviewed earlier.

If Eysenck (1991) is correct about the determinants of creativity, then to maximize creativity, a society must also maximize psychoticism, individualism, or egotism, at least in the organizations or segments devoted to the production of creative ideas. However, given that entrance into such social segments tends to be achieved rather than ascribed, it is hard to see how psychoticism could be segregated to these segments alone. Thus, it would seem that individualism and psychoticism, as opposed to altruism, should pervade the entire society. The abhorrence of creative people for rules, control, and inhibition suggests that the creative society must minimize rules and control and maximize freedom and individuality. Again, it would seem that freedom and "lawlessness" must pervade the entire society, because it cannot be known from where in the society creative geniuses will come. In fact, the proportion of eminent creators coming from the lower class is and always has been extremely small (Sorokin 1927). Thus "lawless" individualism could be confined to the upper and middle classes—thus producing a social Darwinist's utopia or an egalitarian's nightmare—as well as a creative society. Of course, egotism and disregard—or absence—of laws and rules could not be carried too far or the society would collapse into a "war of all against all"—hardly conducive to creativity.

References

Bennett, H. S. 1947. *Chaucer and the Fifteenth Century*. Oxford: Oxford University Press.

Berlyne, D. E. 1965. *Structure and Direction in Thinking*. New York: Wiley.

Berlyne, D. E. 1967. "Arousal and reinforcement." In D. Levine, ed., *Nebraska Symposium on Motivation* (Vol. 15). Lincoln: University of Nebraska Press.

Berlyne, D. E. 1970. "Novelty, Complexity, and Hedonic Value." *Perception and Psychophysics* 8: 279–286.

Berlyne, D. E. 1971. *Aesthetics and Psychobiology*. New York: Appleton-Century-Crofts.

Campbell, D. T. 1974. "Evolutionary Epistemology." In P. A. Schilpp, ed., *The Philosophy of Karl Popper*. LaSalle, ILL: Open Court.

Cavalli-Sforza, L. L., and Feldman, M. W. 1981. *Cultural Transmission and Evolution: A Quantitative Approach*. Princeton, N.J.: Princeton University Press.

Chambers, E. K., ed. 1932. *The Oxford Book of Sixteenth Century Verse*. London: Oxford University Press.

Clignet, R. 1985. *The Structure of Artistic Revolutions*. Philadelphia: University of Pennsylvania Press.

Cohen, J. 1966. *Structure du Langage Poétique*. Paris: Flammarion.

Comeau, H., and Farthing, G. W. 1982. "An Examination of Language Content for Manifestations of Primary and Secondary Process during the Hypnotic and Awake States." Unpublished paper, University of Maine.

Crane, D. 1977. *The Transformation of the Avant-Garde: The New York Art World, 1940–1985*. Chicago: University of Chicago Press.

Darwin, C. 1859. *On the Origin of Species*. London: Watts and Co.

Darwin, D. 1896. *The Descent of Man and Selection in Relation to Sex*. New York: D. Appleton. (Originally published 1871.)

Day, H. I. 1967. "Evaluation of Subjective Complexity, Pleasingness and Interestingness for a Series of Random Polygons Varying in Complexity. *Perception and Psychophysics* 2: 281–286.

Evans, D. R. 1969. *Conceptual Complexity, Arousal and Epistemic Behavior*. Unpublished Ph.D. thesis, University of Toronto.

Eysenck, H. J. 1991. "Measuring Individual Creativity." Paper presented at The Achievement Project Symposium, Ashford, England, December 13.

Farnsworth, P. R. 1969. *The Social Psychology of Music*. Ames, IA: Iowa State University Press.

Fromm, E. 1978. "Primary and Secondary Process in Waking and in Altered States of Consciousness." *Journal of Altered States of Consciousness* 4: 115–128.

Göller, A. 1988. *Entstehung der Architektonischen Stilformen*. Stuttgart: K. Wittwer.

Gottman, J. M. 1981. *Time Series Analysis: A Comprehensive Introduction for Social Scientists*. Cambridge: Cambridge University Press.

Grierson, H. J. C., and Bullough, C., Eds. 1934. *The Oxford Book of Seventeenth Century Verse*. London: Oxford University Press.

Hammond, E. P. 1927. *English Verse between Chaucer and Survey*. Durham, NC: Duke University Press.

Hayward, J., ed. 1964. *The Oxford Book of Nineteenth Century English Verse*. London: Oxford University Press.

Heise, D. R. 1965. "Semantic Differential Profiles for 1000 Most Frequent English Words." *Psychological Monographs* 79: 1–33.

Herdan, G. 1966. *The Advanced Theory of Language as Choice and Chance*. New York: Springer-Verlag.

Holton, G. 1973. *Thematic Origins of Scientific Thought: Keplar to Einstein*. Cambridge, MA: Harvard University Press.

Jakobson, R. 1960. "Linguistics and Poetics." In T. Sebeok, ed., *Style in Language*. Cambridge, MA: MIT Press.

Kamann, R. 1963. "Verbal Complexity and Preferences in Poetry. *Journal of Verbal Learning and Verbal Behavior* 5: 536–540.

Kris, E. 1952. *Psychoanalytic Explorations in Art*. New York: International University Press.

Kroeber, A. 1944. *Configurations of Cultural Growth*. Berkeley: University of California Press.

Kruskal, J. B., and Wish, M. 1978. *Multidimensional Scaling*. Beverly Hills, CA: Sage.

Kubler, G. 1962. *The shape of Time: Remarks on the History of Things*. New Haven: Yale University Press.

Lange, C. 1903. *Sinnesgenüsse und Kunstgenuss*. Wiesbaden: J. F. Bergmann.

Larkin, P., ed. 1973. *The Oxford Book of Twentieth Century English Verse*. London: Oxford University Press.

Laslett, P., and Oosterveen, K. 1973. "Long Term Trends in Bastardy in England." *Population Studies* 27: 255–286.

Laver, J. 1950. *Dress*. London: John Murray.

Lévi-Strauss, C. 1964. *Le Cru et le Cuit*. Paris: Plom.

Martindale, C. 1969. *The Psychology of Literary Change*. Unpublished Ph.D. dissertation, Harvard University.

Martindale, C. 1973a. "COUNT: A PL/I Program for Content Analysis of Natural Language (Abstract)." *Behavioral Science* 18: 1948.

Martindale, C. 1973b. "An Experimental Simulation of Literary Change." *Journal of Personality and Social Psychology* 25: 319–326.

Martindale, C. 1974. "LEXSTAT: A PL/I Program for Computation of Lexical Statistics (Abstract)." *Behavioral Research Methods and Instrumentation* 6: 571.

Martindale, C. 1975. *Romantic Progression: The Psychology of Literary History*. Washington, D.C.: Hemisphere.

Martindale, C. 1976. "Primitive Mentality and the Relationship between Art and Society. *Scientific Aesthetics* 1: 5–18.

Martindale, C. 1977. "Syntactic and Semantic Correlates of Verbal Tics in Gilles de la Tourette's Syndrome: A Quantitative Case Study." *Brain and Language* 4: 231–247.

Martindale, C. 1978. "The Evolution of English Poetry." *Poetics* 7: 231–248.

Martindale, C. 1981. *Cognition and Consciousness*. Homewood, ILL: Dorsey.

Martindale, C. 1984a. "The Evolution of Aesthetic Taste." In K. Gergen and M. Gergen, eds., *Historical Social Psychology*. Hillsdale, N.J.: Erlbaum.

Martindale, C. 1984b. "Evolutionary Trends in Poetic Style: The Case of English Metaphysical Poetry." *Computers and the Humanities* 18: 3–21.

Martindale, C. 1990. *The Clockwork Muse: The Predictability of Artistic Change*. New York: Basic Books.

Martindale, C., Covello, E., and West, A. 1986. "Primary Process Cognition and Hemispheric Asymmetry." *Journal of Genetic Psychology* 149: 79–87.

Martindale, C., and Fischer, R. 1977. "The Effects of Psilocybin on Primary Process Content in Language. *Confinia Psychiatrica* 20: 195–202.

Martindale, C., and Keeley, A. 1988. "Historical Trends in the Content of Twentieth-Century Hungarian and American Short Stories." In C. Martindale, ed., *Psychological Approaches to the Study of Literary Narratives*. Hamburg: Buske.

McClelland, D. C. 1975. *Power: The Inner Experience*. New York: Irvington.

McKellar, P. 1957. *Imagination and Thinking*. New York: Basic Books.

Meyer, L. B. 1956. *Emotion and Meaning in Music*. Chicago: University of Chicago Press.

Miles, J. 1964. *Eras and Modes in English Poetry*. Berkeley: University of California Press.

Mitchell, B. R. 1975. *European Historical Statistics 1750–1970*. New York: Columbia University Press.

Mitchell, B. R., and Deane, P. 1962. *Abstract of British Historical Statistics*. Cambridge: Cambridge University Press.

Mitchell, B. R., and Jones, H. B. 1971. *Second Abstract of British Historical Statistics*. Cambridge: Cambridge University Press.

Mukarovsky, J. 1976. *On Poetic Language*. Lisse: Peter de Ridder. (Originally published 1940.)

Nietzsche, F. 1927. "The Birth of Tragedy from the Spirit of Music." In *The Philosophy of Nietzsche*. New York: Modern Library. (Originally published 1872.)

Osgood, C. E., Suci, G., and Tannenbaum, P. H. 1957. *The Measurement of Meaning*. Urbana: University of Illinois Press.

Paivio, A., Yuille, J. C., & Madigan, S. A. 1968. Concreteness, Imagery, and Meaningfulness Values for 925 Nouns. *Journal of Experimental Psychology Monograph Supplement* 76: 1–25.

Peckham, M. 1965. *Man's Rage for Chaos*. Philadelphia: Chilton.

Perkins, D. 1994. Creativity: Beyond the Darwinian model. In M. Boden, ed., *Dimensions of Creativity*. Cambridge: MIT Press.

Phelps Brown, E. H., and Hopkins, S. V. 1956. "Seven Centuries of the Consumables Compared with Builders' Wage-Rates." *Economica* 23: 296–314.

Pulliam, H. R., and Dunford, C. 1980. *Programmed to Learn: An Essay on the Evolution of Culture*. New York: Columbia University Press.

Reitlinger, G. 1961. *The Economics of Taste*. New York: Holt, Rinehart and Winston.

Renwick, W. L., and Orton, H. 1939. *The Beginnings of English Literature to Skelton*. London: Cresset Press.

Reynes, R., Martindale, C., and Dahl, H. (1984). "Lexical Differences between Working and Resistance Sessions in Psychoanalysis." *Journal of Clinical Psychology* 40: 733–737.

Riegl, A. 1927. *Spätrömische Kunstindustrie nach den Funden in Ostereich-Ungarn*. Vienna: Staatstruckerei. (Originally published 1901.)

Sachs, C. 1946. *The Commonwealth of Art*. New York: Norton.

Schneirla, T. C. 1959. "An Evolutionary and Developmental Theory of Biphasic Processes Underlying Approach and Withdrawal." In M. R. Jones, ed., *Nebraska Symposium on Motivation* (Vol. 7). Lincoln: University of Nebraska Press.

Shklovsky, V. 1969. "Der Zusammenhang Zwischen den Verfahren der Subjetfügang und den Allgemeinen Stilverfahren." In J. Striedter, ed., *Texte der Russischen Formalisten*. Munich: Fink. (Originally published 1919.)

Simonton, D. K. 1983. "Esthetics, Biography, and History in Musical Creativity." *Motivation and Creativity: Documentary Report on the Ann Arbor Symposium on the Application of Psychology to the Teaching and Learning of Music*. Reston, VA: Music Educators National Conference.

Simonton, D. K. 1984. *Genius, Creativity, and Leadership: Historiometric Inquiries*. Cambridge: Harvard University Press.

Sisam, C., and Sisam, K. 1970. *The Oxford Book of Medieval English Verse*. Oxford: Oxford University Press.

Skaife, A. M. 1967. "The Role of Complexity and Deviation in Changing Taste." Unpublished Ph.D. thesis, University of Oregon.

Smith, D. N. 1926. *The Oxford Book of Eighteenth Century Verse*. London: Oxford University Press.

Sokolov, E. N. 1963. *Perception and the Conditioned Reflex*. New York: Macmillan.

Sorokin, P. A. 1927. *Social Mobility*. New York: Harper & Brothers.

Sorokin, P. A. 1937–41. *Social and Cultural Dynamics* (4 vols.). New York: American Book Company.

Stewart, D., and Love, W. 1968. "A General Canonical Correlation Index." *Psychological Bulletin* 70: 160–163.

Stone, P., et al. 1966. *The General Inquirer: A Computer Approach to Content Analysis*. Cambridge: MIT Press.

Tynjanov, J. 1965. "Das Literarische Faktum." In J. Striedter, ed., *Texte der Russischen Formalisten*. Munich: Fink. (Originally published 1924.)

Tynjanov, J. 1967. *Archaisten und Neuerer*. Munich: Fink. (Originally published 1929.)

Tynjanov, J., and Jakobson, R. 1971. "Problems in the Study of Literature and Language." In L. Matejka and K. Pomorska, eds., *Readings in Russian Poetics*. Cambridge: MIT Press. (Originally published 1928.)

Vitz, P. C. 1966. "Preference for Different Amounts of Visual Complexity. *Behavioral Science* 11: 105–114.

Watson, G. 1974. *The New Cambridge Bibliography of English Literature*, Vol. 1. Cambridge: Cambridge University Press.

Werner, H. 1948. *Comparative Psychology of Mental Development*. New York: International Universities Press.

West, A., and Martindale, C. 1988. "Primary Process Content in Paranoid Schizophrenic Speech. *Journal of Genetic Psychology* 149: 547–553.

West, A., Martindale, C., Hines, D., and Roth, W. 1983. "Marijuana-Induced Primary Process Content in the TAT." *Journal of Personality Assessment* 47: 466–467.

West, A., Martindale, C., and Sutton-Smith, B. 1985. "Age Trends in Content and Lexical Characteristics of Children's Fantasy Narrative Productions." *Genetic, Social, and General Psychology Monographs* 111: 389–405.

Wölfflin, H. 1950. *Principles of Art History*. New York: Dover. (Originally published 1915.)

Worringer, W. 1957. *Form in Gothic*. London: G. P. Putnam's Sons.

Yeats, W. B., ed. 1936. *The Oxford Book of Modern Verse*. New York: Oxford University Press.

Young, F. W., Lewyckyi, R., and Takane, Y. 1980. *ALSCAL User's Guide*. Chapel Hill, NC: Psychometric Laboratory, University of North Carolina.

Chapter 8
The Measurement of Creativity
Hans J. Eysenck

Few scientists would doubt the fundamental role that measurement plays in science. As Lord Kelvin said, "One's knowledge of science begins when he can measure what he is speaking about, and express it in numbers." And in a similar vein (and with more attention to syntax), Clerk Maxwell said, "We owe all the great advances in knowledge to those who endeavour to find out how much there is of anything." Many have doubted whether it is possible to measure psychological variables, but most psychologists follow Thorndike in believing that "everything that exists exists in some quantity, and can therefore be measured"—a sentiment he certainly appears to have held, even though it is doubtful if he ever used these precise words. (Joncish 1968).

Theories, however primitive, are an integral part of measurement. Even the use of the hand or the foot as units of length presuppose some theory of (relative) uniformity and durability. Even well-established theories in physics, such as the use of the redshift in determining the speed of recession of stars and galaxies, may be queried, throwing doubt on fundamental discoveries, such as the measuring of the cosmological constant, the expansion of the universe, and the exact distances of galaxies (Field, Arp, and Bahcall 1974; Arp 1987). Uneasy lies the head that wears the apparently best-established scientific theory, and with its demise important changes in our conception of measurement may follow. We may here consider the changes in the conception of length measurement that followed Einstein's theory of relativity, and the equally monumental changes in the measurement and conception of time (Eddington 1935).

These few introductory remarks are intended to reassure readers that the faults, errors, and disputations discovered in our discussion of the measurement of creativity are not peculiar to psychology; they are universal in science, and most noticeable of course in the early days of development of any science. We should certainly not make exaggerated claims for psychology in this respect, but we should equally not be too apologetic because our theories are not perfect and our methods of measurement primitive. How could things be otherwise when our science is so new, our theories of so recent a vintage, and our measurements at the very beginning of development? We have achieved a good deal already, granted the small scope of the work done, but our hope must be that others will build on this foundation and improve our theories and methods beyond recognition.

The Definition of Creativity

There is a good deal of agreement on what we mean by "creativity." Creativity denotes a person's capacity to produce new or original ideas, insights, inventions, or artistic products, which are accepted by experts as being of scientific, aesthetic, social, or technical value (Vernon 1989). In addition to novelty, Vernon suggests we must incorporate in our definition the acceptability or appropriateness of the creative product, even though this valuation may change with the passage of time. Others, like Mednick (1962), define creativity as "the forming of associative elements into new combinations which either meet requirements or are in some way useful" (p. 220).

These definitions immediately raise the problem of differentiating *intelligence* from creativity. Spearman (1923, 1927) defined intelligence in terms of his "neogenetic principles," that is, in terms of generating new knowledge. The education of relations and correlates was the basis of such new knowledge and became the basis of his method of measurement of intelligence; this theoretical view directly inspired the creation of the Raven Progressive Matrices Test, which has a central position in intelligence measurement. Is creativity nothing but high intelligence?

Genius, the most obvious manifestation of creativity, is certainly closely tied to high intelligence. Cox (1926) made estimates of the likely childhood IQ of 300 eminent persons from history, and found an overall average of over 140. She argued convincingly that this was probably an underestimate, attributable to the paucity of information about many cases, and considered the correct figure to be nearer the 160 mark. Gibson and Light (1967) studied 131 university scientists, all of whom had made original contributions, although hardly in the genius class; the average IQ was 126. Roe (1952) found high degrees of ability in the scientists she studied, although patterns of ability differed for verbal, spatial, and numerical ability. It would seem that intelligence is a *necessary* part of creativity; is it a sufficient one? Terman's (1925) famous "Study of Genius," in which he located and followed up some 1,500 children with IQs of 140 and above, gives us the answer. If intelligence equals genius, here we should have had a large supply of geniuses. Follow-up studies (Terman and Oden 1947) showed, alas, that while usually very successful, none of the children grew up into geniuses. Clearly intelligence is not a sufficient condition for great creativity, although in a minor way many of the children were quite creative in poetry, science, and art. (W. Shockley, the Nobel Prize winner, was one of the children originally tested, but did not reach the magic IQ = 140 level!)

Spearman (1931) certainly associated creativity with his neogenetic processes, which he considered as being capable of generating new mental content. As he said, "the final act of creativity must be assigned to the third novel genetic process; that of displacing a relation from the ideas which were its original fundaments to another idea, and thereby generating the further idea which is correlative to the part named, and which may be entirely novel" (p. 83). This principle of correlates is similar to several more recent concepts, such as Guilford's (1967) transfer recall, Mednick's (1962) remote association, Koestler's (1969) "bisociation of matrices," and Rothenberg's (1979) "Janusian thinking," all except Koestler assuming the processes involved to be conscious.

This theory will not do; it fails to discriminate between different conceptions of novelty. Consider a typical Spearmanian test item: Mars is to Aries as Vulcan is to Hermes, Hephaestos, Zeus, Apollo. The correct answer merely shows that the testee knows that the Roman god Vulcan is equivalent to the Greek god Hephaestos, just as Mars is to Aries. No creativity or new knowledge is involved. The use of analogy in science may be a more likely candidate for the use of Spearman's principles in true creativity, but this only indicates that the principles may or may not produce creative content; we are still left with the task of finding the principle that discriminates the one from the other.

Novelty has two quite different meanings, which must be carefully distinguished. One is private novelty—that which I discover and which is new to me. The other is public novelty—that which I discover which is new to everyone. Thus Pascal, as a young boy who had newly become acquainted with geometry, proved entirely on his own initiative, and without a hint from any book, that the sum of the angles of a triangle is equal to two right angles (Bell 1939). (Pascal's sister Gilberte asserted that her brilliant young brother had rediscovered for himself the first thirty-two propositions of Euclid, and that he had found them *in the same order* as that in which Euclid set them forth. This is hard to believe; it means that Pascal would have had to commit all the errors of Euclid, which is unlikely.) However, even if true, the story would demonstrate *private* novelty but not public novelty; millions of people already knew about the angles of a triangle adding to two right angles.

This distinction between private novelty and public novelty is closely associated with the two major definitions and conceptions of creativity. The first of these is *creativity as a trait*, a dispositional variable characteristic of a person leading him to produce acts, items, and instances of private novelty. The second of these is *creativity as shown by productivity*, that is, by actually producing works that are novel in the public sense. The two are by no means identical; many people show private creativity but fail completely to show public creativity. Pascal of course did go on to show great public creativity (although severely hampered by his neurotic illnesses), but that is rare. We will consider the differences and relations between creativity as a trait and creativity defined by achievement and products in the next section.

Creativity as a Trait

The study of creativity involves four components. First, there is the creative process, that is, the production of novel and original content; this process, if repeated regularly by the same person, gives rise to the notion of a *trait*. Second, we have the creative product that may involve the trait of creativity, but also much more. Third, we have the creative person who will show creativity, of course, but also many other characteristics. And finally, we have the creative situation, as defined socially—and some historical periods seem much more likely to produce creative people and products than others. In this section we will discuss creativity as a trait, and its measurement.

The first attempts at such measurement were made by Spearman and his students, under the heading of "fluency." The development of the idea that verbal and imaginative fluency was basic for creativity, and could be measured, has been documented elsewhere (Eysenck 1970a), but essentially this factor was isolated first by Hargreaves (1927) in his studies of "the faculty of imagination." He found that a number of tests calling for a large number of imaginative responses tended to correlate together with an average intercorrelation of .3. These correlations fulfilled the demands of the tetrad criterion and were shown not to be identical with "g" (general intelligence). Some of the tests included were: number of things seen in an inkblot, number of words written, number of different completions to an incomplete picture, and so forth.

Fluency or "f" tests have been found to correlate with intelligence, but to contain something in common over and above intelligence, possibly creativity. These tests were also found to be correlated with extraversion, the more extraverted showing greater fluency. Eysenck (1970a) has summarized the extensive literature concerning "f" in some detail. Fluency tests are an early example of "divergent" as opposed to "convergent" tests of ability. Convergent tests have only one correct answer to the problem set; the series "1 3 5 7 9 ?" inexorably leads to the answer "11." But asking a subject to say how many uses he can find for a brick does not have a single correct answer; it leads to *divergent* responses. (Of course the *quantity* of responses may not be the best score on such tests; we may score for *quality* or for unusualness.) Is there any evidence that fluency is in fact connected with originality and creativity? As an example of what research has discovered, consider an experiment reported by Barron (1963), in which military officers constituted the sample, and originality as assessed by staff members of the Berkeley Institute of Personality Assessment and Research (IPAR) during a living-in period was the criterion. (IQ was partialled out from these correlations.) Total output on a word fluency test correlated .41 with originality. Fluency in a game of charades correlated .28. Fluency of ideas correlated .49. These correlations, particularly when corrected for attenuations—which I have not tried to do, because reliability values for the scores are not given—are definitely suggestive of a real relationship between fluency and originality.

These results suggest the existence of a trait of great productivity of ideas, partly independent of intelligence, and correlated with various traits of personality, all features later verified for other tests of creativity. We shall not pursue the later history of fluency, which as a concept merged with Guilford's (1950) notion of "divergent" ability tests as contrasted with the usual "convergent" type of test familiar from traditional IQ testing. The view of "divergent" or "fluency" tests as measures of creativity has been much criticized. Extraneous factors may determine DT (divergent thinking) performance without measuring DT; any process (instruction, boredom) increasing or decreasing productivity in general would increase or decrease DT scores. Another criticism is that most studies merely count the quantity of answers produced, but it may be quality that is important. However, Hovecar (1979, 1980, 1981) has produced some evidence to show that ideational fluency, in terms of quantity, underlies originality scores, and Campbell (1960) and Simonton (1988) would take a similar view about genuine creativity in science and the arts. Worst of all, there is little evidence that DT tests actually predict creative production (Wallach 1971; Cattell 1971; Brown 1989.) As Barron and Harrington (1981) say in their review, we still do not have a satisfactory answer to "the

vitally important question of whether divergent thinking tests measure abilities actually involved in creative thinking" (p. 447). Indeed,
Barron and Harrington doubted the value of the divergent-convergent
dichotomy altogether (p. 443).

What actually is the degree to which the usual tests of DT correlate
with each other, and do they correlate at all with what we would
ordinarily call "creativity" or "originality"? A study by Barron (1963)
may be used to show the kind of answer we may obtain to such a
question. Subjects of the study were 100 captains in the United States
Air Force, studied in a residential setting by psychologists at IPAR,
whose extensive work in the field of creativity will be mentioned
repeatedly in the survey. Subjects were given eight traditional tests of
creativity-originality, and were given independently ratings on "originality" by staff members who got to know them well during the living-
in process of socializing and testing. Table 8.1 lists the tests used; all,
it will be noted, are tests of divergent thinking or fluency.

Do the tests intercorrelate with each other? Table 8.2 shows their
intercorrelations, as well as their correlations with staff ratings of
originality (9) and correlations with composite test scores, that is, the
sum of all eight tests (10). Clearly, the two Rorschach tests are unreliable and invalid; they do not even correlate with each other, neither
do they correlate with the other tests, or with the staff ratings. This
would have been predicted; the Rorschach test has not been found
useful in any of its many applications (Eysenck 1959). However, the
other six tests correlate together quite well, averaging around .26. All
correlate positively with the staff rating of "originality," and the test
composite score correlates a respectable .55 with the staff rating. Thus
the battery seems to have shown both reliability (it measures well
whatever it does measure), and validity (it does measure what it is
supposed to measure) remarkably so in view of the early date when
the study was done. The results are not untypical of later work,
suggesting that this type of test does have some validity and reliability
(Michael and Wright 1989).

What, then, are the major ways of measuring creativity as a trait?
Hovecar and Bachelor (1989) have given a taxonomy of such measures
as have been used in this context. First and foremost we have tests of
divergent thinking, of which those of Torrance (1974) and Wallach and
Kogan (1965) are perhaps the best known (see Wallach 1986, and
Glover, Ronning, and Reynolds 1989 for review.) Second, they list
attitude and interest inventories, based on the hypothesis that a creative person will express attitudes and interests favoring creative activities. Third in their list are personality inventories, on the
hypothesis that creativity is a set of personality factors rather than a

Table 8.1
Tests used in IPAR study of Air Force captains

1. *Unusual Uses.* This test calls upon the subject to list six uses to which each of several common objects can be put. It is scored for infrequency, in the sample under study, of the uses proposed. Odd-even reliability in the sample is .77.

2. *Consequences B.* In this test, S. is asked to write down what would happen if certain changes were suddenly to take place. The task for him is to list as many consequences or results of these changes as he can. The responses are scored according to how obvious the imagined consequences are, the less obvious responses receiving the higher scores. Interrater agreement is .71.

3. *Plot Titles B.* Two story plots are presented, and S. is asked to write as many titles as he can think of for each plot. The titles are rated on a scale of cleverness from 0 to 5. The number of titles rated 2, 3, 4, or 5 constitutes the cleverness score. Interrater agreement in this study is .43.

4. *Rorschach 0+.* This is a count of the number of original responses given by S. to the ten Rorschach blots and adjudged by two scorers, working separately, to be good rather than poor forms. Standard Rorschach administrative procedure is followed. Interrater agreement is .72, and only those responses scored by both scorers as 0+ were credited.

5. *Thematic Apperception Test: Originality Rating.* Two raters, working independently of one another, rate the TAT protocols of the 100 S.'s on a 9-point scale, using approximate normal curve frequencies for each point along the scale. Interrater agreement is .70. The S.'s score is the average of the two ratings.

6. *Anagrams.* The test word "generation" is used, and the anagram solutions are scored for infrequency of occurrence in the sample under study. If S. offers a solution that is correct and that is offered by no more than two other S.'s, he receives one point for originality. Total score is therefore the number of such uncommon but correct solutions.

7. *Word Rearrangement Test: Originality Rating.* In this test, S. is given 50 words which were selected at random from a list of common nouns, adjectives, and adverbs. He is told to make up a story which will enable him to use as many as possible of the listed words. His composition is rated for originality on a 9-point scale, just as the TAT was. Interrater agreement in this instance is .67.

8. *Achromatic Inkblots.* This is a set of ten achromatic inkblots constructed locally. The S. is asked to give only one response to each blot. Responses are weighted according to their frequency of occurrence in the sample under study, the more infrequent responses receiving the higher weights. Score is the sum of the weights assigned to S.'s responses on all ten blots. Odd-even reliability is .43.

Source: Barron (1963), p. 142.

Table 8.2
Correlations between creativity tests, staff ratings for originality, and composite test originality

Test measures	1	2	3	4	5	6	7	8	9	10
1. Unusual uses	. . .	.42	.37	.08	.17	.29	.06	.17	.30	.60
2. Consequences B	.42	. . .	.46	−.02	.21	.21	.16	.09	.36	.59
3. Plot titles B	.37	.46	. . .	.17	.26	.17	.16	.07	.32	.62
4. Rorschach 0+	.08	−.02	.17	. . .	.21	.03	−.05	.11	.18	.38
5. TAT originality	.17	.21	.26	.21	. . .	.36	.41	.02	.45	.59
6. Anagrams	.29	.21	.17	.03	.36	. . .	.33	.38	.22	.62
7. Word rearrangement originality	.06	.16	.16	−.05	.41	.33	. . .	.09	.45	.51
8. Inkblot originality	.17	.09	.07	.17	.02	.38	.09	. . .	.07	.46
9. Staff rating on originality										.55
10. Composite test originality									.55	

Source: Barron (1963), p. 143.

cognitive trait. Fourth came biographical inventories, hypothesizing that past experience may adumbrate future achievement. Fifth came ratings by teachers, peers, and supervisors. Sixth is the judgment of products, seventh the study of eminent people, and eighth self-reported creative activities and achievements.

A recent paper by Amelang, Herboth, and Oefner (in press) illustrates this last method of measuring creativity. Called a "prototype analysis," the method involves first collecting large samples of creative behavior in ordinary samples, putting these together in a questionnaire, and asking subjects if and how often they have shown each included behavior. Examples of such items are: "When my car broke down, I managed to get it to the next garage by using a basic commodity"; "I described the problems of a difficult situation in a play and put it on stage"; and "I built my own furniture in order to make it more suitable to the apartment and my personal needs." The scale was reliable, and correlated well with peer ratings.

Allied to creativity is the process of "intuition," which theoretically is supposed to be instrumental in mediating creativity. Westcott and Ranzoni (1963) have described a method of measuring intuitive thinking that follows their definition of such thinking as deriving conclusions on the basis of fewer clues than would be used by the average person of similar intelligence—one way of "jumping" at a conclusion! They would offer their subjects a problem that could only be solved by using a number of clues; these would be offered seriatim to the subject, who could, however, guess at an answer at any stage. The "intuitive" subject was the one who attempted an answer when only a small number of clues had been received; there was of course no penalty for using all the clues.

The study resulted in four groups, the intuitive/nonintuitive dichotomy being again divided into those who gave the right answer, and those who did not. (We might think of intuitive thinkers who gave the right answers, like Einstein, and intuitive thinkers who gave the wrong answers, like Freud.) Intuition was found to be a persistent trait of subjects in many different experiments (high reliability), and intelligence would be ruled out as being responsible for producing these correlations. It is unfortunate that Westcott did not correlate "intuition-proneness" with creativity, either as a trait or as achievement; this verification of his theory still lies ahead.

Hovecar and Bachelor (1989) report that the different measures of creativity may not always correlate well together, and indeed sometimes hardly show any degree of correlation at all; furthermore most, with the exception of tests of divergent thinking, show little agreement with a variety of criteria. They conclude that "it is apparent that reliability, discriminant validity, and nomological validity cannot be taken for granted in creativity research" (p. 62). They suggest focusing "on only those studies that include a measure of real-life creativity" (p. 64). The next section will do precisely that.

Creativity as Achievement

Mumford and Gustafson (1988) introduce their review of creativity by pointing out that the lack of integration in creativity research "may be attributed to the fact that, like intelligence, creativity represents a highly complex and diffuse construct" (p. 27). They also remark on the lack of a sound general definition of creative behavior, noting that Guilford (1950) has defined creative behavior in terms of the production of ideas, MacKinnon (1962) as an attribute of personality, Cattell (1971) as a form of problem-solving ability, and yet other writers in terms of actual achievement. Achievement measures, they suggest, may be of three kinds. The first category consists of overt production criteria, such as publication counts or patent awards. "These measures assess creativity in terms of the frequency with which individuals generate innovative products having acknowledged social worth or the quality of their products" (p. 27). Second, they nominate professional recognition criteria, such as awards given to individuals for the production of new ideas or products held to be of some value in an occupational field. Third, social recognition criteria may involve the judgments of knowledgeable others, such as peers or supervisors.

Can we identify these two quite different views of creativity, one as a trait, the other in terms of achievement? There are many fundamental differences that make such identification difficult. The most crucial problem is that of distribution. Creativity as a trait, measured for instance by DT tests, shows a normal, Gaussian type of distribution, and while this may owe something to the distribution of error variance, there is no doubt that it differs profoundly from the distribution observed in the achievement field. Here the distribution of number of contributions, number of citations, number of products, etc., follows the Price (1963) or the rather similar Lotka (1926) law. According to Price, if K represents the total number of contributors to a given field, then $\sqrt{K}$ will be the predicted number of contributors who will generate half of all contributions. This of course implies a highly skewed distribution, with just a few contributors making most of the contributions, and it also suggests that as the discipline expands, the distribution will become ever more elitist (Simonton 1984). Thus in a new discipline with only about a dozen investigators, three (i.e., about 25%) will account for half of all contributions. But if the discipline grows to 100, the bulk of contributions will be made by 10 people, constituting 10% of the whole field! (For confirmation, see Zhao and Jiang 1985.)

Lotka's law attempts to describe the shape of the distribution in some more detail; indeed, his function is similar to Pareto's (1897) law of income distribution. It is this similarity that may contain the answer to our problem of the differences in distribution between our two different concepts of creativity. The problem is similar to that suggested by Pareto; ability is normally distributed (at least roughly so—see Burt 1963), but income is distributed more like a Poissonian, J-shaped curve, although income is supposed to be a derivative of ability. The answer, according to Burt (1943), is that ability is a necessary but not a sufficient causal condition for high income. There are several such causes, and they act synergistically, in other words, their effects multiply rather than add. (Burt also applies this reasoning to citations of educational psychologists, which he shows follow the same distribution as wealth, for the same reasons.)

Basing my argument on published data, I have suggested a possible set of cognitive, personality, and environmental variables that are likely to interact in a multiplicative fashion to produce creative products and achievements (Eysenck, in press). This is given in figure 8.1;

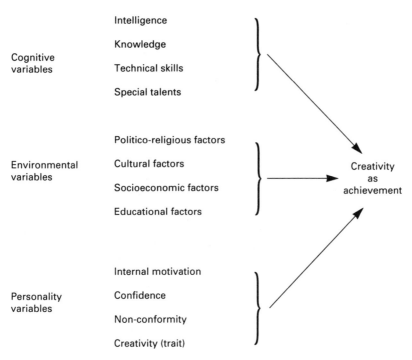

Figure 8.1
The major variables affecting creativity.

it will be seen that creativity (as a trait) is only one among many factors to contribute to creativity, defined in terms of achievement. The normal distribution of the *trait* does not imply a normal distribution of the product; if the contributing variables act multiplicatively (all or some), the resulting effect is likely to show a Poissonian, J-shaped distribution. The model suggested agrees in many ways with a similar general approach suggested by Amabile (1983).

This model also serves to explain the fact that trait creativity does not seem to correlate highly with achievement. A long list of studies demonstrating this is given by Hovecar and Bachelor (1989). Many of these studies can be criticized on various grounds, such as the artificial nature of the criteria used, but it seems well established that the correlation between trait creativity and achievement is not likely to be high. In spite of the lack of identity between the two concepts, Hovecar and Bachelor are not despondent. Asking whether studies that focus on divergent thinking or the creative personality can be discounted, they say "no," for two reasons. First, there is overwhelming evidence that divergent thinking and the creative personality are interesting constructs in their own right and, consequently, deserve attention as distinct and important scientific constructs. And second, there is at least some evidence that these two constructs are potential causes of real-life creativity. If trait creativity is only one element in creative achievement, albeit a necessary one, the relatively low correlations are explicit in our model.

It will be noted that in figure 8.1 intelligence is listed as one of the factors that determine creative achievement, and like creativity, it is a necessary but not a sufficient condition. As we have seen, great achievers have high IQs, but high IQ does not guarantee creative achievement. Heansly and Reynolds (1989) have reviewed the evidence, suggesting that intelligence is an element in the creative process (p. 118), and that the effect of creativity and intelligence is synergistic. It may be surmised that creative achievement is only possible given a relatively high IQ, but that given that there may be little further correlation with achievement, and greater dependence of achievement on trait creativity. For trait measures of creativity, their correlation with IQ is certainly nonlinear, being appreciable below IQ levels of 120 or thereabouts, and low or nonexistent above (Guilford 1981).

Another problem that can be solved by reference to figure 8.1 is that trait creativity is supposedly universal, while creative achievement is nearly always strictly tied to a particular field—creative physicists do not normally produce avant-garde paintings; creative psychologists are not known for their skill in composing novel kinds of music; creative writers seldom contribute important advances to the study of cosmology. Even within a given science or art, creative individuals are usually tied to one special type of problem.

This follows directly from our model. Creative achievement demands special talents (musical, numerative, verbal, visuo-spatial), which serves to localize achievement; it demands special knowledge that may take years to acquire, and does not permit more than very limited transfer; it also demands technical skills (apparatus construction, computer expertise) that are tied to special fields. All of this would make transfer from one field to another unthinkable. We would also expect, in terms of our theory, that universal geniuses (da Vinci, Galton, Leibnitz) would be much more unlikely to emerge at the present time than in previous centuries; the amount of factual information needed to make genuinely creative contributions is so much greater than it once was. Trait tests, however, do not make the same demands, or do so to a much lesser extent, and consequently there may be greater universality.

Creativity as achievement is thus theoretically related to trait creativity, but the evidence is relatively weak. Low correlations between the two are predicted, but of course do not constitute strong support for the theory. I have suggested that to produce such support we have to state the theory in more precise terms, and seek for evidence by way of personality correlates of creativity. These provide another method of measuring creativity (next section), and enable us to forge a link between trait creativity and creativity as achievement (section 6).

The Creative Personality

It is not intuitively obvious that creativity should be related to certain personality traits, but since the days of the ancient Greeks it has been supposed that the supremely creative person was characterized by special traits of personality. In particular, the notion that genius is related to madness is of very ancient origin, going back at least to Plato and Aristotle (Ochse 1991). Many psychiatrists (e.g., Lange-Eichbaum 1932; Prentky 1980) have drawn up lists of mentally disturbed geniuses. Prentky concluded his review by stating that biographers and researchers may have been inexact in classifying the maladies of some creative people, but that in most cases there was ample reason for considering their behavior abnormal. The conclusion that the incidence of mental disorder is higher among creative achievers in the general population is supported by a number of systematic nomothetic studies (Andreasen 1987; Juda 1949; Karlsson 170; and McNeil 1971). The incidence of different types of mental disorder differed according to area of creative endeavor; Juda (1949) found artists to be characterized by schizophrenic disorders more frequently, scientists by manic-depressive disorders.

To give a few examples, Karlsson (1970), on the basis of biographical material, claimed to have found the rate of psychosis to be 30% for great novelists, 35% for great poets, 35% for great painters, 25% for great mathematicians, and 40% for great philosophers; these values are well above those for ordinary people (something like 2%). Similarly, Andreasen (1987), in a controlled study of thirty eminent writers, thirty matched control subjects, and first-degree relatives of both groups, found that no less than 80% of the writers had experienced an episode of affective disorder, whereas only 30% of the controls had done so. In addition, "the families of writers were riddled with both creativity and mental illness, while in the families of the control subjects much of the illness and creativity seems to be randomly scattered" (p. 1290). Ochse also cites an unpublished study in which 38% of 47 eminent British writers had been treated for manic-depressive illness or recurrent depression, while of the poets in the sample, 50% had received psychiatric treatment.

In addition to these studies concerned with psychiatric diagnoses and behavior patterns of gifted and creative individuals, it has been found quite generally that when highly creative subjects are given personality questionnaires, their answers (e.g., on the MMPI) have usually been similar to those of neurotic or psychotic individuals, although usually at a lower level. Barron (1968), Cattell (1971), Gotz and Gotz (1979a, b), MacKinnon (1978), Mohan and Tiwana (1987), and Roe (1953) may be cited in evidence.

While most findings have emphasized a positive relationship between creativity and psychopathology, some have postulated a negative relation (e.g., Kessel 1989; Maslow 1976; Rogers 1976). Others again postulate an absence of any relation, on the grounds that the observed relations are invalid, insignificant statistically, or artificial (Becker 1978; Nicolson 1947; Gedo 1978). Ochse (1990) gives a good account of this controversy. Like most controversies in psychology, this one rests on certain major misunderstandings.

The first of these is that the presence of psychopathology makes the appearance of positive personality characteristics impossible; that is obviously not so, except in very severe cases, and then only during the actual attack. Creative people may, in addition to certain psychopathological characteristics, have others which are much more positive. Thus Dellas and Gaier (1970) conclude their evaluation of more than two dozen studies of personality characteristics of creative persons by saying that their "evidence points up a common pattern of personality traits among creative persons, and also that these personality factors may have some bearing on creativity in the abstract, regardless of field" (p. 65). The major thirteen traits they found associated with creativity were: (1) Independence in attitude and social behavior; (2) dominance; (3) introversion; (4) openness to stimuli; (5) wide interests; (6) self-acceptance; (7) intuitiveness; (8) flexibility; (9) social presence and poise; (10) an asocial attitude; (11) concern for social norms; (12) radicalism; (13) rejection of external constraints.

Similarly, Welsh (1975), on the basis of his own work, gives a list of the personality characteristics of students not having any overt psychopathology, which includes both socially positive and negative items. Creative as opposed to noncreative students are unstable, irresponsible, disorderly, rebellious, uncontrolled, self-seeking, tactless, intemperate, rejecting of rules, uncooperative, impulsive, and careless—surely all negative traits socially, and positively indicative of psychopathology. But they were also original, adventurous, liberal, refined, tolerant, candid, subtle, spontaneous, interesting, flexible, and artistic—all rather positive variables. Perhaps one side of the coin implies the other; it is impossible to possess all of a number of contradictory virtues.

MacKinnon (1962, 1965, 1978), in discussing the very large-scale research of his group into creativity, extending over many years and including external criteria of achievement as well as internal ratings, again and again draws attention to the high scores of his creative subjects on some of the MMPI scales related to psychosis—schizophrenia, depression, psychopathic deviance, paranoia, and the like. "On the eight scales which measure the strength of these descriptions in the person, our creative subjects earn scores which, on the average, are some 5 to 10 points above the general population's average score of 50" (MacKinnon 962, p. 488). A difference of 10 points is equal to a whole standard deviation, and is certainly not negligible, particularly when it is remembered that his sample (successful architects) comes from a socioeconomic and educational group whose mean scores on these scales is usually well below 50 (Friedman, Webb, and Lewak 1989; Dahlstrom, Lachar, and Dahlstrom 1986). MacKinnon adds that "in the self-reports and in the MMPI profiles of many of our creative subjects, one can find rather clear evidence of psychopathology, but also evidence of adequate control mechanisms, as the success with which they live their productive and creative lives testifies" (p. 488). Possibly it is the creative tension set up by these contradictory personality traits that is responsible for the outstanding success of MacKinnon's subjects.

Even more important than this misconception is another fundamental error in the interpretation of the theory linking personality and creativity, namely the assumption that psychiatric abnormality is categorical rather than dimensional. As I have argued repeatedly (Eysenck 1970b; Eysenck, Wakefield, and Friedman 1983), the psychiatric habit of using categorical diagnostic labels (schizophrenia, hysteria, manic-depressive illness) goes counter to a great deal of evidence that favors continuity along certain dimensions, in particular that of "psychoticism." Figure 8.2 illustrates the point. The abscissa denotes a hypothetical dispositional trait, "psychoticism," a genetic predisposition to develop psychosis under appropriate stress. The normal curve suggests the distribution of this trait in the population, curve P_A suggests the increase in probability of developing diagnosed psychosis, with increased psychoticism, and the notations underneath the abscissa indicate mental disorders or personality traits defining the continuum. This is a diathesis-stress model of disease in which the diathesis (psychoticism) can be measured as a personality trait

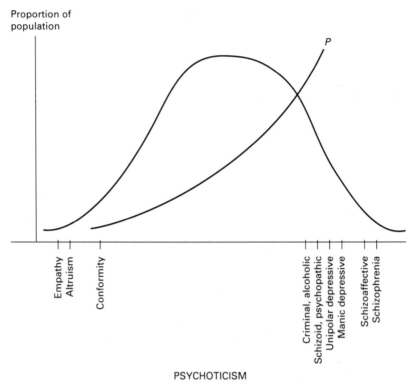

Figure 8.2
Normal curve suggesting the distribution in the population of psychoticism. The *P* variable suggests the increase in the probability of psychotic illness with increase in psychoticism.

(Eysenck and Eysenck 1976). Close to the target group (psychotics) we have individuals with personalities similar to those of psychotics, but not themselves psychotic; such persons would be called schizoid, or sociopaths, or personality disordered (Eysenck and Eysenck 1977), with these so-called spectrum disorders shading gradually into less odd and psychopathological types.

It has been objected that "psychosis" is too broad a concept, and that there may be little or nothing in common between, say, schizophrenic and manic-depressive psychosis. Crow (1986) has recently argued for the existence of a psychotic continuum, giving psychiatric support for the idea of a personality dimension of "psychoticism." This is not the place to argue the case; let us merely state that much of the debate about creative geniuses being or not being "psychotic" can be easily aborted by disregarding the false dichotomy of the categorical system of classification, and simply allocating a position on the continuum of psychoticism to any particular creative individual. Some will be found to fall into the psychotic group at the right hand of the continuum, but the majority will probably be found to fall short of this extreme, and rather show evidence of schizoid, depressed, psychopathic, and antisocial tendencies, without actually being certifiably insane (Eysenck, in press).

This dimensional model of abnormality satisfies the large literature showing considerable correlation between measures and indices of abnormality and creativity, without going to the rather contradictory position of declaring creative people or geniuses in particular to be "mad." Our model, then, suggests some similarity between psychotic and creative people with respect to certain personality traits, but certainly does not claim identity; it agrees with Dryden that "great wits are sure to madness near allied, and thin partitions do their bounds divide." This puts the case very neatly; not identity, but "near alliance," with their bounds being divided by thin partitions maybe, but partitions nevertheless.

Having argued that there are certain features that psychoticism and creativity have in common, we next have to face the task of showing what these features are. It will be found that such a task requires us to construct a broader model of creative thinking than has been done hitherto, on the Kantian principle that "theory without practice is lame, practice without theory is blind."

The Creative Personality and Preference for Complexity

Most measures of (trait) creativity use some form of fluency/divergent thinking measures, which have two major defects. In the first place, such forms of measurement nearly always use *verbal* material, so that nonverbal types are handicapped; numerical or visuo-spatial ability would possibly make such people appear more creative if the tests incorporated material geared to their cognitive strengths. In the second place, use of verbal material almost guarantees some correlation with g; especially at the lower levels, because to be creative verbally you have to have a large vocabulary, which is highly correlated with IQ—at least verbal IQ. Hence particular interest has attached to a very different method of testing creativity, associated with the names of Welsh (1975) and Barron (1953, 1969); see also Barron and Welsh (1952).

Essentially, Barron and Welsh are concerned with a perceptual preference factor that seems to have considerable generality in human behavior. It "opposes a preference for perceiving and dealing with

complexity to a preference for simplicity, when both of these alternatives are phenomenally present and when a choice must be made
between them" (Barron 1953, p. 163). Such a perceptual factor was
originally discovered by Eysenck (1941), who also provided measures
of it (for summaries of this work, see Eysenck 1981).

Welsh started out by developing a 400-item Figure Preference Test
(WPFT), in which simple line drawings were presented to the subject,
who had to respond with either "Like" (L) or "Don't like" (DL) (Welsh
1959). Observation on this WFPT, supported by factor analyses, suggested a dimension opposing liking for complex to liking for simple
figures, and because of interesting correlations with personality, relevant items were put together to form the Barron-Welsh Art Scale
(BW), consisting of 62 items of the original 400. Scores on this scale
are referred to as measures of "origence," because of the correlation
of preference for complex designs with originality and creativity; origence was found uncorrelated with "intellectence," as measured by
IQ tests (Welsh 1975). In this book Welsh summarizes an enormous
amount of research, indicating that high origence scorers (1) can be
shown to be creative in real life, and (2) have a personality similar to
that which has been found to be characteristic of creative people, as
defined by their creative achievements. Of all the material available,
only some of the most important studies can be cited.

Much of the early work was done in the Governor's School in North
Carolina, which runs a special summer program for talented and gifted
high school students. (Note that the independence of origence and
intellectence in this high-IQ group does not necessarily mean that no
correlation would be found in less gifted children. There is a paucity
of evidence for below-average IQ groups.) Welsh administered a great
variety of personality scales to these students, and arrived at results
that are remarkably similar to those reported by Dellas and Gaier
(1970), whose summary of earlier work has been quoted in the last
section. Welsh does, however, indicate that differences in intelligence
may produce differences in the expression of creative and noncreative
personalities. The dull but high-origence student seems extraverted
in temperament, rejects people who impose some standards of performance on him or criticize his behavior, is inclined toward rebellion
for its own sake rather than for an ideological principle, and rejects
authority both personally and in terms of formal social values.

By contrast, the bright high-origence scorer shows rather a different
pattern, much closer to the Dellas and Gaier model. Barron describes
him thus:

> The second personality type, high on origence and on intellect-
> ence, is contrastingly introversive in temperament and intro-

spective by nature. Where the first type looked outward he looks inward and responds to his own subjective feelings and attitudes, rejecting at the same time the views and opinions of others. Although he may have a few intimate friends, he is generally asocial and is uninterested in having people around him. He is more inclined to act impersonally and to express his views indirectly by writing than by face-to-face interaction; likewise he would rather read what someone has to say than to hear it directly from the person himself. There is an isolative and withdrawing tendency that leaves him to his own devices intellectually and emotionally.

He is planful and persistent and can work toward his own distant goal independently. He rejects the help of others just as he is so preoccupied with his own views that he cannot accept ordinary social values and conventional morality. He would rather do things his own way than to yield to others although he may respond to rational and logical argument of an intellectual kind. He is not affected by emotional appeals unless they coincide with his own values and attitudes. Similarly, he cannot understand why others do not accept his views and ideas as he fails to recognize the need for emotional or social appeals to other persons. He may appear tactless and stubborn because he expects others to recognize as obvious the conclusions that he has arrived at by his own insights which seem so compelling to him. This leads to further estrangement from the social world around him and to greater self-involvement. He becomes convinced of the correctness of his own views and is not afraid to take risks because he has confidence in his own ability. If he fails, it is others who do not understand him or appreciate what he is trying to do—they should change, not he. (p. 104)

The dull low-origence type also tends to extraversion, like the dull high-origence type. (It should be remembered that the measure used to measure intelligence was the Terman Concept Mastery Test, which is probably more a measure of crystallized than of fluid ability, and hence would favor introverts—see Wankowski 1973). He is characterized by bland conformance and conventionality. He does not recognize the extent to which his attitudes have been formed by those around him, nor the degree of his dependency on externally imposed rules and regulations. He is a follower, relies on authority figures, prefers the tried and true, and rejects anything new or unproven.

Most interesting is the behavior of the bright low-origence student, as compared with the bright high-origence student quoted above. Welsh characterizes him as

The fourth personality type which is high on intelligence but low on origence is somewhat introversive like the second, but does not seem quite so withdrawn and asocial in orientation, nor is he so introspective by nature. He is much more objective in outlook and responds to people in the world around him and to their attitudes and ideas, although he tends to maintain some social and personal distance from them. Most of his responses are intellectualized or rationalized and he seldom acts impulsively as the first type often does. He seems to believe that the world is an orderly place and that there are rules and regulations to be followed both in daily conduct and in solving problems that may appear. For this reason he finds mathematics and the physical sciences congenial since they are impersonal in nature but challenging intellectually.

He respects his own accomplishments as well as those of other persons but expects them to follow protocol strictly and is resistant to the flashes of insight or the intuitive solutions that the second type may achieve. The nonlogical does not fit into his systematic approach to problems. He follows a well-specified code of ethics and expects others to act in the same manner; perhaps he may sometimes seem to be overly strict in his interpretation of moral behaviour. He seems to be more optimistic in outlook than the second type, possibly because of a belief that a desirable and worthwhile outcome may be achieved through hard work and the application of comprehensible principles. (pp. 105–106)

Relying primarily on the differences between bright high- and low-origence students, Welsh states that his findings agree with the Dellas and Gaier summary on eleven of thirteen points. High origence involves independence of attitude and social behavior, dominance, introversion, openness to stimuli, wide interests, self-acceptance, intuitiveness, asocial attitude, unconcern for social norms, radicalism, and rejection of external controls. Two traits, flexibility, and social presence and poise, Welsh fails to find in his high-origence students; possibly their youth has something to do with this. As he says, "those who fall into type two, high origence/high intellectence, resemble to a striking degree the composite picture of the creative person inferred from the thirteen-point summary. The prediction seems justified that Governor's School students of this type can be considered to be potentially creative from the standpoint of personality" (p. 107). Of course, several of the eleven traits characteristic of high origence are also found in the low intellectence group, such as independence, asocial attitudes, unconcern for social norms, and rejection of external controls. These may be the most basic correlates of origence. (We should bear in mind that "low intelligence" in this group is relative, even the low scorers on intellectence would be above the population mean.)

Using samples of university students, Barron (1953) studied his subjects not only by inventories, but also by staff assessment of various behavior patterns observed in personal contact. Complexity on the Barron-Welsh scale correlated .50 with present tempo, .29 with verbal fluency and −.42 with constriction; "thus, the Complex person is more intensely expressive, expansive, and fluent in speech than the Simple person. The Simple person, on the other hand, is seen as being more natural and likeable, and also as more straightforward and lacking in duplicity" (p. 166). Complexity was found to correlate −.44 with naturalness, −.27 with likeability, and .56 with deceitfulness, as rated by the staff. Good judgment and adjustment were also lacking in the Complex person, with r values of −.39 and −.31. (Adjustment was defined as "getting along with the world as it is, adequate degree of social conformity, capacity to adapt to a wide range of conditions, ability to fit in.")

Originality was also rated by the staff, every subject being rated on the degree of originality he had displayed in his work. The Complex person was seen as more original, both by the assessment staff and by the faculty of his department, with a correlation of the criterion ratings on originality of .30. A specially designed mosaic construction test was also administered and rated for artistic merit, the rating correlated with Complexity .40.

Other correlations for Complexity were for flexibility ($r = −.35$ with rigidity defined as "inflexibility of thought and manner, stubborn, pedantic, unbending, firm.") Impulsiveness showed a correlation of .50 with Complexity, and several MMPI scales of psychopathology showed a correlation of .37 (schizophrenia) and .36 (psychopathic deviate). "Thus Complexity goes along both with lack of control of impulse (the Pd Scale) and with the failure of repression which characterizes the schizophrenic process" (p.167). Anxiety was also correlated with Complexity ($r = .34$). Social nonconformity is another correlate of Complexity, staff ratings giving a correlation of −.47 with Complexity, and self-ratings one of −.53. Submissiveness was not characteristic of Complex persons ($r = −.29$), but holding socially dissident and deviant opinions was (r with the MMPI F-scale = .36).

Independent judgment was tested by means of the Asch (1956) test. This consists of an experimental social situation in which the subject is put under pressure to conform to a group opinion that is false. There are from eight to sixteen ostensible subjects, only one of whom, however, is naive; the rest are employed by the experimenter. The task is to judge which of three lines of variable lengths meets a standard line. The subjects, one by one, announce their judgments publicly. The naive subject is so placed as to be one of the last to announce his judgment. On the critical trials, the hired majority gives a prearranged false answer. The experimental variable is called "yielding," which is defined as agreeing with group opinion when it is in error. Complexity was significantly and negatively correlated with yielding in two separate samples.

Those findings were replicated on several other samples of students and adults, cited by Barron (1953) and Welsh (1975), but we must now turn to consider evidence that the BW test actually measures creativity. A special study was conducted at IPAR on a sample of 129 architects who had been rated for professional creativity by their peers. Sample I had been nominated as the most outstanding creative practitioners in the United States by other architects and various experts; forty of these took part in the living-in assessment. A second sample (II) consisted of forty-three subjects matched for age and geographic location of practice who had at least two years of working experience with the originally nominated creative architects. A third group, Architects III, was selected as being representative of architects in general; they had no connection with the creative architects. Scores on origence were transformed into T scores, that is, scores with a mean of 50 and a standard deviation of 10 for the boys at the Governor's School. Architects I, the ones judged particularly creative, had a mean of 56.90 and a S.D. of 5.73; Architects II, less creative but above the mean, had a score of 50.70, S.D. 6.97; Architects III, the least creative as rated, had a score of 47.71, S.D. 5.36. Thus degree of professional creativity (creative achievement) was mirrored by origence scores, the most creative architects scoring about twice their own S.D. above the least creative (who of course would be well above the large group of architects who would fall below the mean for achievement—architects III did not contain any failures or poor performers). Overall mean creativity ratings for the individual architects was significantly correlated with origence scores, $r = -.47$ (p < .001). This correlation of course underestimates the "true" (i.e., unattenuated) value. Using estimates of $-.75$ for reliability of measurement for origence and creativity, the corrected value is in excess of $-.62$—very respectable indeed. (It is only fair to mention that in results for a much smaller group of forty-five unselected scientists there was little agreement of ratings and origence score, but apparently none were especially creative or noncreative. This sample should be seen as being in the middle range of the Lotka-Price continuum, and hence showing too little variance to expect large correlations between ratings and creativity and origence, although even here the group of scientists rated most creative had had a mean score of 49.47, as compared with the rest at 46.76.)

The many well-planned and well-executed studies carried out at IPAR have been summarized by MacKinnon (1961, 1962, 1965) and Barron (1969); there is too much to discuss in detail, although I shall come back to this work in conjunction with my discussion of the Word Association test as a measure of creativity in the next section. The IPAR studies are without a doubt the most concerted, effective, and illuminating experiments ever done in the field of creativity, and should be familiar to every student of this field.

Psychoticism and Creativity

We have seen that many studies of creativity in passing show a relationship between creativity and traits that suggest mental abnormality or psychoticism. In this section we will look in more detail into this relationship, featuring particularly work developed specifically to test this hypothesis. In the next section we will then examine the causal features of the model, i.e. try to explain just what it is psychologically that accounts for the observed relationship.

Some of the early studies linking psychoticism and creativity have been discussed elsewhere (Eysenck and Eysenck 1976). Thus Farmer (1974) found two factors, fluency and originality, in a factor analysis of correlations between divergent thinking tests. P had a small loading of .24, but a very high one on originality ($r = .74$). Kidner (1978; see pp. 186–187 in Eysenck and Eysenck 1976) used IQ and divergent thinking tests, creating an "index of creativity" by subtracting the standardized sum of the IQ tests from that of the creativity tests; this correlated .31 with P. The correlation with E (extraversion) was .21. In another experiment he replicated the correlation of P with creativity, and also found P correlated with overinclusiveness of thinking and slowness in categorization; aspects of schizophrenic thinking discussed in later sections.

I will concentrate on two studies, one concerned with *trait* creativity, the other with *achievement* creativity. These two studies have been selected for detailed discussion because they bring out particularly well certain points of theoretical interest. The first is by Woody and Claridge (1977), and was designed especially to test the hypothesis of a strong relationship between creativity and psychoticism. The tests used were the Eysenck Personality Questionnaire, or EPQ (Eysenck and Eysenck 1975), the Wallach-Kogan (1965) creativity tests, and the Nufferno Speed Test as a measure of intelligence (Furneaux 1956). Subjects were 100 Oxford University students, sampling widely from the various fields of specialization; mean age of the group was twenty years, standard deviation two years.

Consider first the correlation of P with the five tasks constituting the creativity test: instances, pattern meanings, uses, similarities, and line meanings. For each of these divergent tests, there are two scores, one for numbers of suggestions (fluency) and the other for consequences (originality); correlations with P were .32, .37, .45, .36, and .38 for number score, and .61, .64, .66, .68, and .65 for uniqueness. Overall the correlations with extraversion and neuroticism were quite insignificant, but those for L (Lie Scale) were significant and in the $-.20$ region. (For groups such as this, L probably measures social conformity rather than lying, and correlates negatively with P.) It is worth noting that the ten indices of creativity were all highly intercorrelated, correlations ranging from .37 to .83; thus it appeared that the tests were tapping a unitary factor. Correlations between the creativity and personality variables, on the one hand, and intelligence, on the other, were insignificant.

Using all ten tests of creativity predicted P at a high level (multiple $R = .84$). While no doubt replications would give a lower value for R, using the same prediction formula, the fact that the R is higher than the reliability of P does suggest an astonishingly close relationship between the two variables, and thus supports the original theory. Of course these results refer only to creativity as a trait, they say nothing about creativity in terms of achievement.

This problem has been tackled by Gotz and Gotz (1979a, b), two internationally known German painters who were successful, because of their inside position, in getting 147 male and 110 female artists of renown to return completed forms of the EPQ. Painters and sculptors were included in this sample. Mean age was forty-seven years, with a range of 29 to 78 years. 300 male and 300 female controls were also tested, with a similar age range (mean 41 years, range 21 to 79 years). Testing was done individually or in small groups.

Male but not female artists were more introverted than respective controls; perhaps women need more dominance and surgency to compete! Male but not female artists were more neurotic than respective controls. Most important from our point of view, male artists had higher P scores than male controls (6.53 vs. 5.79), and female artists had higher P scores than female controls (6.18 vs. 4.32). The standard deviations were around 3.00. Both differences were highly significant, and are in the predicted direction. Note the exceptionally high P score of the female artists; this is expected on the basis of the double threshold hypothesis (Eysenck and Gudjonsson 1988), and is similar to findings concerning P scores for male and female criminals. For L, there is no difference for males, but a large one for females ($p < .001$). It should be noted that comparisons between artists and controls may as stated appear less significant than they really are because P declines with age (Eysenck 1987a), and the artists were significantly older by six years.

In Gotz and Gotz (1979b), sixty well-known artists were divided by experts into thirty-seven more and twenty-three less successful ones. The more successful ones had significantly higher P scores. Some artists who were successful had low P scores, but these tended to be in the high age group, where P scores tend to drop. Altogether, being a successful artist correlates well with P, and distinguishes artists from nonartists. This is very much in line with our theory. These two studies are thus complementary in linking P with both definitions of creativity.

Would we expect *psychotics* to show high creativity? Hebeison (1960), Kidner (1978), and Soueif and Farag (1971) have found significantly *depressed* performance of schizophrenics on tests of creative thinking. As we shall argue, creativity demands a combination of high P and high ego strength; there is considerable evidence for the necessity of combining these two apparently antithetical properties. Rawlings (1985) has suggested a theoretical resolution to this problem, using an experiment involving dichotic listening. As he points out, the problem is similar to that of reaction time, where P correlates with *quick* reactions, while psychotics are generally *slow*. Psychosis adds a new element to high psychoticism, eliminating individuals with high ego strength who would not succumb to actual psychotic illness, and influencing performance in a negative direction. Psychosis should never be identified with psychoticism; the former is an illness, the latter a predisposition. It may be more illuminating to consider persons with the psychotic *Erbkreis*, but who are not themselves psychotic.

This can be done by looking at relatives of psychotics, to see if they show unusual amounts of creativity (Eysenck 1983). Thus Heston (1966) studied offspring of schizophrenic mothers raised by foster parents and found that although about half showed psychosocial disability, the remaining half were certainly successful adults, pursuing artistic talents and demonstrating imaginative adaptations to life to a degree not found in the control group. Karlsson (1968, 1970) found in Iceland that among relatives of schizophrenics there was a high incidence of individuals of great creative achievement. McNeil (1971) studied the occurrence of mental illness in highly creative adopted children and their biological parents, discovering that the mental illness rates in the adoptees and in their biological parents were positively and significantly related to the creativity level of the adoptees. Such findings give powerful support to a link between psychoticism and creativity.

As we shall suggest in the next section, schizophrenic thinking is characterized by a cognitive style that has been variously called over-inclusive, allusive, loose, or characterized by the term "mental slippage." Such overinclusiveness would seem to be similar in nature to the gentler slope of the associative gradient, or the broader associative horizon often suggested to be crucial in accounting for creativity.

Our theory would demand that some good and appropriate measure of "overinclusion" should (1) be commonly found in schizophrenics and/or in other psychotic patients; (2) correlate with measures of psychoticism in normal people; and (3) correlate with creativity. The obvious choice for such a test must be one of word association, because it has been known for a long time that unusual associations are highly characteristic of schizophrenic patients; I have reviewed the literature elsewhere (Eysenck, in press). Does the giving of unusual word associations correlate with creative performance? An excellent test of this hypothesis comes from the work of IPAR. MacKinnon (1962, 1965) has described the study in detail; I have already referred briefly to the groups of creative, somewhat creative, and non-creative architects (n = 124) who made up the sample.

MacKinnon (1962) starts his account with a reference to a study by Bingham (1953), who tested Amy Lowell, the poet, with (among other tests) the word association test and found that "she gave a higher proportion of unique responses than those of anyone outside a mental institution" (p. 11.) With his architects, MacKinnon found the same; the unusualness of responses correlated .50 with the rated creativity of the architects. Thus group I (the most creative) scored 204; Architects II scored 128; and Architects III, the least creative, scored 114. They postulated association between creativity and "overinclusion," at least as measured by this test. The overall correlation between creativity and overinclusion was .50.

Gough (1976) has reported on a similar study done with sixty engineering students and forty-five industrial reward scientists. The subjects were rated for creativity and given two word association tests, one general and one using a scientific word list. Both correlated with creativity, but the scientific word list gave rather higher correlations. This is an intriguing finding that ought to be followed up in future research.

Similar results have also been reported by Miller and Chapman (1983), using the Chapman and Chapman (1980) scales as measures of schizotypal behavior. Using a continuum word association test, they found that subjects with high scores in Perceptual Aberration/ Magical Ideation gave a larger number of idiosyncratic responses. It is also relevant that Griffiths, Mednick, Schulsinger, and Diderichsen (1980) reported more deviant associations in the children of schizophrenic parents.

Finally, we come to the predicted association between unusual word associations and psychoticism. The most relevant study is one by Upmanyu and Kaur (1986) in which 140 university students were tested on the Kent-Rosanoff Word Association Test (WAT) and the Eysenck Personality Questionnaire (Eysenck and Eysenck 1975). Unique responses correlated .32 with P; E, N, and the Lie Scale failed to show any correlation, as did intelligence. The reliability of the WAT was .72, that of the P scale was .68; correcting for attentuation gives us a correlation between P and unique responses of .46. Ward, McConaghy, and Catts (1991) reported similar results. The third requirement of our theory seems to be fulfilled.

It is possible to add three other predictions to those considered above. If creativity is correlated with P, then groups having *low P* should be less creative. Two such groups are (1) older people and (2) women. It may be useful to look at the relationship between creativity, on the one hand, and age and sex on the other.

I have summarized the evidence to indicate that P declines linearly with age (Eysenck 1987a); it remains to show that so does creativity. Simonton (1988) gives a lengthy discussion of the evidence, and presents a figure that graphs the decline of creative potential with age. He also gives a formula for the relation between age and output: $p(t) = c(e^{-at} - e^{-bt})$, where $p(t)$ is creative productivity at time t; a is the ideation rate; b is the elaboration rate; and e is the exponential constant. Elaboration rate is the second stage in a cognitive process beginning with "creative ideations"; the second step consists in progressively translating these ideations into actual "creative contributions," that is, what he calls "communication configuration" for publication in the established journals. Whatever the value of the actual $p(t)$ figures, there is no doubt that the literature does show a decline in creative potential with age (Beard 1874; Lehman 1953; Mumford 1984; Simonton 1977).

Turning next to gender, we find that women have P scores about half those of men (Eysenck and Eysenck 1976); they are also well known to be much less well represented among geniuses and outstanding scientists, mathematicians, composers, painters, and politicians than men. Bell (1939), in his test of outstanding mathematicians, found only one woman to include (Sonya Kowalewski), and she entered the Hall of Fame only because of her connection with the more famous Weierstrass. Folgman (1933), in his list of favorite classical composers, found no women to include. Lists of the most renowned painters also lack any women's names. The roll call of Nobel Prize winners is almost exclusively male (Moulin 1955; Berry 1981; see Wilson 1989), and the membership of the Royal Society, and the Russian or American Academy of Science, is very largely so. The reasons for this disequilibrium are of course in dispute (for example, the cultural conditioning of women may lead them to be relatively conformist in their thinking, and low expectations on the part of society may lead to lack of recognition of their creative ideas). But the facts themselves can hardly be gainsaid. We thus find that our two predictions are in line with factual observation. They are less impressive than our empirical data previously considered because social phenomena have many associated causes and require complex interpretation; hence their evidential value in support of a general theory must remain problematical.

There is one venue of research which links schizophrenia and psychosis with creativity and general excellence, which is difficult to evaluate (Eysenck and Nias 1982, p. 104). We are here concerned with the simple fact that outstandingly successful individuals, but also schizophrenics, tend to be born with very significant frequency, in the February–March period of the year, as compared with the commonality (Eysenck and Nias 1982). It is not suggested that this simple physical fact is linked with astrology, or supports it in any way. It is simply suggested that there is a fairly strong correlation, of unknown origin; whether it is relevant to our main theory is also at present unknown. (For references, see Huntington 1938 and Kaulins 1979 for eminence, and Dalen 1968, Hare 1978, and Hare, Price, and Slater 1974 for psychosis.) IQ is not the cause; for intelligence there is in fact an opposite trend (Pintner and Forlano 1943; Forlano and Ehrlich 1941).

The coincidence is certainly notable but difficult to explain. Lewis and Griffin (1981) tried to argue the case away by suggesting that the schizophrenia data were based on a statistical fallacy, but this explanation is not widely accepted. It must remain uncertain whether these data can be accepted as support for the theory linking psychoticism and creativity. It may be "merely corroborative detail, intended to give artistic verisimilitude to an otherwise bald and unconvincing narrative" as the Mikado has it, but I would suggest that this rather startling correlation deserves closer scrutiny.

Psychoticism and the Creative Process

Measurement always implies a theory and a model, however primitive, and the only model to lend itself to scientific testing, and to have received such testing, is the one that views creativity as an associative process (Mednick 1962). According to Mednick, the creative thinking process may be defined as "the forming of associative elements into new combinations which either meet specified requirements or are in some way useful. The more mutually remote the elements of the new combination, the more creative the process or solution" (p. 221). Mednick postulated an "associative hierarchy," a way in which people produce associations to words or problems; creative people have a shallow gradient, extending much further than the steep gradients of less creative people. These gradients resemble generalization gradients, and may be measured by Mednick's (1962) Remote Associates Test (RAT).

As a measure of creativity the RAT is a failure; as reviews in Buros (1972, 1978) make clear, the test correlates well with IQ but poorly if at all with actual creative productivity. Nevertheless, the underlying idea is probably along the right lines, although the test is too much weighted in the direction of convergent thinking; Wallach and Kogan (1965) adapted the testing procedure to produce a much more promising test. What is certain is that this approach has given rise to what Lakatos and Musgrave (1970) would call a "progressive research programme," as opposed to Freudian theory, also frequently used for creativity, which in this as in other fields has turned out to be a "degenerating research programme" (Eysenck 1985).

Mednick was concerned with the steepness of the associative gradient, or what I would call the extent of the associative horizon (Eysenck, in press). But that has to be set in a more inclusive associative framework, such as that provided by the Campbell (1960)-Simonton (1984) and the Furneaux (1960)-Eysenck (1953) models. Both postulate something like a chance configuration theory, according to which random variations in associate-formation occur in response to a perceived problem, with certain successful combinations being selected for retention. The Furneaux (1960) model is much more explicit statistically, and permits direct testing (Frearson, Eysenck, and Barrett 1990). I have suggested that both formulations make the unlikely assumption that the production of associates is *truly* random (Eysenck, in press); this is inherently unlikely and contradicted by a wealth of experimental studies. I have postulated instead that associations are restricted to a class that may be considered "relevant," although it is also postulated that the criterion of relevance varies from person to person, with creative people having a less stringent criterion. This, in turn, gives rise to the less steep association gradient, or wider association horizon, of the creative person.

In this associative process, the *speed* with which new associations are formed would seem a crucial factor (Eysenck 1953, 1967, 1982, 1986a, b), which in turn seems to depend on the degree to which transmission of information across the cortex is error-free (Eysenck 1986a, 1987b). Degree of error-proneness, and hence speed of mental activity, and IQ generally, are dependent on certain measurable physiological properties of the cortex (Eysenck and Barrett 1985; Barrett and Eysenck, in press). Greater speed of mental functioning (fluid intelligence) is likely to produce greater knowledge (crystallized ability); thus the theory accounts for most of the traditional factors in intelligence measurement.

How does creativity fit into this model? As already suggested, I have postulated that creativity is related to, or is a function of, psychoticism as a personality variable (Eysenck and Eysenck 1976; Eysenck 1983; in press). What is needed is to specify how precisely psychoticism can produce original and creative solutions.

The answer may lie in considering the nature of psychotic (mainly schizophrenic) thinking. If the theory is correct, or at least along the right lines, then there should be some connection between what characterizes such thinking, and original and creative cognition. It may be useful to start with a well-established theory, namely Cameron's notion of "overinclusion" (Cameron 1939a, b, 1947; Cameron and Margaret 1950, 1951). Cameron believes that schizophrenics' concepts are overgeneralized. Schizophrenics are unable to maintain the normal conceptual boundaries, and incorporate into their concepts elements, some of them personal, which are merely associated with the concept but are not an essential part of it. Cameron used the term "overinclusion" to describe this abnormality, and reported that in working on the Vigotsky test and a sentence completion test, schizophrenics were unable to preserve the "conceptual boundaries" of the task. In solving a problem, the schizophrenics "included such a variety of categories at one time, that the specific problems became too extensive and too complex for a solution to be reached" (Cameron 1939a).

A fair number of experiments have been carried out to investigate this theory. These have been reviewed elsewhere (Payne 1960; Payne and Hewlett 1960; Payne, Matussek, and George 1959). The results obtained have consistently supported the theory (e.g., Moran 1953; Epstein 1953; and White 1949; see also Chapman 1956 and Chapman and Taylor 1957.

Payne et al. (1959) have suggested that it is possible to reformulate Cameron's theory of overinclusion in a slightly more general way so that a number of predictions follow from it. Concept formation can be regarded as largely the result of discrimination learning. When a child first hears a word in a certain context, the word is associated with the entire situation (stimulus compound). As the word is heard again and again, only certain aspects of the stimulus compound are reinforced. Gradually the extraneous elements cease to evoke the response (the word) having become "inhibited" through lack of reinforcement. This inhibition is in some sense an active process, as it suppresses a response that was formerly evoked by the stimulus. Overinclusive thinking may be the result of a disorder of the process whereby inhibition is built up to circumscribe and define the learned response (the word or concept). In short, it could be an extreme degree of stimulus generalization.

The same theory can be expressed in different terms. All purposeful behavior depends for its success on the fact that some stimuli are attended to and some other stimuli are ignored. It is a well-known fact that when concentrating on one task, normal people are quite unaware of most stimuli irrelevant to the task. It is as if some filter mechanism cuts out or inhibits the stimuli, both internal and external, that are irrelevant to the task at hand, to allow the most efficient processing of incoming information. Overinclusive thinking might be only one aspect of a general breakdown of this filter mechanism.

The notion of overinclusion and allusive thinking as being characteristic of normal as well as schizophrenic thinking ultimately derives from Rapaport's (1945) suggestion that at least two quite different types of formal thought disorder contributed to the disturbances of thinking found in schizophrenics, neither of which was in fact specific to schizophrenia. One of these defects, demonstrated clearly in object-sorting tests, consisted in a tendency to function more at a concrete than an abstract level (Vigotsky 1934). The other consisted of a "loosening of the concept span," in that schizophrenics included objects in the various groups of the test to which they did not strictly belong. This "looseness of thinking" is what others have called overinclusive or allusive thinking, and it occurs in normal people as well as in schizophrenics. Looseness of thinking, as measured by sorting tests, correlates well with clinical assessments of that behavior (Lovibond 1954). "Looseness" may be suggested to be a normal type of thinking related to psychoticism, and fundamental to creativity; concrete thinking is characteristic rather of psychosis, and has no link with creativity, but rather precludes it.

A similar concept of overinclusion is that of "allusive" thinking, characteristic of many schizophrenics on object sorting tests. Mc-Conaghy and Clancy (1968) demonstrated that this type of thinking existed widely in less exaggerated forms in the normal population, showed similar familiar transmission in schizophrenics and nonschizophrenics, and was akin to creative thinking. Dykes and McGhie (1976) actually demonstrated that highly creative normals scored as highly on the Lovibond object sorting test as do schizophrenics. The low creative normals tended to produce conventional, unoriginal sortings, while the highly creative normals and the schizophrenics tended to give an equal proportion of unusual sortings. "This supports strongly that a common thinking style may lead to a controlled usefulness in normals and an uncontrollable impairment in schizophrenics" (Woody and Claridge 1977).

An interesting study that demonstrates the *dependence* of creativity (as shown by fluency and unusualness of word associations) on psychosis and also the relevance of bipolar disorders, is the work of Shaw, Mann, and Stokes (1986). They found that lithium *decreases* both the number of productions and the idiosyncrasy of production. Thus the link with creativity need not be via schizophrenia, but may be via psychotic depression.

Whatever may be the most appropriate name for the thinking characteristics which link schizophrenics and highly creative normals (overinclusiveness, allusive, etc.); there clearly is a marked similarity. Furthermore, this view supports the notion of schizophrenia as a genetic morphism (Huxley, Mayr, Hoffer, and Osmond 1964), whose frequency results from a balance between selectively favorable and unfavorable properties.

The term overinclusion has long since been replaced, and new theories and experiments developed to include what are essentially similar ideas and conceptions; I have discussed these in some detail elsewhere (Eysenck, in press).

One often-voiced criticism of the concept of "psychoticism" has been that the behavior so characterized is more akin to psychopathic and indeed criminal behavior, and that in fact psychopaths and criminals have very high P scores (Eysenck and Gudjonsson 1988). As already mentioned, in our conception psychopathy lies close to schizophrenia on the psychotic-normal continuum, and such high scores would be expected, and had been predicted (Eysenck and Eysenck 1976).

The psychopathic personalities are among the most persistently reported group among close relatives of schizophrenics; and certain forms of these vaguely defined disorders appear to be, not only structurally but also developmentally connected with schizophrenic psychosis. Planansky (1972) traces the history of this association from Kahlbaum (1890), through Kraepelin (1913) to Schafer (1951), and Delay, Deniker, and Green (1957), and summarizes the empirical literature by saying, "There is an abundance of reports concerning incidence of schizoid psychopathic personality in families of schizophrenic probands [patients]." Mostly, these studies have started from the psychotic patient, but of equal interest are studies starting at the other end, using psychopathic patients. These studies have dealt with so-called schizoid psychopathic personalities; however, there is also a considerable agglomeration of nonschizoid psychopathic personalities in relatives of schizophrenics. The most important study in this field is Heston's (1966), in which children of schizophrenic mothers were removed immediately after birth and raised by foster parents. Nine of forty-seven children were diagnosed sociopathic personalities with antisocial behavior of an impulsive kind, and with long police records. Only four of these forty-seven children developed schizophrenia, demonstrating that the incidence of psychotic and nonpsychotic abnormalities is very high in the progeny of schizophrenics, under conditions when direct environmental determination is ruled out. There was also a high incidence of creative children among schizophrenic offspring.

Along more experimental lines is more recent work that also agrees in finding distinct congruence between psychosis, schizoid behavior, and psychopathy (Raine, in press). Thus this criticism of the concept of "psychoticism" can hardly be regarded as crucial.

We may conclude that the evidence supports on the whole not only a relationship between psychoticism, psychopathy, and creativity, but also the suggestion that the important cognitive variable involved is some loosening of associative thinking, some broadening of the associative horizon, a quality of overinclusiveness, a failure of inhibition that allows less relevant thoughts to intrude into the problem-solving process. In terms of the Campbell-Simonton-Furneaux model of random variation, the concept of *relevance* becomes crucial; for the psychotic or creative individual, this concept is broadened, and ideas and associations become relevant that would not appear to be so for the ordinary person. Creative thinking is distinguished from schizophrenic thinking by a more critical assessment of the products of such thinking (what Furneaux [1960] has called the "comparator"; see also Eysenck 1986a). Fluency produces more associations, creativity enables one to retain only the most fruitful ones.

Discussion and Summary

This chapter may seem to be an example of the overinclusive or allusive thinking that I have argued characterizes psychotic and creative thinking. The reason for such an impression is probably the simple fact that creativity is a very complex subject (Glover, Ronning, and Reynolds 1989; Ochse 1990) that does not easily lend itself to simplification. Even concentrating on measurement is not possible without linking it with theory, and theory insists on bringing in concepts like intelligence and personality, which require separate discussion. Terms like "psychoticism," "fluency," or "overinclusiveness" cannot be introduced without some indication of the provenance or distinctive meaning of the concepts involved, and these inevitably enlarge the compass of the discussion. Nevertheless, the final outcome is perhaps more positive than might have been expected from reading the preface of the Glover, Ronning, and Reynolds *Handbook of Creativity*, to the effect that this was a field that "had come to be a large-scale example of a 'degenerating' research program" (p. xi).

What do we find? Creativity can be measured directly as a trait, but this only correlates moderately with creative achievement; it is a necessary but not a sufficient ingredient. It interacts in a probably multiplicative fashion with other variables like intelligence, motivation, and personality. Creativity is indexed by certain cognitive styles (overinclusiveness, allusive thinking, looseness or "slippage" of ideation), which increases fluency and originality. This type of cognitive style is closely related to psychoticism, and accounts for the many links between psychosis and creativity. Psychosis as such is of course likely to *prevent* creative achievement, in spite of being related to the trait of creativity; it constitutes a negative factor in the multiplicative relationship between the factors making for creative achievement.

Psychoticism is linked directly with both trait creativity (e.g., Woody and Claridge 1977) and achievement creativity (e.g., Gotz and Gotz 1979a, b), the link being overinclusiveness. This common origin suggests a strong link between trait creativity and achievement creativity, as suggested in figure 8.3; the arrows drawn solid suggest well-substantiated links, the broken arrow has less substantial direct support. The model clearly suggests the importance of personality as a causal feature in creativity.

The reader is likely to agree that some such cognitive style as overinclusiveness is characteristic of psychotic-schizophrenic-paranoid thinking, and also of creative thinking; he may wonder why such a thinking style should be linked also with some of the behavioral characteristics of the psychotic or high P scorer. These would seem to

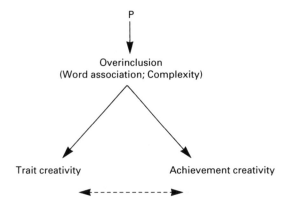

Figure 8.3
The relation between Psychoticism (*P*), Overinclusion, and Creativity.

fall into two groups, one of which is clearly linked with originality—creativity; traits in this group are imaginative, unconventional, rebellious, individualistic, independent, autonomous, flexible, and intuitive. These, one might say, are in some ways almost synonymous with originality and creativity, and the association causes no surprise.

But there is another set of characteristics that seem to have no such obvious connection. The creative individual is also conceited, cynical, disorderly, egotistical, hostile, outspoken, uninhibited, quarrelsome, aggressive, asocial, and, in the extreme, psychopathic. Why this association between traits and behaviors that show little a priori connection? My suggestion has been that we are here dealing with pleiotropic effects, that is, with genetic associations produced by certain genes having effects on more than one phenotypic trait or character (Eysenck, in press). Pleiotropic effects can be determined by major genes, and are then relatively easy to study; such effects have been known since 1915, when Sturtevant described the effect of the gene yellow in Drosophila in mating behavior (Royce and Mos 1979). Pleiotropic effects may also be determined by polygenes, which are much more likely to be involved in the determination of human traits (Eaves, Eysenck, and Martin 1989). Carson (1975), Caspari (1979a), and King (1976) have recently revived this notion, originally suggested by Mather but dropped at the time in the absence of confirmatory evidence. As Caspari (1979b) has pointed out, "pleiotropic action of genes is one of the main ways in which we can explain correlations between different behavioural characters" (p. 668).

Why has evolution produced this association between creativity and contrariness, whether through pleiotropy or not? The reason may simply be that the creative individual, because of his originality, is likely to upset the mediocre majority rigidly clinging to preconceived notions, and hence forced to fight for his ideas as best he can. Barber (1961) has given a historical review of what he calls "resistance by scientists to scientific discovery," and Gotz and Gotz (1979a, b) have argued similarly as far as creativity in the visual arts is concerned. When this hostility to new ideas by fellow scientists is added to the well-documented hostility on religious (Galileo, Darwin) and political grounds (Einstein in Germany, the Lysenko persecution of Mendelian geneticists), it will be clear why the creative scientist or artist, in order to succeed, has to have a strong character that fits him to fight for his ideas, overcome all opposition, and persevere in the face of hostility, derision, and persecution. Originality without this often apparently antisocial type of behavior is likely to wither on the vine, and not lead to creative achievement. Creativity is a threat to the great uncreative majority, and hence severely penalized and suppressed; quite often in history the delinquents are imprisoned or killed (Medvedev 1969).

Given the obvious difficulties inherent in "fuzzy" concepts like "creativity," measurement becomes even more crucial in giving such concepts "a local habitation and a name." Progress has been quite reasonable, and we certainly have a much better understanding now of the general outline of the field than we did fifty years ago. We also have a better understanding of the problems involved in measurement, some of which at least may be nearing a solution. Progress is likely to be swift if we confine ourselves to scientific problems, and do not follow the primrose path of premature application of imperfect measures to practical and social problems. This has been the sad fact of intelligence testing, which has left us with a useful technology searching for scientific status. Measurement and theoretical advance are mutually dependent and reinforcing; we have now reached a point where real advances in understanding seem possible. Creativity lies at the crossroads of intellect and personality; its understanding and measurement both rely on advances in these two fields and feed back results of empirical studies. It deserves greater attention than it has received.

References

Amabile, T. M. 1983. "The Social Psychology of Creativity: A Componential Conceptualization." *Journal of Personality and Social Psychology* 45: 357–376.

Amelang, M., Herboth, G., and Oefner, I. In press. "A Prototype Strategy for the Construction of a Creativity Scale."

Andreasen, N. C. 1987. "Creativity and Mental Illness: Prevalence Rates in Writers and Their First-Degree Relatives." *American Journal of Psychiatry* 144: 1288–1292.

Arp, H. 1987. *Quasers, Redshifts and Controversies.* Berkeley: Interstellar Media.

Asch, S. E. 1956. *Studies of Independence and Conformity:* I: A uniformity of one against a unanimous majority. Psychological Monograph, 70. (Whole No. 546.)

Barber, B. 1961. "Resistance by Scientists to Scientific Discovery." *Science* 134: 596–602.

Barrett, P., and Eysenck, H. J. 1992. "Brain Electrical Potential and Intelligence." In A. Gale and M. W. Eysenck, eds., *Handbook of Individual Differences: Biological Perspectives.* New York: Wiley, 255–286.

Barron, F. 1953. "Complexity-Simplicity as a Personality Dimension." *Journal of Abnormal and Social Psychology* 48: 163–172.

Barron, F. 1963. "The Disposition toward Originality." In C. W. Taylor and F. Barron, eds., *Scientific Creativity: Its Recognition and Development,* 139–152.

Barron, F. 1968. *Creativity and Personal Freedom.* Princeton: van Nostrand.

Barron, F. 1969. *Creative Person and Creative Process.* New York: Holt, Rinehart and Winston.

Barron, F., and Harrington, D. M. 1981. "Creativity, Intelligence, and Personality." *Annual Review of Psychology* 32: 439–476.

Barron, F., and Welsh, G. S. 1952. "Artistic Perception as a Possible Factor in Personality Style: Its Measurement by a Figure Preference Test." *Journal of Psychology* 33:199–203.

Beard, G. M. 1874. *Legal Responsibility in Old Age.* New York: Russell.

Becker, G. 1978. *The Mad Genius Controversy: A Study in the Sociology of Deviance.* Beverley Hills: Sage.

Bell, E. T. 1939. *Men of Mathematics.* London: Camelot Press.

Berry, C. 1981. "The Nobel Scientists and the Origins of Scientific Achievement." *British Journal of Sociology* 32: 381–391.

Bingham, M. T. 1953. "Beyond Psychology." In *Homo sapiens auduboniensis: A tribute to Walter Van Dyke Bingham,* 5–29. New York: National Audubon Society.

Brown, R. T. 1989. "Creativity: What Are We to Measure?" In J. A. Glover, R. R. Ronning, and C. R. Reynolds, *Handbook of Creativity,* 3–32. New York: Plenum Press.

Buros, O. K., ed. 1972. *The Seventh Mental Measurement Yearbook.* Highland Park: Gryphon Press.

Buros, O. K., ed. 1978. *The Eighth Mental Measurement Yearbook.* Highland Park, Gryphon Press.

Burt, C. 1943. "Ability and Income." *British Journal of Educational Psychology* 13: 83–98.

Burt, C. 1963. Is Intelligence Distributed Normally? *British Journal of Statistical Psychology* 16: 175–190.

Campbell, D. T. 1960. "Blind Variation and Selective Retention in Creative Thought as in Other Knowledge Processes." *Psychological Review* 67: 380–400.

Cameron, N. 1939a. "Deterioration and Regression in Schizophrenic Thinking." *Journal of Abnormal and Social Psychology* 34: 265–270.

Cameron, N. 1939b. "Schizophrenic Thinking in a Problem-Solving Situation." *Journal of Mental Science* 85: 1012, 1035.

Cameron, N. 1947. *The Psychology of Behavior Disorders.* Boston: Houghton Mifflin.

Cameron, N., and Margaret, A. 1950. "Experimental Studies in Thinking: I. Scattered Speech in the Responses of Normal Subjects to Incomplete Sentences. *Journal of Experimental Psychology* 39: 617–627.

Cameron, N., and Margaret, A. 1951. *Behavior Pathology.* Boston: Houghton Mifflin.

Carroll, J. B. 1941. "A Factor Analysis of Verbal Abilities." *Psychometrika* 6: 279–308.

Carson, H. C. 1975. "The Genetics of Speciation at the Diploid Level." *American Naturalist,* 109, 83–101.

Caspari, E. 1979a. "Evolutionary Theory and the Evolution of the Human Brain." In M. Hahn, ed., *Development and Evolution of Brain Size: Behavioural Implications.* New York: Academic Press.

Caspari, E. 1979b. "The Goals and Future of Behavior Genetics." In Royce, J. R., and Mos, L. P., eds., *Theoretical Advances in Behavior Genetics,* 661–679. Germantown, MD: Sijthoff and Noordhoff.

Cattell, R. B. 1971. *Abilities: Their Structure, Growth, and Action.* Boston: Houghton Mifflin.

Chapman, L. J. 1956. "Distractibility in the Conceptual Performance of Schizophrenics." *Journal of Abnormal and Social Psychology* 53: 286–291.

Chapman, L. J., and Chapman, J. P. 1980. "Scales for Rating Psychotic and Psychotic-like Experiences as Continua." *Schizophrenia Bulletin* 6: 476–489.

Chapman, L. J., and Taylor, J. 1957. "Breadth of Deviate Concepts Used by Schizophrenics." *Journal of Abnormal and Social Psychology* 54: 118–123.

Cox, C. M. 1926. *The Early Mental Traits of Three Hundred Geniuses.* Stanford: Stanford University Press.

Crow, T. J. 1986. "The Continuum of Psychosis and Its Implications for the Structure of the Gene." *British Journal of Psychiatry* 149: 419–429.

Dahlstrom, W. G., Lachar, D., and Dahlstrom, L. E. 1986. *MMPI Patterns of American Minorities.* Minneapolis: University of Minnesota Press.

Dalen, P. 1968. "Month of Birth and Schizophrenia." *Acta Psychiatrica Scandinavica* 203: 55–60.

Dalen, P. 1975. *Season of Birth: A Study of Schizophrenia and Other Mental Disorders.* New York: Elsevier.

Dalen, P. 1988. "Schizophrenia, Season of Birth, and Maternal Age." *British Journal of Psychiatry* 153: 727–733.

Delay, J., Deniker, P., and Green, A. 1957. Le Milieu Familial des Schizophrenics." *Encephale* 46: 189–204.

Dellas, M., and Gaier, E. L. 1970. "Identification of Creativity: The Individual." *Psychological Bulletin* 73: 55–73.

Dykes, M., and McGhie, A. 1976. "A Comparative Study of Attentional Strategies of Schizophrenic and Highly Creative Normal Subjects." *British Journal of Psychiatry* 128: 50–56.

Eaves, L., Eysenck, H. J., and Martin, N. 1989. *Genes, Culture and Personality: An Empirical Approach.* New York: Academic Press.

Eddington, A. 1935. *The Nature of the Physical World.* London: J. M. Dent & Sons.

Epstein, S. 1953. "Overinclusive Thinking in a Schizophrenic and a Control Group." *Journal of Counseling Psychology* 17: 384–388.

Eysenck, H. J. 1941. ""Type"-Factors in Aesthetic Judgments." *British Journal of Psychology* 31: 262–270.

Eysenck, H. J. 1953. *Uses and Abuses of Psychology.* London: Pelican.

Eysenck, H. J. 1959. "The Rorschach Test." In O. Buros, ed., *The Fifth Mental Measurement Yearbook,* 276–278. Highland Park, N.J.: Gryphon Press.

Eysenck, H. J. 1967. "Intelligence Assessment: A Theoretical Experimental Approach." *British Journal of Educational Psychology* 37: 81–98.

Eysenck, H. J. 1970a. *The Structure of Human Personality.* London: Methuen.

Eysenck, H. J. 1970b. "A Dimensional System of Psychodiagnostics." In A. R. Mahrer, ed., *New Approaches to Personality Classification and Psychodiagnosis.* New York: Columbia University Press.

Eysenck, H. J. 1972. "An Experimental and Genetic Model of Schizophrenia." In A. R. Kaplan, ed., *Genetic Factors in "Schizophrenia",* 504–515. Springfield: C. C. Thomas.

Eysenck, H. J. 1981. "Aesthetic Preferences and Individual Differences." In D. O'Hare, ed., *Psychology and the Arts*, 76–101. Brighton: Harvester Press.

Eysenck, H. J., ed. 1982. *A Model for Intelligence.* New York: Springer Verlag.

Eysenck, H. J., 1983. "The Roots of Creativity: Cognition Ability or Personality Trait?" *Roeper Review* 5: 109–12.

Eysenck, H. J. 1985. *The Decline and Fall of the Freudian Empire.* London: Viking.

Eysenck, H. J. 1986a. "The Theory of Intelligence and the Psychophysiology of Cognition." In R. J. Sternberg, ed., *Advances in the Psychology of Human Learning*, 1–34.

Eysenck, H. J. 1986b. "Intelligence: The New Look." *Psychologische Beitrage* 28: 332–365.

Eysenck, H. J. 1987a. "Personality and Aging: An Exploratory Analysis." *Journal of Social Behavior and Personality* 3: 11–21.

Eysenck, H. J. 1987b. "Speed of Information Processing, Reaction Time, and the Theory of Intelligence." In P. A. Vernon, ed., *Speed of Information Processing and Intelligence*, 21–68. Norwood, N.J.: Ablex.

Eysenck, H. J. 1988. "Personality and Scientific Aesthetics." In F. H. Farley and R. W. Neperud, eds., *The Foundations of Aesthetics, Art, and Art Education*, 117–160. New York: Praeger.

Eysenck, H. J. 1990. *Rebel with a Cause.* London: W. H. Allen.

Eysenck, H. J. 1993. Creativity and Personality: A Theoretical Perspective. *Psychological Inquiry* 4: 147–178.

Eysenck, H. J., and Barrett, P. 1985. "Psychophysiology and the Measurement of Intelligence." In C. R. Reynolds and V. Willson, eds., *Methodological and Statistical Advances in the Study of Individual Differences*. New York: Plenum Press.

Eysenck, H. J., and Castle, M. 1970. "A Factor-Analytic Study of the Barron-Welsh Art Scale." *Psychological Record* 20: 523–525.

Eysenck, H. J., and Eysenck, M. W. 1985. *Personality and Individual Differences: A Natural Science Approach.* New York: Plenum Press.

Eysenck, H. J., and Eysenck, S. B. G. 1975. *Manual of the Eysenck Personality Questionnaire.* London: Hodder & Stoughton, San Diego: EDITS.

Eysenck, H. J., and Eysenck, S. B. G. 1975. *Psychoticism as a Dimension of Personality.* London: Hodder & Stoughton.

Eysenck, H. J., and Eysenck, S. B. G. 1977. "Psychopaths, Personality and Genetics." In R. D. Hare and D. Schalling, eds., *Psychopathic Behavior: Approaches to Research.* London: Wiley.

Eysenck, H. J., and Gudjonsson, G. 1988. *The Causes and Cures of Criminality.* New York: Plenum Press.

Eysenck, H. J., and Nias, D. K. B. 1982. *Astrology: Science or Superstition?* London: Maurice Temple Smith.

Eysenck, H. J., Wakefield, J. A., and Friedman, A. F. 1983. "Diagnosis and Clinical Assessment: The DSM-III." *Annual Review of Psychology* 34: 167–193.

Farmer, E. W. 1974. "Psychoticism and Person-Orientation as General Personality Characteristics of Importance for Different Aspects of Creative Thinking." Glasgow: Unpublished B.Sc. thesis, quoted in Eysenck and Eysenck, 1976.

Field, G. B., Arp, H., and Bahcall, J. V. 1974. *The Redshift Controversy.* New York: W. A. Bergania.

Folgman, E. C. 1933. "An Experimental Study of Composer-Preference of Four Outstanding Symphony Orchestras." *Journal of Experimental Psychology* 16: 709–724.

Forlano, G., and Ehrlich, V. Z. 1941. "Month and Season of Birth in Relation to Intelligence, Introversion-Extraversion, and Inferiority Feelings." *Journal of Educational Psychology* 32: 1–12.

Franks, F. 1981. *Polywater.* Cambridge: MA: The MIT Press.

Frearson, W., Eysenck, H. J., and Barrett, P. 1990. "The Furneaux Model of Human Problem-Solving: Its Relationship to Reaction Time and Intelligence." *Personality and Individual Differences* 11: 239–257.

Friedman, A. F., Webb, J. T., and Lewak, R. 1989. *Psychological Assessment with the MMPI.* Hillsdale, N.J.: Lawrence Erlbaum.

Furneaux, W. D. 1956. *Manual of Nufferno Speed Tests.* London: National Foundation for Educational Research.

Furneaux, W. D. 1960. "Intellectual Abilities and Problem-Solving Behaviour." In H. J. Eysenck, ed., *Handbook of Abnormal Psychology*, 167–192. London: Pitman.

Gedo, J. E. 1978. "Nietzsche and the Psychology of Genius." *American Image* 35: 37–91.

Gibson, J., and Light, F. 1967. "Intelligence among University Students." *Nature* 213: 441–442.

Glover, J. A., Ronning, R. R., and Reynolds, C. R. 1989. *Handbook of Creativity.* New York: Plenum Press.

Goldberg, S. C., Schooler, N. R., and Mattson, M. 1908. "Paranoid and Withdrawal Symptoms in Schizophrenia: Relationship to Reaction Time." *British Journal of Psychiatry* 114: 1161–1165.

Gotz, K. O., and Gotz, K. 1979a. "Personality Characteristics of Professional Artists." *Perceptual and Motor Skills*, 49, 327–334.

Gotz, K. O., and Gotz, K. 1979b. "Personality Characteristics of Successful Artists." *Perceptual and Motor Skills* 49: 919–924.

Gough, H. G. 1976. "Studying Creativity by Means of Word Association Tests." *Journal of Applied Psychology* 61: 348–353.

Griffiths, J. J., Mednick, S. J., Schulsinger, F., and Diderichsen, B. 1980. "Verbal Associative Disturbances in Children at High Risk for Schizophrenia." *Journal of Abnormal Psychology*, 89, 125–131.

Guilford, J. P. 1950. "Creativity." *American Psychologist* 5: 444–454.

Guilford, J. P. 1967. *The Nature of Human Intelligence.* New York: McGraw-Hill.

Guilford, J. P. 1981. "Potentiality for Creativity." In J. C. Gowan, J. Khatena, and E. P. Torrance, eds., *Creativity: Its Educational Implications* (2nd ed., 1–5). Dubuque: Kendall, Hunt.

Hare, E. A. 1978. "Variations in the Seasonal Distribution of Births of Psychotic Patients in England and Wales." *British Journal of Psychiatry* 132: 155–158.

Hare, E. H., Price, J. S., and Slater, E. 1974. "Mental Disorder and Season of Birth." *British Journal of Psychiatry* 124: 81–86.

Hargreaves, H. L. 1927. "The "Faculty" of Imagination." *British Journal of Psychology*, Monograph Supplement, 10, 74.

Heansly, P., and Reynolds, C. R. 1989. "Creativity and Intelligence." In J. A. Glover, R. R. Ronning, and C. R. Reynolds, eds., *Handbook of Creativity*, 111–132. New York: Plenum Press.

Hebeison, A. A. 1960. "The Performance of a Group of Schizophrenic Patients on a Test of Creative Thinking." In E. P. Torrance, ed., *Creativity: Third Minnesota Conference on Gifted Children.*

Heston, L. L. 1966. "Psychiatric Disorders in Foster-Home-Reared Children of Schizophrenic Mothers." *British Journal of Psychiatry* 112: 819–825.

Hovecar, D. 1979. "Ideational Fluency as a Confounding Factor in the Measurement of Originality." *Journal of Educational Psychology* 71: 191–196.

Hovecar, D. 1980. "Intelligence, Divergent Thinking, and Creativity." *Intelligence* 4: 25–40.

Hovecar, D. 1981. "Measurement of Creativity: Review and Critique." *Journal of Personality Assessment* 45: 450–464.

Hovecar, D., and Bachelor, P. 1989. "A Taxonomy and Critique of Measurements Used in the Study of Creativity." In J. A. Glover, R. R. Ronning, and C. R. Reynolds, eds., *Handbook of Creativity*, 53–75. New York: Plenum Press.

Huntington, E. 1938. *Season of Birth: Its Relation to Human Abilities*. New York: Wiley.

Huxley, J., Mayr, E., Hoffer, H., and Osmond, A. 1964. "Schizophrenia as a Genetic Morphism." *Nature* 204: 220–221.

Joncish, G. 1968. *The Sane Positivist*. Middletown, CO: Weslyan University Press.

Juda, A. 1949. "The Relationship between Highest Mental Capacity and Psychic Abnormalities." *American Journal of Psychiatry* 1106: 296–307.

Kahlbaum, R. 1890. "Uber Heboidophrenie." *Allgemeine Zeitschrift fur Psychiatrie* 40: 461–489.

Karlsson, J. I. 1968. "Generalogic Studies of Schizophrenia." In D. Rosenthal and S. S. Kety, eds., *The Transmission of Schizophrenia*. Oxford: Pergamon Press.

Karlsson, J. I. 1970. "Genetic Association of Giftedness and Creativity with Schizophrenics." *Hereditas* 66: 177–182.

Kaulins, A. 1979. "Cycles in the Birth of Eminent Humans." *Cycles* 30: 9–15.

Kessel, N. 1989. "Genius and Mental Disorder: A History of Ideas Concerning Their Conjunction." In P. Murray, ed., *Genius: The History of an Idea*, 195–212. Oxford: Blackwell.

Kidner, D. W. 1978. "Personality and Conceptual Structure: An Integrative Model." London: Unpublished Ph.D. thesis.

King, J. L. 1976. "Progress in the Neutral Mutations–Random Drift Controversy." *Federation Proceedings* 35: 2087–2094.

Koestler, A. 1969. *The Act of Creation*. New York: Macmillan.

Kraepelin, E. 1913. *Psychiatrie*, Vol. III, Leipzig: Barlts.

Lakatos, I., and Musgrave, A. Eds. 1970. *Criticism and the Growth of Knowledge*. Cambridge: University Press.

Lange-Eichbaum, W. 1932. *The Problem of Genius*. New York: Macmillan.

Lehman, H. C. 1955. *Age and Achievement*. Princeton: Princeton University Press.

Lewis, M. S., and Griffin, P. A. 1981. "An Explanation for the Season of Birth Effects in Schizophrenia and Certain Other Diseases." *Psychological Bulletin* 89: 509–596.

Lotka, A. J. 1926. "The Frequency Distribution of Scientific Productivity." *Journal of the Washington Academy of Sciences* 16: 317–323.

Lovibond, S. H. 1954. "The Object Sorting Test and Conceptual Thinking in Schizophrenics." *Australian Journal of Psychology* 6: 52–70.

McConaghy, V., and Clancy, M. 1968. "Familial Relationships of Allusive Thinking in University Students and Their Parents." *British Journal of Psychiatry* 114: 1079–1087.

McNeil, T. F. 1971. "Prebirth and Postbirth Influence on the Relationship between Creative Ability and Recorded Mental Illness." *Journal of Personality* 39: 391–406.

MacKinnon, D. W., ed. 1961. *The Creative Person*. Berkeley: University of California Press.

MacKinnon, D. W. 1962. "The Nature and Nurture of Creative Talent." *American Psychologist* 17: 484–495.

MacKinnon, D. W. 1965. "Personality and the Realization of Creative Potential." *American Psychologist* 20: 279–281.

MacKinnon, D. W. 1978. *In Search of Human Effectiveness*. New York: Creative Educational Foundation.

Maslow, A. 1976. "Creativity in Self-Actualizing People." In A. Rothenberg and C. R. Hausman, eds., *The Creativity Question*, 86–92. Durham, NC: Duke University Press.

Mednick, S. A. 1962. "The Associative Basis of the Creative Process." *Psychological Review* 69: 220–232.

Medvedev, Z. A. 1969. *The Rise and Fall of T. D. Lysenhov*. New York: Columbia University Press.

Michael, W. B., and Wright, C. R. 1989. "Psychometric Issues in the Assessment of Creativity." In J. A. Glover, R. R. Ronning, and C. R. Reynolds, eds., *Handbook of Creativity*, 33–52. New York: Plenum Press.

Miller, E. N., and Chapman, L. J. 1983. "Continued Word Association in Hypothetically Psychosis-Prone College Students." *Journal of Abnormal Psychology* 92: 468–478.

Mohan, J. L., and Tiwana, M. 1987. "Personality and Alienation of Creative Writers: A Brief Report." *Personality and Individual Differences* 8: 449.

Moran, L. J. 1953. *Vocabulary Knowledge and Usage among Normal and Schizophrenic Subjects*. Psychological Monograph, 67, No. 20 (Whole No. 370).

Moulin, L. 1955. "The Nobel Prizes for Sciences from 1901–1950: An Essay in Sociological Analysis. *British Journal of Sociology* 6: 246–263.

Mumford, M. D. 1984. "Age and Outstanding Occupational Achievement: Lehman Revisited." *Journal of Vocational Behavior* 25: 225–255.

Mumford, M. D., and Gustafson, S. B. 1988. "Creativity Syndrome: Integration, Application and Innovation." *Psychological Bulletin* 103: 27–43.

Nicolson, H. 1947. "The Health of Authors." *Lancet*, II, 709–714.

Ochse, R. 1990. *Before the Gates of Excellence: The Determinants of Creative Genius*. Cambridge: Cambridge University Press.

Ochse, R. 1991. "The Relation between Creative Genius and Psychopathology. An Historical Perspective and a New Explanation." *South African Journal of Psychology* 21: 45–53.

Pareto, V. 1897. *Cours d'Economic Politique*. Paris: Armand.

Payne, R. W. 1960. "Cognitive Abnormalities." In H. J. Eysenck, ed., *Handbook of Abnormal Psychology*, 193–261. London: Pitman.

Payne, R. W., and Hewlett, J. H. G. 1960. "Thought Disorder in Psychotic Patients." In H. J. Eysenck, ed., *Experiments in Personality*, 3–104. London: Routledge and Kegan Paul.

Payne, R. W., Matussek, P., and George, E. I. 1959. "An Experimental Study of Schizophrenic Thought Disorder." *Journal of Mental Science* 105: 627–652.

Pintner, R., and Forlano, G. 1943. "Season of Birth and Mental Differences." *Psychological Bulletin* 40: 25–35.

Planansky, K. 1972. "Phenotypic Boundaries and Genetic Specificity in Schizophrenics." In A. R. Kaplan, ed., *Genetic Factors in "Schizophrenia,"* 141–172. Springfield: C. C. Thomas.

Prentky, R. A. 1980. *Creativity and Psychopathology: A Neurocognitive Perspective*. New York: Praeger.

Price, D. 1963. *Little Science, Big Science*. New York: Columbia University Press.

Raine, A. C. In press. "Schizotypal and Borderline Features in Psychopathic Criminals." *Personality and Individual Differences*.

Rapaport, R. 1945. *Diagnostic Clinical Testing*. Chicago: Year Book Publishers.

Rawlings, D. 1985. "Psychoticism, Creativity and Dichotic Shadowing." *Personality and Individual Differences* 6: 737–742.

Roe, A. 1952. *The Making of a Scientist*. New York: Dodd, Mead.

Roe, A. 1953. *A Psychological Study of Eminent Psychologists and Anthropologists, and a Comparison with Biological and Physical Scientists*. Psychological Monograph: General and Applied, 67, Whole No. 352.

Rogers, C. A. 1976. "Toward a Theory of Creativity." In A. Rothenberg and C. R. Hausman, eds., *The Creativity Question*, 296–305. Durham, NC.: Duke University Press.

Rothenberg, A. 1979. *The Emerging Goddess: The Creative Process in Art, Science, and Other Fields*. Chicago: University of Chicago Press.

Royce, J. R., and Mos, L. P. 1979. *Theoretical Advances in Behavior Genetics*. Germantown, MD: Sijthoff and Noordhoff.

Schafer, R. 1951. *The Clinical Application of Psychological Tests*. New York: International University Press.

Shaw, E. D., Mann, J. J., and Stokes, P. E. 1986. "Effects of Lithium Carbonate on Creativity in Bipolar Outpatients." *American Journal of Psychiatry* 143: 1166–1169.

Silverman, A. 1969. "The Scanning Control Mechanism and "Cognitive" Filtering in Paranoid and Non-paranoid Schizophrenics." *Journal of Consulting Psychology* 28: 385–393.

Simonton, D. K. 1977. "Creative Productivity, Age, and Stress: A Biographical Time-Series Analysis of 10 Classical Composers." *Journal of Personality and Social Psychology* 35: 791–804.

Simonton, D. K. 1984. *Genius, Creativity and Leadership*. Cambridge: MA: Harvard University Press.

Simonton, D. K. 1988. *Scientific Genius*. Cambridge: Cambridge University Press.

Soueif, M. I., and Farag, S. E. 1971. "Creative Thinking Aptitudes in Schizophrenia: A Factorial Study." *Scientific Aesthetics* 8: 51–60.

Spearman, C. 1923. *The Nature of "Intelligence" and the Principles of Cognition*. London: Macmillan.

Spearman, C. 1927. *The Abilities of Man*. London: Macmillan.

Spearman, C. 1931. *Creative Mind*. New York: Appleton.

Terman, L. M. 1925. *Genetic Studies of Genius: Vol. 1. Mental and Physical Traits of a Thousand Gifted Children*. Stanford: Stanford University Press.

Terman, L. M., and Oden, M. H. 1947. *Genetic Studies of Genius, Vol. IV. The Gifted Child Grows Up*. Stanford: Stanford University Press.

Terman, L. M., and Oden, M. H. 1951. "The Stanford Studies of the Gifted." In D. C. Welty, ed., *The Gifted Child*. Boston: Heath.

Terman, L. M., and Oden, M. H. 1959. *Genetic Studies of Genius. Vol. V. The Gifted Groups in Midlife*. Stanford: Stanford University Press.

Torrance, E. P. 1974. *Torrance Tests of Creative Thinking: Norms—Technical Manual*. Lexington, MA: Ginn.

Upmanyu, V. V., and Kaur, K. 1986. "Diagnostic Ability of Word Association Emotional Indicators." *Psychological Studies* 32: 71–78.

Venables, P. H., and O'Connor, N. 1959. "A Short Scale for Rating Paranoid Schizophrenia." *Journal of Mental Science* 105: 815–818.

Vernon, P. E. 1989. "The Nature-Nurture Problem in Creativity." In J. A. Glover, R. R. Ronning, and C. R. Reynolds, eds., *Handbook of Creativity*, 93–110. New York: Plenum Press.

Vigotsky, L. S. 1934. "Thought in Schizophrenia." *Archives of Neurology and Psychiatry* 31: 1063–1077.

Wallach, M. A. 1971. *The Intelligence/Creativity Distinction*. New York: General Learning Press.

Wallach, M. A. 1986. "Creativity Testing and Giftedness." In F. D. Horowitz and M. O'Brien, eds., *The Gifted and Talented: Developmental Perspectives*. Washington, D.C.: American Psychological Association.

Wallach, M. A., and Kogan, N. 1965. *Modes of Thinking in Young Children.* New York: Holt, Rinehart & Winston.

Wankowski, J. A. 1973. *Temperament, Motivation and Academic Achievement.* Birmingham: University of Birmingham Educational Survey and Counseling Unit.

Ward, P. B., McConaghy, N., and Catts, S. V. 1991. "Word Association and Measures of Psychosis-Proneness in University Students." *Personality and Individual Differences* 12: 473–480.

Welsh, G. S. 1959. *Preliminary Manual, the Welsh Figure Preference Test.* Palo Alto: Consulting Psychologists Press.

Welsh, G. 1975. *Creativity of Intelligence: A Personality Approach.* Chapel Hill, N.C.: University of North Carolina Press.

Westcott, M., and Ranzoni, J. 1963. "Correlates of Intuitive Thinking." *Psychological Reports* 12: 595–613.

White, M. 1949. "A Study of Schizophrenic Language." *Journal of Abnormal and Social Psychology*, 44, 61–74.

Wilson, G. 1989. *The Great Sex Divide.* London: Peter Owen.

Woody, E., and Claridge, G. 1977. "Psychoticism and Thinking." *British Journal of Social and Clinical Psychology* 16: 241–248.

Zhao, H., and Jiang, G. 1985. "Shifting of World's Scientific Center and Scientists' Social Ages." *Scientometrics* 8: 59–70.

Index

Analogy, 10, 76, 97–103
Arousal potential, 172–176, 188
Artificial intelligence, 84–112

Combination theories, 75–76
Composite variability index, 173–176
Computational psychology, 84–116, 121, 139, 144–145
Computer models, 6–7, 84–112
Conceptual spaces, 6–7, 8, 10, 75–118, 120, 124–125. *See also* Klondike spaces
Context of discovery, 3, 13–52, 71–72, 119–142
Creativity tests, 199–234

Discovery, 3–5, 13–52, 71–72, 119–142

Evaluation, 3–5, 13–52, 75–76, 77, 161–163, 231
Evolutionary explanations, 6–7, 33, 106–112, 119–130, 138–140, 159–168
Exemplary creators, 8, 147–150

Fruitful asynchrony, 153–154

Genetic algorithms, 106–112

Heuristics, 5–6, 53–74, 82–83, 104–106

Inventors, 130–140

Klondike spaces, 7, 119–142. *See also* Conceptual spaces

Measurement of creativity, 7, 112–116, 135–138, 159–234
Motivation, 8, 11, 143–158, 211–234
Multiple discoveries, 17, 32–36

Overinclusiveness, 10–11, 199–234

Personality, 8, 11, 143–158, 211–234
Physiological factors, 11, 228–230
Pleiotropic effects, 233
Primordial content, 163–165, 177–186
Priority disputes, 32–36
Psychometrics, 10–11, 159–198, 199–234
Psychopathology, 211–215, 226, 228–234
Psychosis, 214–215, 223–224, 226, 229–234
Psychoticism, 11, 193, 213–215, 221–234

Representational redescription, 91

Schizophrenia. *See* Psychopathology; Psychosis
Scientific discovery, 13–34
Social context, 143–158, 188–193
Social support, 8, 143–158
Stylistic change, 159–198. *See also* Conceptual spaces; Klondike spaces

Tools-to-theories heuristic, 5–6, 53–74